BEYONCÉ: RUNNING THE WORLD

BEYONCÉ: RUNNING THE WORLD

The Biography

Anna Pointer

CORONET

First published in Great Britain in 2014 by Coronet
An imprint of Hodder & Stoughton
An Hachette UK company

First published in paperback in 2015

1

A CIP catalogue record for this title is available
from the British Library

Paperback ISBN 978 1 473 60735 4
Ebook ISBN 978 1 473 60732 3

Typeset by Hewer Text UK Ltd, Edinburgh
Printed and bound by CPI Group (UK) Ltd, Croydon CR0 4YY

Hodder & Stoughton policy is to use papers that are natural,
renewable and recyclable products and made from wood grown in
sustainable forests. The logging and manufacturing processes
are expected to conform to the environmental regulations
of the country of origin.

Hodder & Stoughton Ltd
Carmelite House
50 Victoria Embankment
London EC4Y 0DZ

www.hodder.co.uk

'I now know that, yes, I am powerful . . . I'm more powerful than my mind can even digest and understand.'

Beyoncé

Chapter One

As the thunder of applause dies away, the little girl takes centre stage and grins back at the hundreds of rapturous faces packing the theatre auditorium. Although she's only seven years old and can barely see over the wooden stand to speak into the microphone, she knows exactly what she wants to say. It seems this is where she belongs. In a shiny party dress, her hair carefully arranged in ringlets, she has just sung her heart out to win a major national talent show. She takes a deep breath and begins to speak, thanking her parents and the judges for crowning her winner. Then, as if she's been in the spotlight for years, she raises her hand to her mouth and blows the audience a kiss. The gesture is full of charm – a flash of youthful showbiz flair and natural empathy with the crowd, who rise to their feet amid more deafening cheers and applause. The ability to captivate an entire concert hall is a gift that has stayed with her all her life and become a hallmark of her success.

Fast forward a year, and the little girl has blossomed into a real performer. There is polish and poise in each movement, and total confidence as she hits every note. No longer a competitor, she has returned to the Houston theatre to make a guest appearance at the same talent show she had won so convincingly the year before. Taking to the stage once again, she delivers such a knockout performance that there can be no doubt she has a glittering future ahead. Beyoncé Knowles is well on her way to becoming the biggest female singing star in the world.

She was born with music running through her veins. 'My dad tells me that, as a baby, I would go crazy whenever I heard music, and I tried to dance before I could even walk,' she revealed in the Destiny's Child autobiography *Soul Survivors*. 'He has the embarrassing videos to prove it!' Her father, Mathew Knowles, would surely not describe the home movies as embarrassing but as one of his most treasured possessions. He was always the proud dad of his elder daughter and never more so than on 4 September 1981, when Beyoncé Giselle Knowles made her grand entrance into the world at Park Plaza Hospital in Houston.

'My mom claims that it was an easy and relatively painless birth – unlike some of my other entrances,' Beyoncé wrote in *Soul Survivors*. 'The deal my parents made before I was born was that my dad would pick my middle name and my mom would choose my first name. So Beyoncé comes from her – it's actually her maiden name.'

In fact, Beyoncé is a derivative of her mother's family name. Tina was born Celestine Ann Beyincé, and in an effort to keep the surname going when she got married, she came up with the name Beyoncé – which did not go down too well with her own father, Lumiz Beyincé. 'My family was not happy,' Tina told *Rolling Stone* magazine. 'My dad said, "She's gonna be really mad at you because that's a last name."' Lumiz was right: as a young child Beyoncé did indeed hate her name. 'Through the years, I have grown to love it, but when I was little, it was just another reason for kids to pick on me,' she said in *Soul Survivors*. 'Every morning when the teacher would take roll call, I wanted to crawl under my desk.'

But, of course, before she began school Beyoncé had no idea that her name was unusual and there was nothing to cloud her first few years. At home she was nicknamed 'Bey' or simply 'B' – both of which stayed with her into her adult years. Early pictures show her as a smiling, happy toddler with an adorably round face and a shock of dark curls. As soon as she was walking she would dance to songs on the radio or to her parents' records, which included Michael Jackson, Luther Vandross and Prince. Mathew and Tina had both loved singing since they were very young and had taken part in talent shows, while Tina had also sung in a pop group called the Beltones, who were modelled on Diana Ross and the Supremes and wore costumes that she designed herself. The house was always full of music and Beyoncé has fond memories of family sing-songs with her dad on keyboard.

One of her earliest recollections is singing her mother a number she had been taught at school. 'I was in first grade when my mom asked me what I learned at school that day and I said, "A song." She was standing at the sink washing dishes, but then she wiped her hands on her apron, turned around and looked at me. "Well, that's nice," she said. "Let's hear it." I was sitting at the kitchen table, and I stood up to sing it for her just like my teacher had taught me. I'll never forget that feeling,' she reflected in *Soul Survivors*. 'I loved performing for my mom – it was a rush. Even before that, my parents used to sing to me all the time.'

While music had always been an important part of Mathew and Tina's lives, they both had a natural aptitude for business and a determination to achieve financial success against all odds. Mathew, now sixty-three, was born in Gadsden, Alabama, in 1951, when racial intolerance and segregation between black and white people was still strong. The family were poor and lived in a tiny, ramshackle house without an indoor bathroom. But his parents were hard-working and resourceful. His father, also called Mathew, was a truck driver, who persuaded the owners of the vehicle to allow him to use it at night to sell the scrap metal he had collected from old cars and houses. Mathew's mother worked as a maid for a white family and in her spare time made and sold quilts and canned goods. His grandfather, who was half Cherokee, owned 300 acres of land that he leased out to a paper mill.

The example set by his parents and grandfather inspired Mathew's ambition to become a businessman, and he started his first venture when he was still at school by buying sweets at a discount and selling them on at a profit. 'I always wanted to be a businessman. I would go and buy a dollar's worth of candy and make that dollar turn into three dollars,' he told *Empower* magazine. 'I didn't really know what I was doing, but it worked.'

His parents not only fostered his entrepreneurial spirit but were also keen to encourage his education – and his love of music. Mathew recalls that after the family's Sunday dinner, he would regularly act as a DJ while his mum and dad danced around the living room. 'My dad was six foot four and three hundred twenty pounds, but could really dance for a big guy. I always loved music,' he said. He was in a choir and a boy band at school, but he revealed that while growing up Beyoncé used to beg him: 'Don't sing, Daddy. Please, don't you sing.'

Mathew won a basketball scholarship to the University of Tennessee but then transferred to Fisk University in Nashville where he studied economics and business administration. While he was a student at Fisk he began thinking about developing musical acts with the help of the local radio station. After graduating in 1974, his interest in promoting music was put on hold as he concentrated on building a career in sales, which included working for life insurance and medical equipment companies. He joined Xerox as a salesman in their medical imaging division and was so successful that by the time his elder daughter was born in 1981 he was earning six figures, while he and Tina were living in a comfortable home in Houston, Texas.

Tina, now sixty, was also from a poor background. The youngest of seven children, and of Louisiana Creole descent, with African, Native American, French and Irish ancestry, Tina grew up in Galveston, Texas. She was sent to private fee-paying Catholic schools that her mother Agnèz helped fund by making clothing for society folk. 'My mother paid part of the tuition by making robes for altar boys, cloaks for the priests and altar cloths for the church,' Tina told *Ebony* magazine. 'She was really talented. People would come to her for prom dresses and fancy gowns.'

In the mid-seventies Tina worked at a bank and met Mathew at a party, but it wasn't until a year later that they started dating. They married in 1979, a successful and glamorous young couple with an enviable lifestyle, thanks to Mathew's Xerox salary. They had a beautiful house, cars and money, so it was not surprising that they soon began to think about starting a family. By Christmas 1980 Tina was pregnant with their first child.

The year after Beyoncé was born Tina left the bank and, with her savings, opened a hair salon called Headliners. It became the go-to place for well-to-do African Americans in Houston and would often seat twenty-four clients during its peak. It was so successful that the family were able to move to a six-bedroom house on a leafy street called Parkwood Drive in a predominantly African-American community called the Third Ward. Memories of her childhood home have always been fundamentally important to Beyoncé, so much so that she later named her management team Parkwood. In 1986, Tina gave birth to a second daughter, Solange. The sisters were five years apart but they developed a strong bond. As the elder child, Beyoncé was very nurturing of Solange and used to enjoy playing 'mommy' to her. She loved holding her as a baby and was always on hand to help out with bathing, feeding and changing her. To that end she was a great help to Tina, who says squabbles were rare even as her daughters got older. 'There was a period where Solange got on Beyoncé's nerves because she was in all her stuff, the typical things kids go through, but they have always been very protective of each other and very close,' she told *Access Hollywood*. 'There's never been this rivalry stuff that sometimes people try to make out. They're just sisters like any other sisters and they love and support each other.'

Peace was kept between them largely because Solange says she refused to compare herself to her big sister. 'My family always called me the rebel,' she explained to *Texas Monthly* magazine. 'I'd always dress differently. I never defined myself by my sister.'

Tina has always described herself as being very family-oriented and her daughters grew up enjoying all the traditional treats of childhood. Christmas was a particularly happy time, with carols, a glittering tree, turkey and all the trimmings. Another red-letter day in the family calendar was the Houston Livestock Show and Rodeo. The girls would look forward to the occasion every year. 'It was like the biggest family picnic. We'd eat fried Snickers,' Beyoncé later remembered in *Essence* magazine.

Nowadays, a mother at twenty-eight, Solange also looks back at their childhood with affection, insisting it wasn't very different from most people's upbringing. 'My sister and I were not allowed expensive clothes. We so badly wanted these Fila sneakers as kids but my mother took us down to the flea market and got imitation ones,' she said in the *Guardian*. 'Look at the early Destiny's Child videos. You'll see!'

Even if the must-have trainers were out of bounds, the sisters were always the cutest of kids, Beyoncé's shyness balanced by Solange's cheek. One early picture shows them in matching tartan dresses: Beyoncé is gazing serenely into the camera while Solange sticks out her tongue and waves her hands in front of her face.

To earn pocket money, Beyoncé would sweep the floors and sing for tips in Tina's salon, which mostly went towards paying for her season ticket to the famed Houston theme park Six Flags AstroWorld. Although the attraction closed in October 2005, it had the world's first river rapids ride and a roller-coaster called Greezed Lightnin', which Beyoncé adored. She and Solange would add to their funds by putting on shows together at home and selling tickets. 'No one wanted to come to our house because we literally would make stages out of whatever we could find,' Beyoncé told NBC. 'Stacking up stuff. Tore up all the furniture.

Had the boom box sky high . . . And we would make them buy tickets. And they were, like, five dollars. So we had a lot of nerve.'

Aware that both their daughters loved nothing more than performing, Tina and Mathew had a deck built at the back of the house, complete with different levels so that it formed a sizeable stage for the girls. They would try to put on shows every day. Tina says: 'That was a big part of their lives. That was what they loved to do.' Solange also says her sister would be forever practising in front of her mirror. 'I have very, very early-on memories of her rehearsing on her own in her room,' she told *GQ*. 'I specifically remember her taking a line out of a song or a routine and just doing it over and over and over again until it was perfect and it was strong . . . When everybody else was ready to say, "Okay, I'm tired, let's take a break", she wanted to continue – to ace it and overcome it.'

When she was five, Beyoncé's parents took her to a life-changing event – a Michael Jackson show. 'I was five years old – it was my first concert,' she later said on the Australian TV show *Sunday Night*. 'That night I decided exactly my purpose. He's the reason I do what I do. I would have never experienced that magic if it wasn't for him.'

Filmed at around the same time, old home-video footage shows a gap-toothed Beyoncé staging a mini rap about herself, exuding a self-assurance that is alien to most children her age. Clicking her fingers and moving neatly to the rhyme, she sings:

> '*I think I'm bad*
> *Beyoncé's my name*
> *Love is my game*

So take a sip of my potion and do it in slow motion
She thinks she's bad
Baby, baby don't make me mad.'

Mathew and Tina were highly religious and Sundays would always involve a visit to church – where Beyoncé sang in the choir from the age of seven. Initially the family went to a Catholic church, but later switched to St John's United Methodist Church, which became their regular place of worship. Young Beyoncé loved singing gospel too and once told VH1: '[It's] able to touch you and touch emotions that words can't touch. It's so powerful, it affects you. It's the most beautiful music there is.'

When school was over for the year, the girls got together with their cousin Angie Beyincé, to whom they were very close. 'The last day of school, Aunt Tina would pick me up,' Angie told the *Observer*. 'I'd spend the entire summer at [their] house, and then be dropped back home the night before school started again. Beyoncé and Solange loved Janet Jackson,' she remembered. 'We'd talk all night and watch *Showtime at the Apollo*, and my snake, Fendi, would just be crawling around. He'd sit on our heads while we watched TV.' Angie would prove to be a vital part of the 400-strong team behind Beyoncé in future years, becoming vice president of operations at her Parkwood enterprise and also helping her write many of her songs.

Another of Beyoncé's favourite shows was the movie *A Star Is Born* – she was later asked to appear in a remake. 'It's when I became a fan of Barbra Streisand. And I then saw Judy Garland's version of *A Star Is Born* and I realised every twenty to thirty years a new star is born and a new talent represents that generation and era. I didn't think that I would ever get the opportunity to be the star,' she said.

While she was happy and secure at home, Beyoncé's intense shyness made life difficult at school, St Mary's Elementary in Fredericksburg, Texas. The teasing that started over her name sparked insecurities about her appearance and she became a quiet, withdrawn child, afraid even to put up her hand in class. 'I was the type of child always that if someone didn't like me, it killed me,' she once told MTV. 'My whole thing was to wonder why and to fix it.'

Beyoncé was aware that some of the girls resented her because the boys thought she was cute, even though she avoided talking to them. She was so shy she would walk away from them rather than risk having a conversation. She was especially quiet and nervous in class and struggled in many of her subjects. 'Some kids don't have to study hard. I definitely had to study in school,' she wrote in *Soul Survivors*. Maths was a particular bugbear and she added: 'I was scared of the numbers – they intimidated me. So did this boy who sat next to me. He used to call me dumb, and stupid, and ugly. I was already shy, and so I just believed it. I wore boy clothes all the time because I was chunky. He made me feel self-conscious.'

Beyoncé had no idea at this time just how striking she really was. As well as believing she was overweight, she was also convinced that her ears stuck out like Dumbo's. She tried hard to fade into the background and chose clothes that would help her seem invisible. In one school snap, she wears a pinafore dress with a long-sleeved white jumper underneath – a world apart from some of the raunchy costumes she wears on stage today. 'I did everything I could to not draw attention to myself. People form opinions of you no matter who you are and how you look,' she said. 'People thought I was stuck-up . . . Some people misunderstand quietness and shyness – they think you're full of yourself. They don't even give you a chance.'

In an effort to boost their daughter's confidence, Tina and Mathew hired a tutor to help with academic studies and encouraged her to attend school dance classes. Those lessons proved to be the first step on her path to superstardom because her teacher, Darlette Johnson, recognised her potential. Beyoncé has a clear memory of the day when Darlette first heard her sing and revealed in a TV interview: 'She said, "Baby, sing for me. I heard you over there singing to the track. Sing for me." And I did, and she was, like, "You can really sing!" She told me to perform at a talent show and I fell in love with the stage. I owe a lot to her.'

Meanwhile, Darlette recalled: 'I knew she was a star, I knew it. She was at the studio and she was the last one. I was singing a song out of tune and Beyoncé finished the song for me and she hit a note and I said, "Sing it again." She was maybe six or seven and her parents came to pick her up and I said, "She can sing! You know she really can sing!" I put her in some singing and dancing competitions and it's been history ever since. When I heard her sing for the first time I knew she was special.'

It was Darlette who encouraged Beyoncé to take part in a school show singing John Lennon's 'Imagine'. She was just seven years old and so daunted by singing in front of an audience that she almost froze with fear. She was terrified that she wouldn't be able to speak, let alone sing, but as soon as the music started her nerves melted away like magic. 'I was terrified, I didn't want to do it, and she's [Darlene], like, "C'mon, baby, get out there." I remember walking out and I was scared but when the music started, I don't know what happened . . . I just changed.'

Beyoncé had simply found her voice and it sounded as sweet as honey. She blew away the other kids taking part, who included fifteen- and sixteen-year-olds, and brought the audience to their feet in a standing ovation. 'I decided all the world would be my stage,' she said. 'I only felt comfortable singing or dancing. I wanted to be a performer. I was a shy girl until I was performing.'

Hearing her sing 'Imagine' with such power and confidence at the talent show changed something in her parents too. It was then that they truly realised the extraordinary talent their daughter possessed. As Mathew told *Billboard* magazine: 'Her mother and I looked at each other and said: "That can't be our Beyoncé. She's shy and quiet." We didn't know. We were just there to support her, but she was a different person on stage, she wasn't the same Beyoncé that we knew as parents.' Tina also told CBS: 'On stage she came alive and she had all this confidence and I was like, "Wow, who is that?" That's kind of how it started. We encouraged her to do this because it brought out her personality.'

Beyoncé herself explained to *Billboard* how much her world altered when she discovered she could sing. 'I got lost when I got on stage. It was like the most comfortable hour, a place where I could not be shy.' She had found her calling in life, which inspired the whole family. Mathew and Tina entered her in at least thirty talent competitions. Some of these shows were part talent show, part beauty contest – an aspect she didn't much enjoy as she was a natural tomboy. But by now she had become more comfortable with her self-image and won each contest. The shelves in her bedroom were soon groaning under the weight of shiny trophies in all shapes and sizes. 'She never came in second, always first,' said Mathew, proudly. And, as she eloquently put it years later in *USA Today*, she didn't even have to try. 'Everything I've done has come naturally to me. I was in my first talent show at five. I was writing songs at nine . . . It was just in me. I feel like if you were born for certain things, and certain things are in your heart, why not do as much as you're good at, as much as you can?'

Chapter Two

The electrifying moment when she won her first national competition in a Houston theatre happened in 1988 and set the rest of her life in motion. The contest was run by the People's Family Workshop, a high-profile organisation set up to promote the arts in Houston. Winning the Baby Junior Talent category, for the 'seven and unders', was a huge achievement, but Beyoncé took it in her stride. In old video footage of her acceptance speech, her little face peers over the top of the podium as she says, in her strong Texan accent: 'I would like to thank the judges for picking me, my parents who I love. I love you, Houston.' With those final words she blew that kiss into the auditorium as if she were a seasoned pro.

When she returned to the same competition in a guest slot one year later, the show's presenter told the audience of the astounding impression Beyoncé had made previously. 'Every time I said her name I got a terrific round of applause,' she said. And when Beyoncé stepped onto the stage for her guest appearance, she was hardly recognisable as the child of twelve months earlier. As she sang 'Home', a far-from-easy song from the musical *The Wiz*, she wore a Dorothy-inspired costume of blue-sequined pinafore dress over a puff-sleeved white blouse, with full makeup, glittering earrings and her hair glossy and curled. She appeared every inch the young star in the way she looked and sang, especially when she pirouetted and twirled across the stage without getting a note wrong.

Although her talent spoke for itself, Mathew and Tina thought it would be a good idea for Beyoncé to have professional vocal coaching to make sure her voice was tuned correctly and that she did not pick up bad habits. In 1989 they contacted a man called David Lee Brewer, an international opera tenor, who worked with the Houston Ebony Opera and had just started offering private lessons. Unsurprisingly, Beyoncé, whose own voice was classified as mezzo-soprano – a mid-range pitch, the most common female singing voice – wowed David instantly. 'Beyoncé was an eight-year-old cherub when we first met,' he wrote on his website. Tina asked David if he would listen to her daughter sing, which he happily agreed to. When that audition took place a few days later, he was astounded by what he heard. 'The little girl, in a frilly dress and anklets to match, slowly breathed in, and then opened her mouth to start. What she let loose was one of the most impressive sounds I'd ever heard from a child.

'Something about it grabbed me and wouldn't let me go. The sound was molten gold, with a distinguished timbre. What's more, Beyoncé possessed a seemingly innate physical connection to the music. This was more than just a voice, I thought, it was a spirit. She and I bonded instantly over our mutual passion for singing.'

At one stage, David even moved into an apartment above the

family's garage and, with his expert guidance on tap, Beyoncé's voice became even more polished. Her parents bought her a kara-oke machine with which she attempted to better the efforts of some of her R&B inspirations. 'Karaoke was my joy,' she revealed to the *Guardian*. 'I would be with it all day and tape myself over other people's songs and occasionally rewrite the words.'

But as she began performing more frequently on the talent-show network, she needed a way of dealing with the nerves that always plagued her before going on stage. That was when her alter-ego, Sasha Fierce, was born. An imaginary persona she would adopt whenever she sang in public, Sasha was a gutsy, no-nonsense figure, whose voice was richly powerful and who was immune to the harshest of critics. Her cousin Angie came up with the name, and Beyoncé confessed in a TV interview with ABC News how the tactic saved her from the intense pressure she was under as a child. 'Sasha is so confident and is fearless and can do a lot of things that I can't do,' she later explained. 'She protects me. In my mind I'm saying, "Okay, take over, take over, take over. I'm Sasha, I'm Sasha." I have to psych myself out when I'm terri-fied.' Crucially, Sasha was to be an ever-present part of Beyoncé's life until 2010, when she made the big decision to 'kill her off'.

Beyoncé continued to scrape by at school, where one of her key roles was to look out for her kid sister Solange, who was several years below. 'I can't tell you how many boys and girls [in junior high school] can say Beyoncé came and threatened to put some hands on them if they bothered me,' Solange confided in *GQ*.

Such a bond may be rare, but Beyoncé has frequently spoken of her feelings for her sibling, telling *Harper's Bazaar*: 'I have always been the big sister. I am five years older than Solange and just always felt the need to love and protect her. I never had it in me to fight with my sister. We are very different in what we like and how we do things but those differences added to our friendship. The love I have for her is indescribable.'

'She has always – since I was a baby – been such a nurturer and caretaker, and so protective of me,' Solange said.

'Disrespect my sister, and I will go completely crazy on you,' agreed Beyoncé.

In 1990, nine-year-old Beyoncé enrolled at Parker Elementary School in Houston, which was famed for nurturing musical talent in its students. But while most of her peers were more concerned with handing in their homework on time than planning a music career, Beyoncé was of a different species entirely: she had already made up her mind that she would be a famous singer. Not content to stay in the little league of local talent contests and beauty pageants, her starry ambitions began to accelerate rapidly when she struck up a close bond with a classmate called LaTavia Roberson. 'We met up in elementary school, and basically grew up together,' LaTavia told *Black Beat* magazine.

The pair loved singing together, and when they heard about auditions for a new kids' band for girls in the city, Mathew and Tina took them to try out. After wowing the judges with their infectious harmonies, Beyoncé and LaTavia were put in a group with three other girls and given the title 'Girls Tyme'. LaTavia told MTV many years afterwards: 'There were a lot of girls – I mean a lot of girls – but out of sixty-five girls, Beyoncé and I made it.' Completing the line-up were LaTavia's cousins, sisters Nikki and Nina Taylor, and another girl called Ashley Támar Davis. The structure of Girls Tyme changed regularly over the following months, with different girls swapping in and out, but perhaps inevitably it was Beyoncé who took the role as lead vocalist.

When the band was put together, an enterprising woman called Andretta Tillman chose to invest some money in the girls in exchange for managing them. Soon afterwards, LaTavia introduced another friend to the Girls Tyme equation. She was called Kelly Rowland and would not only turn out to be a key member of the group but one of the most important figures in Beyoncé's life to date. LaTavia and Beyoncé regularly began meeting up with Kelly and the girls would head to the local pool, play Barbies or build tents in their backyards. Kelly was a big Whitney Houston fan and would always launch into her songs as they played together. It was on hearing her tuneful voice that LaTavia suggested Kelly audition for Beyoncé's parents and, when she did, she was swiftly recruited into Girls Tyme.

Kelly, whose birth name was Kelendria, had recently moved to Houston from Atlanta with her mother. Seven months older than Beyoncé, she had shown a similar early aptitude for singing after joining a church choir aged just four. And, just like Beyoncé, she dreamed of being famous, like her idol Whitney Houston. But Kelly hailed from a difficult background: her mother, Doris, had walked out on her heavy-drinking father, Christopher, because of his ferocious temper. Money was always tight, and Doris struggled to make ends meet as a live-in nanny. After relocating to Houston, Kelly rarely saw Christopher and she later spoke of her sadness over their separation. 'I would look at kids at school and see their dads pick them up and that was something I missed. Every little girl wants to be a daddy's girl,' she told the *Daily Mail*.

'Music was my escape. It still is. I probably felt like I missed out not having a father.'

Still, Kelly was warmly welcomed into the bosom of the Knowles clan and it wasn't long until she was staying over several nights a week. She and Beyoncé would be up late into the night, giggling and swapping stories, and the pair enjoyed regular sing-alongs with Mathew and Tina. Writing in the Destiny's Child autobiography many years later, Kelly revealed that sharing a room with Beyoncé was like having a slumber party every single night – although she pointed out that it was always a rather noisy one.

With Kelly on board and Andretta's encouragement, Girls Tyme began practising together whenever and wherever they could, fitting high-intensity rehearsals around their school time-tables. Singing and rapping to pop and R&B tunes, they managed to break several of Mathew and Tina's precious artefacts and even a glass cabinet door as they high-kicked and leap-frogged around the family's front room. The girls also tested their high-octane routines on Tina's clients at her Headliners salon on Montrose Boulevard, occasionally receiving generous tips for their efforts. As Tina cut her clients' hair, Mathew would direct the girls' moves, then ask the customers for honest feedback. 'The customers sometimes didn't want to listen,' Tina confided in *Texas Monthly*. 'The girls would call out, "Put your hands together!" Customers would be rolling their eyes. That was a tough audience.'

Always eager to learn new steps, the girls spent their spare time watching old music videos to pick up tips from the likes of the Jackson Five and the Supremes. And realising that image was key, if they were to catch the beady eye of any music executives, Tina stepped in to style them at Headliners, while also designing colourful costumes for them. They were becoming the perfect little pop package.

Although it was hard work, Beyoncé has always been keen to stress that the focus was then on having a good time, insisting that her parents weren't overbearing or as pushy as many have since suggested. 'I thought of rehearsing as fun,' she wrote in *Soul Survivors*. 'It was my time to create dance routines and vocal arrangements. It seemed like playtime.'

In 1991, Kelly moved in permanently with the Knowles family and began calling Tina 'Aunt' and Mathew 'Dad'. It was an arrangement that suited everyone. 'My mom was working as a live-in nanny,' she later told *Interview* magazine. 'We were rehearsing every day, and with my mom's schedule, she couldn't really take me back and forth to all the rehearsals. So in order to make it work, my mom asked Tina, "Could Kelly stay with you for the summer?" And the summer turned into . . . how long? But it was like a big ol' happy family because my mom came over every night to kiss me good night. I say I have three parents – Tina and Mathew and my mom – three wise people to help me.'

Clearly, Beyoncé's parents adored Kelly as one of their own, and Tina admitted later: 'Kelly has been a great joy in my life. I'm going to be so sad the day that she moves out.' Despite incessant claims that she and Mathew had adopted Kelly or become her legal guardians, Tina always denied this. 'All those rumours are so crazy,' she scoffed, in *Ebony* magazine. 'Kelly's mom had a key to our house and to our car. Most weekends she stayed with us. She has been a part of Kelly's life every day.'

Beyoncé was now closer than ever to her best friend. 'We were sleeping in the same bed, waking up every morning, singing all day and loving every minute of it,' she told *Blender* magazine. They also got up to no end of mischief, and in an appearance on Graham Norton's chat show when she was much older, she giggled while telling the host: 'We were bad little kids but we had fun . . . We took all the mattresses out of the house and made slides, and made swings out of the curtains. We would try to trap little kittens in the house – my mom came home and there was like twenty cats running round the house!'

The pair fuelled each other's aspirations and it was around this time that Beyoncé voiced a detailed list of her future goals on a home video. Rather than simply stating that she wanted to be a pop star, she declared, in surprisingly technical detail for one of her age, that her aim was to make a gold album, record a platinum follow-up, then write and produce a third album. Nobody – not even Mathew and Tina – could ever have foretold that she would achieve all three wishes before she was twenty-one.

Certainly, her peers at school had no idea about the secret plans bubbling away in her mind, because she chose to keep her talents hidden from her classmates. As a pupil at Welch Middle School, she was as shy as ever and quietly knuckled down to her subjects, even if they did not engage her brain. She was keen to stay out of the limelight after her cousin Angie had starkly warned her that other girls might feel threatened by her and cut off her long hair if they found out about her sideline in singing. This had such an effect on Beyoncé that she wore her hair in a bun for the first six months at the school. It was only after lessons ended and she dashed to rehearse with Girls Tyme that her true personality came out.

Outside school, devout Beyoncé still found time to drop in at St John's United Methodist Church every week, and it was there, in 1993, that Kelly introduced her to a handsome boy called Lyndall Locke. At thirteen, he was a year older, but the pair got on instantly and began meeting up after school whenever her rehearsal schedule would allow. Almost every night they would chat on the phone at length before going to sleep, often nodding off with the receiver still in hand. At weekends, they loved going to watch the latest movies, or would just hang out at her house, watching music videos and playing Connect Four. After a year of friendship, Lyndall formally asked Beyoncé to be his girlfriend and she happily agreed – although little changed as their 'dates' remained very innocent. In the end, they were an item for seven years and Beyoncé said later: 'At that age, that was a long time. I've always been very loyal and a little more mature.'

Meanwhile, Lyndall told the *Sun* just how smitten he had been, likening her to an angel and calling her the most beautiful girl he had ever seen.

But in the early stages, Beyoncé decided not to tell Lyndall about her double life as a singer, fearing he might think her arrogant or ridiculous. 'She was just so shy, she was a bit of an outcast at school and didn't even sing in the choir. For two years I didn't know she could sing,' he said. Still, he had worked out that she was a good dancer after watching her and Solange try out endless routines at the family home.

Although they might have been love's young dream at the time, Beyoncé played down their relationship in later years, saying her first kiss with him 'sucked'. She told *Elle* magazine: 'It was terrible. I was gritting my teeth shut so he couldn't stick his tongue down my throat . . . I told Kelly that it was the worst thing in life.' Lyndall's recollection of the kiss could not have been more different. He later told the *Sun* he had taken Beyoncé to a concert when he dropped a tub of popcorn on the floor. 'As we both went down to grab it, we bumped heads and locked into our first kiss. We both just looked at each other, realising there was this incredible spark of fireworks between us. It was that fairytale kiss you only hear about in the movies. That was the first feeling of true love between me and Beyoncé. Still, to this day, I've never had another kiss as passionate as that one.'

Regardless of his memories, Beyoncé was less than complimentary about Lyndall in an interview with *COSMOgirl* magazine. 'My first boyfriend sucked. He just wasn't right. We talked on the phone, and it was like, "Hello?" "Hello." "What are you doing?" "Nothing." It really stank. He was boring and didn't have any ambition.'

Although she was fond of Lyndall in the early years, Beyoncé refused to let him get in the way of her bigger plan. And while her parents were fairly relaxed about her having a boyfriend, they were strict about what went on under their roof. Ever since the girls were born, the Knowleses had always drummed a keen sense of morality into Beyoncé and Solange, which was reflected in their musical projects. In those early days, Tina was adamant that there were to be no profanities or any sexual behaviour when they sang.

After many more months of intensive practice and a level of dedication that belied their years, Girls Tyme landed a series of low-key gigs, including a slot at the Miss Black Houston Metroplex Pageant. And it was around this time that they began to get noticed. Crucially, an R&B producer called Arne Frager flew into the city to see them and was highly impressed with the girls' commitment, as well as their vocals and slick dance moves. Notably, it was Beyoncé's voice and personality that most intrigued him. After whisking the group to his Californian base, he decided they needed large-scale public exposure if they were to win a record deal, so signed them up for a major national TV talent show called *Star Search*. As a forerunner to shows like *The X Factor* and *American Idol*, *Star Search* was broadcast throughout the eighties and nineties and saw a panel of four judges awarding stars to competing acts. As well as Beyoncé and her Girls Tyme bandmates, other wannabe performers on the show over the years included a very young Alanis Morissette, Britney Spears, Justin Timberlake and Jessica Simpson, who all went on to achieve enormous worldwide success.

Wearing brightly coloured macs with matching shorts and shiny, customised boots, Girls Tyme sashayed and rapped across the stage, but in the end something did not gel and they were not up to scratch. They were narrowly beaten, losing out by just one star to a craggy metal band called Skeleton Crew. They were, of course, despondent, and Beyoncé later recalled their agony in the face of the rival act: 'We bit back our tears and wore the fakest smiles on our lips,' she said. After the show ended, it all proved too much to take and the girls ran backstage and burst into floods of tears. But on watching back their performance, they were all saying: 'We messed up.' LaTavia later suggested that the choice of song had been wrong for their young voices. 'They made us do a rap song, although we wanted to sing,' she said. 'They even made a new hip-hop category for us. Looking back on it now, though, it was a learning experience we'll never forget.'

Beyoncé reflected on that pivotal day much later, in a video she released simultaneously with her 2013 album *Beyoncé*, saying: 'It was a really defining moment in my life as a child. In my mind, we would perform on *Star Search*, we would win, we would get a record deal, and that was my dream at the time. There's no way in the world I would have imagined losing as a possibility. I was only nine years old, so at that time you don't realise that you could actually work super-hard and give everything you have, and lose. It was the best message for me.'

She added: 'The reality is, sometimes you lose. You're never too good to lose; you're never too big to lose; you're never too smart to lose. It happens. And it happens when it needs to happen. You have to embrace those things.'

Following that defeat, the girls could have been forgiven for thinking that their dream was over before it had even got going. But ever-optimistic Mathew had very different ideas. He had seen a glimpse of a dazzling future for his daughter and was not prepared to give up without a fight. During a lecture at Thornton School of Music at the University of Southern California in 2011, he said: 'For some reason, the ones that lose on *Star Search* re-dedicate, change their organisation, and they go on to be successful.'

To make this a reality, he decided he had to be more involved and begged Andretta to let him co-manage the girls. While she was initially reluctant, it has been said that Mathew threatened to withdraw Beyoncé from the group unless she relented. Andretta passed away some years later, having suffered from lupus for many years, but her brother Lornonda Brown says she had no choice but to agree to share the management responsibilities with

25

Mathew. 'She knew she had to,' he said. 'Mathew's daughter was his trump card.'

Now he was at the helm, Mathew knew he needed to start from the very beginning with the band – especially as they had recently gained a new recruit in the shape of LeToya Luckett, a girl in Beyoncé's class at elementary school who had talent. In an interview with the *Independent*, LeToya said: 'Bey found out I could sing when we were both auditioning for *Pinocchio*. We shared the lead part in the school play and learned the songs and the little dance routines together.'

With the new member offering the group a fresh dimension, Mathew and Andretta decided on a drastic cull of the original line-up. Scaling back from seven to just four members, the new-look group consisted of Beyoncé, LeToya, Kelly and LaTavia. Each girl showed off a different quality and at last they had the whole vocal spectrum covered. Kelly had a broad range, which worked well on upbeat numbers; LaTavia could hit the bottom notes with her rich voice; LeToya's soprano was capable of reaching giddy heights; as for Beyoncé, she had cultivated powerful, soulful tones that sent a shiver down the spine of anyone within earshot.

As they got to grips with life as a foursome, the real hard work commenced. Mathew meant business from the word go: this was no longer about a group of girls simply having fun. Over the following eighteen months he worked them extremely hard on mini 'bootcamps' and would send them to Houston's parks before school, where they would sing while jogging so they could learn not to become breathless during physical exertion. They began following low-fat diets, and Beyoncé would typically eat frozen

Lean Cuisine meals and sugar-free Jell-O for dinner instead of the calorific fried foods she adored. The girls were also instructed to practise their energetic dance routines in high heels, leading to a few twisted ankles. 'Every time he pushed me, I got stronger,' Beyoncé said later of Mathew's regime. She also told how they had to make many sacrifices, such as giving up cheerleading. As for social events with school friends, there was little chance. 'My life was work. I didn't really even go to a prom,' she told the *Daily Telegraph*. 'Well, I went to my boyfriend's prom, as his date. But I didn't know anyone there, and I had to be home early!'

As part of his grand plan, Mathew worked with the girls on composing their own songs as well as singing covers. For Beyoncé, the inspiration for writing lyrics came from Tina's hair salon, where she would eavesdrop on the clients' conversations about their wayward men. 'Women in a hair salon are more open than men in a barbershop,' she told *Elle*. 'They'll look at fashion magazines and listen to Anita Baker and talk about men cheatin' on them. That's juicier than any barbershop.' Mathew also made it compulsory for them to perform at a local venue, such as a school, church or fashion show, at least once a week – and more often in school holidays. 'There was nothing too small or too large,' he said in *Forbes* magazine. 'Repetition, repetition. Beyoncé has always had such passion about music that she never complained about doing it again.'

They even performed at Beyoncé's favourite theme park, Six Flags AstroWorld, on several occasions – though she had one of the most humiliating experiences of her life while on stage there. Reliving the torturous moment with chat-show presenter Graham Norton, she said: 'I had my peers in the audience and it was freezing cold, and my face was numb. Before you know it, I can see something kind of blowing up. My nose is really red . . . and it's a huge snot bubble. It was in the middle of the performance and I ran off stage to fix myself up, but all my friends saw it. It was terribly embarrassing.'

But while many have claimed Mathew worked the girls too hard, Beyoncé maintains that it was always her choice, telling *Scholastic Action* magazine: 'When I was younger, a lot of people were going to parties. I was focused in the studio. When other kids were out playing, I wanted to be inside writing songs and practising dancing.'

Using his growing book of contacts, Mathew managed to convince a highly influential A&R woman from Columbia Records, Teresa LaBarbera Whites, to fly from New York to Houston to listen to them sing at a Jewish community centre. But it did not go according to plan: the girls had gone swimming together the day before and had nasal vocals as a result. During a video of their performance for Teresa, unhappy Mathew can be heard stopping them mid-song before chiding them: 'I don't really care if Teresa is here. See the price you're paying for going swimming?'

In later years, LeToya revealed how difficult she had found the regime. 'It was demanding to be in a serious band so young,' she told the *Independent*. 'We had to go to singing lessons at six a.m. and we sacrificed part of our childhood. We were pulled out of school in the sixth grade, so we didn't get to go to the prom or do any of that homecoming-queen stuff. It was exciting, though. We were very keen and focused for a bunch of kids.'

All equally devout, the girls held joint prayer sessions to ask God to help them get a record deal, echoing the famously strict beginnings of the Jackson Five. 'We used to call [Mathew] Joe Jackson,' LaTavia once confessed. 'He was very strict. Beyoncé was the only one brave enough to stand up to him.' Perhaps the most scathing of all the girls about their regime, she also said: 'We worked really hard. It was rehearse, rehearse, rehearse. It would be the four of us and he was like a drill sergeant. When summertime came he would start a camp at his house in Houston. He would make us wake up early in the morning and take us to Herman Park. There was a three-and-a-half-mile track and we would sing while we jogged around it. Then we would go to the house and rehearse. That's what our days consisted of, seven days a week. Looking back, working that hard did cost us our childhood. But at the time we were just focused on living out our dreams.'

Chapter Three

At the age of thirteen, Beyoncé had enrolled at the prestigious Houston School for the Performing and Visual Arts, where pictures from her yearbook show she was blossoming into a naturally beautiful young woman. With flawless skin, a gleaming white smile and braided hair, she could have passed for a model.

But to her, music always mattered far more than appearance, and as she and the other girls continued their academic studies, Mathew was frantically trying to bag them support-act gigs for more established R&B groups on the live music scene. Eventually his work paid off: they were invited to audition for several labels, including Elektra, where they met a producer called Darryl Simmons. Grainy video footage from that audition shows the four girls wearing beige jeans and black vest tops, performing a neatly choreographed routine to their song 'Wide Open'. Crucially, their vocals sounded much tighter than in the past and the effect was more polished and grown-up. After years of plugging away, the girls and Mathew were thrilled when Darryl reported back to Sylvia Rhone, a key figure at Elektra, who had previously signed the hugely successful group En Vogue. As with most others who heard the girls sing, Sylvia found that Beyoncé's voice stood out and she instructed Darryl to sign them up, with Beyoncé the band's focal point.

Shortly afterwards, the group was flown some eight hundred miles to Atlanta, where Darryl was based, and taken to a studio where they started laying down vocals for an album. They lived together in a small house, with Darryl's assistant, and the trip had the feel of summer camp, but it meant the girls missing a lot of school. This was a worry for all of their parents and, for the first time, private tutors were brought into the mix. However, after a few months, catastrophe struck. No release date for any album had been discussed and it seemed that Elektra was dragging its heels. In the end, a letter arrived from a senior figure at the label, advising them that the band was being dropped. *Essence* magazine reported that the executives had had a dramatic change of heart and now thought the girls were 'too young and underdeveloped' to progress.

The frustration of being axed so prematurely was heartbreaking, and Beyoncé told *Q* magazine many years later: 'We thought the world was at an end.' At the height of their global domination in 2002, Kelly looked back on it more humorously: 'I hope whoever worked at Elektra and made the decision to let us go watched the 2000 Grammy Awards.'

Back in Houston, the disappointing news sparked a major reaction in Mathew: he resigned from his six-figure pharmaceutical sales job so he could manage the band full time. 'That was the defining moment, when they were dropped by Elektra,' he said. 'I quit my job and everyone thought I was nuts.' Mathew's commitment to his profession had been waning for some time. 'I was in corporate America for twenty years and eighteen of those years were phenomenal,' he told *Empower*. 'But the last two years, I didn't have the passion for it any more and knew I was transitioning.' His choice to leave that world behind was made easier for him when it emerged that his co-manager, Andretta, was becoming increasingly weakened by lupus.

He also made another vital decision about the band's future. Believing 'Girls Tyme' sounded too young, it was time to reinvent the group with a new name. Among the suggestions were 'Somethin' Fresh' and 'Borderline', but they failed to stick, as did 'Cliché' and 'Da Dolls'. Then 'Destiny' was suggested – but that had already been taken. Finally, they chose 'Destiny's Child', with Beyoncé revealing how it came about: 'Whenever I'm confused about something I ask God to reveal the answers to my questions, and he does. That's how we found our name – we opened up the Bible, and the word "destiny" was right there,' she told *Interview* magazine.

LaTavia elaborated: 'One day Beyonce's mom was about to read the Bible and she opened it up to read a scripture in Isaiah. Our picture fell out. Under our picture in bold-faced print was the word "destiny". We felt that God was sending us this name. We found out that a lot of groups had the name, so we had "child", as a rebirth of destiny.'

Although everyone was excited about their new direction, Mathew's sudden walk-out from his job had severe implications for the Knowleses' financial situation. But such was his devotion to Beyoncé's cause that he and Tina mutually agreed to sell the family home to ease the burden on themselves. 'We downsized our house to an apartment,' Beyoncé said. 'We downsized our three cars to two and then to one.'

Tina found the strain on the family hard to cope with, revealing in a frank interview with CBS: 'It was very stressful, because we went from having two really great incomes to having one. We had to scale down our house, sell our cars. It was a really tough time for us.' Unsurprisingly, many of the couple's friends questioned their decision, and she admitted: 'People thought we were nuts, they really thought we were crazy.'

There was yet more bad news when the family got hit with tax problems. 'Everything kinda came crashing down,' Tina told *Rolling Stone* magazine. 'We had to sell our house for way less than we could've gotten if we'd had time to sell it right. It was very emotional, because my kids grew up in that house, and they were not happy at all.' There was more turmoil prior to moving into the new apartment when Mathew found out that the previous tenant had committed suicide in the bathroom.

Recalling the new domestic set-up at the Knowleses', LaTavia later said: 'Mathew and Tina would share one room and Beyoncé, her sister Solange and Kelly would share the other. They had two single beds with pull-outs underneath. Looking back, it must have been stressful for the family.'

To bring in a little more cash, Tina upped her hours at the hair salon, while Mathew went away for several months to undertake a course in artist management – later enabling him to set up his own multi-million dollar firm, Music World Entertainment. Mathew's decision to manage his daughter and her friends had been inspired by a story he'd heard about Berry Gordy, the president of Motown Records. Berry had achieved incredible success by doing everything in-house at his own studio in Detroit – managing his artists, recording and releasing their music, and marketing them. He did it all. He also focused on teaching his acts how to behave, dress and move. In effect, he showed them exactly how to become superstars.

But the battle to get Beyoncé's career off the ground was all-consuming and led to Mathew and Tina temporarily splitting up. Tina told CBS: 'We separated because at that point I felt like he was a little too driven. I was never in doubt that it would happen but I was like, "You can't just stop life and do this and not take care of the family."' Analysing their situation in more detail in *Rolling Stone*, she added: 'At that point we were just not getting along. I felt like Mathew was obsessed and should go get a job . . . We were just miserable.'

Just as it is for any child, her parents' break-up was traumatic for Beyoncé, and she later admitted: 'It was such a painful time that I erased a lot of those memories from my head.' She turned to her church group for comfort and was often seen crying at St John's as she prayed. When it all got too much, she had learned a mantra, which she would recite over and over, to help her cope: 'God has a plan and God is in control of everything.' It settled her mind, calmed her down and became a motto she used throughout her life.

Her Christian beliefs also helped her cope with the band's numerous ups and downs, and she once told *COSMOgirl* magazine of the time she first felt God's presence. 'I was like the group mother – if there was tension or if someone lied or hurt someone's feelings, it affected me really bad,' she said. 'I was stressed because I knew the group was going crazy. I couldn't sleep and my face was breaking out. One day in church I was crying, and all of a sudden I just let go of everything. It was as though God was saying, "Give it to me." All the stress just lifted off me . . . Afterward I was so at peace for twenty minutes. I felt like I was floating.'

Despite her sadness, Mathew and Tina's split made Beyoncé more determined than ever to get Destiny's Child the recognition they all craved. And it was a trip to San Francisco in 1996 to record a set of demo tapes that finally sparked their breakthrough. With the tapes mailed to dozens of key industry figures, a musician called D'wayne Wiggins from Oakland in California had liked what he heard and immediately signed the group to his company, Grass Roots Entertainment. In a later interview with Soul Train website, D'wayne spoke about that all-important decision to give the band a chance. 'The biggest experience of my life, in terms of the business, was the signing and developing of Destiny's Child,' he said. 'These young ladies were some grown women in young-girl bodies. They were focused and could see the light.'

As part of his investment in the girls, D'wayne moved them into a six-bedroom house in Oakland near his studios, enabling them to start writing and recording. As before, school was out of the question and tutors were hired so they could fit their studies around the music.

Instantly proving herself a natural in such an environment, Beyoncé could not fail to impress D'wayne. Speaking to Soul Train, he recalled a time when he was arranging vocals in the studio, with eager Beyoncé on the microphone. Pitching her a harmony, she responded with a stream of melodies that D'wayne said blew his mind, while she was also 'dancing and throwing her hair like she was in a concert.' He added: 'I was the production and a fan. I loved the experience of meeting the family – Tina, Mathew and

Solange – and I felt the trust and respect. I always felt like, "Wow, they trusted me with their children to look after and produce, as well as making sure that their education was in place."'

Despite D'wayne's commitment to their continued learning, Beyoncé never got her high-school diploma because the band took over her life. Still, it was a small price to pay for what lay ahead. With D'wayne's interest in the group giving them added credibility, Destiny's Child flew to New York in 1997 to try out for a second time with Teresa LaBarbera Whites, who was still at Columbia Records, which had the likes of Bruce Springsteen, Michael Jackson and Mariah Carey on its books. As Beyoncé later admitted in *Soul Survivors*, this was their very last chance and they simply could not afford to throw it away.

Things didn't bode well when the conference room allocated for the audition was not big enough for musical instruments as well as the four girls, so they faced the daunting challenge of sing-ing a cappella. Fortunately, their renditions of 'Ain't No Sunshine' by Bill Withers and their own track, 'Are You Ready?', were note perfect – although Teresa gave them no hint as to how their performance had gone. They headed back to Houston with their fate still horribly uncertain. Teresa had been bowled over, though, and many years later told Songwriter Universe website: 'Beyoncé is an amazing artist, songwriter, producer and performer – she does it all. I've known her since she was a child and have watched her mature into the legendary musical force that she has become. I'm not sure if there's anything much cooler than that.'

An agonising wait over the next few weeks left Beyoncé and the girls distracted and unable to think of much else. Fittingly, they were at Tina's hair salon when they heard the news that

Columbia was to offer them a deal. Tina had playfully hidden the record label's letter in an envelope marked with the logo of a local diner called Luby's, so when she handed it over, Beyoncé was convinced it was merely a voucher for free food. On reading the contents of the envelope, she could barely breathe, let alone speak. 'We started screaming and crying right in the middle of the salon,' she recalled in *Soul Survivors*. 'The ladies with their heads under the dryers looked at us like we were crazy because they couldn't hear what all the yelling was about. We ran around the shop, jumping up and down, holding our contract in the air for all the customers to see.'

Unlike with Elektra, the momentum picked up from the instant they signed on the dotted line. With plenty of songs already written and ready to be brought to life after so many days in studios, the band went to work straight away and their first song was released in July 1997. Called 'Killing Time', it was a ballad, which featured on the soundtrack to the Will Smith film *Men in Black*. They were also assigned their first ever publicist at Columbia, Yvette Noel-Schure – who went on to become a vital part of Team Beyoncé later down the line. Recalling the day she first met the singer at the studios, Yvette told *Out* magazine: 'I saw a very meticulous fourteen-year-old girl. To be so in-the-know at that age – I remember saying: "This is my project. I'm gonna have the time of my life with these girls."' She added: 'This is what I'm always gonna remember about Beyoncé: She takes you in. She looks you straight in the eyes when she's talking to you . . . In those days she was, "Yes, ma'am, yes, ma'am," to me, but she looked me right straight in the eye, didn't blink, it seemed. She really takes you in . . . I saw the boldness of her. To this day, when you talk to her, it's the same thing. And I always say, "Wow, you still do that."'

They also began work on their debut album, to be called *Destiny's Child*, and release dates were eagerly plotted. Knowing their image was vital, Teresa instructed her team to search far and wide for suitable tracks that would not sound too 'girlie' or juvenile. Mathew was also keen for the girls not to be seen as a teenage act, and for many months they pretended to be two years older than they really were. When asked their age in an interview in 1998, Beyoncé even told *Black Beat* magazine: 'We don't know. I'm just kidding! Actually, we're teenagers. The only reason that we don't tell is because older people aren't so interested when they find out how old we are. Our music is diverse, and older people can enjoy it, so we'd rather not be labelled.'

One of the early numbers they recorded, 'No, No, No', was mooted as the first single release from the album, but was then judged too slow. Respected rapper Wyclef Jean, of the Fugees fame, was drafted in to provide an edgier sound, and on its release in early 1998, the renamed song, 'No, No, No Part 2', charted at number three in the US, going platinum, while hitting number five in the UK and number seven in Canada. It was deemed pretty impressive for a brand new group starting out in an intensely competitive field. Beyoncé later told an amusing anecdote about hearing the single on the radio for the first time when she was out with Kelly and her sister, Solange: the two bandmates stopped the car, jumped out and began running around the vehicle as they sang along. Solange was puzzled, Beyoncé recalled, but then 'She dropped her bag and books and started running around the car, too. It was a really cool experience.'

Meanwhile, the welcome change in luck also meant the pressure on Beyoncé's parents eased and they were reconciled, with Mathew moving back into the family's cramped apartment. Delighted as she was with the breakthrough, Tina now had her work cut out in styling the girls, as new outfits were needed on a weekly basis. But on wardrobe matters, there was a distinct clash with the record label. 'I always wanted the girls to be glamorous,' Tina told *Texas Monthly*. 'But for the longest time, nobody at Columbia got us. They'd say, "Tina, these girls, they're so Texas. Can you lay off the makeup and the big hair and high heels?" But I love big hair and makeup. We here are different than anywhere else in the world. Women here are so well put together.'

Styling issues aside, Tina was determined that her daughter's blossoming fame would not go to her head. Such motherly concern led to an amusing public showdown that the Knowles clan would for ever more refer to as 'The Slap'. It happened during a family trip to a record store, during which 'No, No, No Part 2' began playing on the radio. As Beyoncé started singing along loudly to drown out her mother's attempts to talk to her, Tina was furious. Appearing on Piers Morgan's CNN chat show later, Beyoncé recalled: 'She smacked the crap outta me and sent me to the car.' Tina then blasted her: 'I don't care what song you have on the radio. You are my child and you will not disrespect me.' Recalling what happened next, Tina told *Elle* magazine: 'My husband came up and said, "Tina! She's got the number-one record on the radio!" I said, "I don't care!"' Echoing her own mother's words of advice, Tina added: 'You got to be cute on the inside.' Looking back on the encounter, Beyoncé eventually told the *Daily Telegraph*: 'It was the best thing she could have ever done to me because for the first time I realised I was losing sight of what was important.'

With her stark lesson learned, the *Destiny's Child* album eventually hit the shelves in February 1998, some thirty-six months after they had first started working on their debut material. And despite all the gut-wrenching efforts that had gone into such a landmark event, Beyoncé was still just sixteen. She told *Black Beat*: 'It took us two and a half years to do the album. We recorded thirty-three tracks to get thirteen for the album.' She added: 'Before, we would wonder why everything was taking so long. And then we realised that God had a plan for us. Now, unlike most groups, we have grown up together and we love each other. We're sisters at heart.'

Although reviews were mixed, the critics appeared to welcome the latest addition to the R&B scene and the album shifted half a million copies. Such a figure was never going to set the world alight, but it was more than enough to justify Columbia hanging on to them.

The next few months were a whirlwind for the band. As well as touring with Wyclef Jean and playing shows with Dru Hill, LL Cool J and Run-DMC, they were introduced to the concept of international travel, luxury hotels and a clutch of adoring fans – who quickly took to calling the band 'DC' for short. But the biggest sign of their growing stature came when they were invited by the late Whitney Houston to perform at her thirty-fifth birthday party in New York in August 1998. Scrabbling together all their money, the girls bought matching new outfits and when they got to the party, many guests pointed out their similarity to the Supremes, a huge compliment for the girls. Further encounters with megastars followed, including the ultimate R&B diva Mariah Carey – a meeting that Kelly confessed left them all 'in shock'. The girls had always idolised Mariah, with Beyoncé once telling VH1: 'I feel like Mariah Carey's voice comes from God.' The singer's smash hit, 'Vision Of Love', had deeply affected Beyoncé, who was aged just eight on its release in 1990. 'I heard all of these riffs and I was like, "How does she do that?" The amount of notes she could squeeze into one little bar was fascinating to me and that's when I started trying it. She completely inspired me.'

Another hit single came in 1998 with 'Get On The Bus', featuring rapper Timbaland, which appeared on the soundtrack for the film *Why Do Fools Fall in Love*, starring Halle Berry. Then the phenomenally successful Boyz II Men asked Destiny's Child to support them on the first leg of their sold-out Evolution tour. LaTavia recalled: 'Being on tour was very intense. We were girls, we were going through puberty. Hormones were crazy. The schedule would be challenging . . . late nights and early days.' Still getting used to being away from home for extended periods, the girls would switch hotel rooms, according to moods and arguments. 'One week I would be with Beyoncé, the next with Kelly, then LeToya,' said LaTavia. And of the girls' different temperaments, she said: 'LeToya was the jokester, I was the sassy one, Beyoncé was the mamma and Kelly the sensitive one. Watching movies, she'd be the first to cry.'

In fact, Kelly was so gentle-natured that she found the pressure at the top hard to handle at first – especially if she didn't measure up to ever-demanding Mathew's standards. After one very early gig in Atlanta, in which she missed a series of dance steps during one of their routines, he apparently gave her a mammoth dressing-down: 'Where were you tonight, Kelly? I watched you mess up twelve dance steps.' Kelly was distraught, and LaTavia told the *Daily Mirror*: 'Mathew did not mince his words and it can be tough to take that kind of criticism when you are a little girl. We would try not to let it break us. But Kelly was the sensitive one, and sometimes she would go to her room and cry.'

Still, his often brutal management technique did not affect Kelly's loyalty to him and she told *Vibe* magazine: 'He's my hero. Mathew has sacrificed so much for us. He didn't have to take me in. He didn't have to sell his house and his cars for us. He didn't have to give up his life for Destiny's Child.'

Sensing the big-time was just around the corner, Columbia worked with the band to record their follow-up album, *The Writing's On the Wall*, in just two months. Taking the role as band talisman and thriving under intense pressure to get it done on time, Beyoncé wrote and co-produced seventeen tracks, with artists including She'kspere, Timbaland and Missy Elliott. With writing credits on almost every track, her more mature views were starting to come through, with many of the songs focused on empowering women – a key theme for the future. After asking 'Why is it that men can go do us wrong?' in the song 'Hey Ladies', she stressed in a promo interview: 'This album really spells out what will happen in a relationship if people treat each other a certain way. It really shows what's going on.'

Reflecting on how the girls changed between each album, she told *Texas Music* magazine: 'There's a huge growth between sixteen and eighteen when we recorded the albums. That's when you go from being a girl to a young woman. It was natural for us to mature, and you hear it in the music.' Interestingly, on the *Destiny's Child* album cover released just a year before, Beyoncé is positioned at the far edge of the photograph, looking faintly unsure of herself, while the other three girls grin broadly at the camera. However, on the artwork for *The Writing's On the Wall*, she stands at the front, dominating the shot and looking far more confident.

Released in July 1999, the new CD pulsated with a blend of R&B beats and daring harmonies, which resulted in them being likened to En Vogue – a group they'd always loved. 'They're comparing us, which is wonderful,' Beyoncé told the *Washington Post*. 'They had great songs, great routines. We would sit and watch them and pretend to be them.'

Happily for Destiny's Child, *The Writing's On the Wall* was a worldwide triumph, debuting at number six on the *Billboard* chart and selling 132,000 copies in its first week of release. Before the end of 1999, it notched up a further 1.5 million sales and earned the girls a total of six Grammy nominations – of which they won two, for Best R&B Performance by a Group with Vocals and Best R&B Song. Not only that, but *Billboard* later ranked it at number thirty-nine in its rundown of the top 200 albums of the entire decade. The album went on to sell 3.8 million copies in 2000, while it also spawned a succession of four hit singles, including 'Say My Name' and 'Bills, Bills, Bills' – a critique of men using women for money by maxing out their credit cards and using up the petrol in their cars.

Although things were going so well, one source of irritation for the girls was the common assumption that they had found stardom almost overnight. Keen to set the record straight, Beyoncé said in one interview at the time: 'Most people don't realise that we really have dedicated our lives to this. Some people in Houston used to say we were crazy trying to get a record deal because no one's ever really done it from there before. But we are proof that whatever you put your mind to you can achieve. This is just the start for us, believe me.'

With Beyoncé and the girls seemingly on such a high, it would have been hard to foretell that major trouble was brewing, or that after such a short time at the top of their game, *The Writing's On the Wall* would be the last ever work for the band in that guise.

Chapter Four

Peace was well and truly shattered between late 1999 and early 2000, a period that Beyoncé has since referred to as 'The Change'. It began two weeks before the girls were due to shoot the video for 'Say My Name', which, ironically, went on to be their biggest hit yet. Totally out of the blue, LeToya and LaTavia – who had recently turned eighteen – wrote letters to Mathew on 14 December, saying they no longer wanted him to be their manager. The letters allegedly stated: 'As of this moment, please do not transact any further business on my behalf, individually or as a member of Destiny's Child. You do not have any authority to do so.' It was widely reported that they accused him of failing to pay them an equal share of the band's profits and that they felt he was giving preferential treatment to Beyoncé and Kelly. There was a clear fracture between the two girls who lived at the Knowles family home and the two who did not.

Attempts to resolve the spat amicably failed, Beyoncé later telling *Q* magazine: 'We tried everything. Counselling with our church, our youth pastor. Rotating rooms. But it was two and two. Our vision of the group was different from theirs.'

Beyoncé always strongly maintained that each member of the band did in fact receive a fair 25 per cent split of profits, and in the end LaTavia appeared to concede this was true. 'I'm not saying pay cheques were any different,' she eventually told the *Daily Mirror*, '[but] things seemed unfair. Beyoncé and Kelly had cars . . . Matthew used to say a lot of crazy things like, "Y'all should be glad I'm giving you money."'

With the damage done, it was decided that LeToya and LaTavia would leave the band – although Mathew insisted he had not fired them and simply concluded that their 'asking to leave [the manager] was asking to leave Destiny's Child'. Inevitably, eighteen-year-old Beyoncé was badly shaken by this shock development. 'It was a stressful time for Kelly and I,' she told *Q*. 'We were very depressed and hurt.' Having always been nicknamed the group's 'mom' and peacemaker, she admitted that she was so upset about losing her childhood friends that she fell to pieces. 'For two weeks I literally stayed in my room and did not move. I felt like I could not breathe,' she told *Vibe* magazine the following year. 'I had a nervous breakdown, because I just couldn't believe it. And it hurt so bad.'

However, with a new single imminent and a video shoot in the diary, there was no time to waste. New recruits – former backing singer Michelle Williams, nineteen, and Farrah Franklin, eighteen, who had danced in the band's 'Bills, Bills, Bills' video – were swiftly ushered in to replace LaTavia and LeToya. The reshaped group went ahead and filmed the video for 'Say My Name', but that was by no means the end of the matter: LeToya and LaTavia said they only realised they'd been ejected from the band when they first saw the finished video five weeks later. As a result, the pair filed a lawsuit against Beyoncé, Kelly and Mathew, claiming a breach of partnership and financial duties.

Speaking to MTV just weeks after they left the group, LeToya said: 'It's just a real weird feeling, to be with somebody since you were like nine or ten, and then be separated so suddenly.' LaTavia implied there had been problems for a while: 'It was something that had been going on. It was things that we were noticing . . . There were things that were going on that we would look at, and we would talk about it and be like, "That's not right." We'd be, like, "This shouldn't be this way. We should not feel that there is a conflict in interest."' She also told the music channel of their disappointment when they saw how quickly they were replaced in Destiny's Child. 'I was in a car when I got that news, and I was, like, dumbfounded . . . We were told that things were going to be put on hold until everything got settled. Next thing we know . . . Oh, my God, there are two new girls in the group.'

Although Beyoncé and Kelly said little about the incident initially, there was much mud-slinging over the coming months. In the pair's jaw-droppingly candid interview with *Vibe* the following February, Beyoncé stuck the knife in deep: 'LeToya was, like, tone deaf,' she claimed, with Kelly adding that their former bandmate was a rapper, not a singer.

The stinging remarks did not end there, and Beyoncé even let slip that the girls had not seen eye to eye for two years. Although the foursome had been as close as sisters in the beginning days, when things began to sour they had to carry on as normal, knowing their growing rift must not leak out into the media. As a result, Beyoncé admitted they could not reveal they were unhappy in any interviews. They were so desperate not to let their fans down they made a pact not to say anything 'It was like being in a bad marriage when you have kids and you act like you're happy,' she said.

Beyoncé also told *Vibe* that she had written LeToya and LaTavia a letter in the midst of the spat, which read: 'I have shared some of the best moments in my life with the two of you by my side. I have also shared some of the worst . . . I never complained when you didn't sing one note on numerous songs on the album. I've never complained that when I was working my butt off in the studio, as I did on the last album, the two of you were both either sleeping or on your phones approximately 80 per cent of the time.' The magazine said she ended the letter: 'Approximately every three weeks (or less) there is "drama" caused by one or both of you! It has been this way for at least the past two years and I don't deserve this!'

LeToya was furious about being branded idle and hit back: 'We weren't lazy. When it was time to write, when it was time to sing, we were ready to go. I want to put someone on the stand with a Bible and have them say that we didn't work.'

As the insults flew, Kelly told *Q* magazine: 'They were very negative and jealous . . . They weren't able to do leads by themselves. We went to voice lessons because we wanted strong vocals. They wouldn't do that.' In the same interview, Tina Knowles also pointed the finger at LaTavia and LeToya. 'They were late for interviews and photo shoots,' she claimed. 'That's not the philosophy of Destiny's Child. The group is serious about what they do. Nothing comes before DC but God.'

With a lawsuit hanging over the family, months of unpleasant legal wrangling ensued. LaTavia and LeToya eventually agreed to drop their case against Beyoncé and Kelly but continued to pursue it against Mathew. Finally it was settled out of court, with the two ex-band members reportedly receiving $850,000 each and relinquishing all claims to Destiny's Child. Beyoncé attempted to put a positive spin on the whole sorry saga, telling *Newsweek* that it had boosted their record sales enormously. 'Destiny's Child was always very talented,' she said. 'But I think the thing we were lacking was controversy. I think in order for your group to be successful your story has to be interesting. Our story was very squeaky clean, so I thank God for the controversy. I'm happy because it helps me sell records.'

Away from the turmoil behind the scenes, the girls were thrilled when the singer Christina Aguilera invited them to be her opening act during her first headline tour in spring 2000. They leaped at the chance, but disaster struck when Kelly suffered an excruciating injury halfway through one of their sets, breaking several of her toes. Luckily, Solange was able to fill in temporarily. Beyoncé recalled in *Teen* magazine: 'Our costume changing booth was so far away from the stage it was hazardous. Kelly was running full speed, and it was dark, and she ran into a ramp right in the middle of our performance. We heard her screaming and crying, and we were, like, "Oh, my God, she really hurt herself!"'

After a brief respite from scandal, there was yet more upheaval for the group when replacement singer Farrah left in August 2000, just five months after joining them. Gossip columns were filled with reports that being in a world-dominating pop group had become too much for her. When she failed to show up for an

MTV show in Sacramento, citing stomach flu, it was swiftly announced that she had 'moved on'. Disappointed, Beyoncé told *Q*: 'That was such a huge thing for us. It took us nine years to get on MTV. We'd worked so hard to get to that point.'

Like LeToya and LaTavia, Farrah was keen to put across her side of the story and revealed that she had been unhappy at being told to change her image by Beyoncé's mother. 'I had to dye my hair red when it was sandy brown with blonde streaks,' she told *Sister 2 Sister* magazine. 'I hated it.' Farrah also claimed she had been instructed to change her name – ironically from Destiny, saying: 'My middle name is Destiny and I've been going by Destiny my whole life. I never went by Farrah. I had to go by Farrah to be in DC.' She told the same publication that she was instructed to have tanning sessions to deepen her skin tone, Tina reportedly telling her: 'You look prettier darker.'

What's more, she echoed LaTavia and LeToya's comments that the weighting of the group was always in Beyoncé and Kelly's favour: 'It was never equal. Regardless of how much anyone wants to say there's no favouritism, there is going to be favouritism when your whole family is running the show.'

Tackling Farrah's grievances a little later, the band's other new signing, Michelle, branded her claims 'very unnecessary bullcrap that's absolutely ridiculous'. She was also scathing about the issue of image change, saying in *Vibe* magazine: 'You're travelling every day, flying first class, staying in the best hotels, and you're tripping about a hair colour and your name?'

Beyoncé was hugely grateful that Michelle at least was offering Destiny's Child unwavering loyalty; she and Kelly quickly established a very close and long-lasting connection with her. It helped that Michelle had already had experience of the industry: she had been a backing singer for Monica, the teen R&B singer, who enjoyed moderate success Stateside. While she was growing up, Michelle's family had worked in healthcare and she had originally wanted to be an obstetrician. Describing herself as a 'nerdy' child, she told *Cross Rhythms* magazine: 'Growing up, I experienced a lot of hurt. When you try so hard to be accepted, before you know it you're being someone that you're not and that's crazy. I was ridiculed and bullied for being a good student and person. Kids were really cruel. I was skinny and under-developed.'

It was while Michelle was studying at the University of Illinois that music took over her life and she dropped out. She went to audition for Destiny's Child, whom she had met while touring with Monica. 'We were looking mostly for personality, and when Michelle walked in she was perfect,' Beyoncé told *Texas Music*. 'She was beautiful, she went to church, and above all she could sing.' Right away, Michelle was welcomed into the Knowles home, even sharing beds with Beyoncé and Kelly. Then, under Tina's supervision, she started work on cultivating a pop-star look. 'I got my moustache waxed for the first time,' she reminisced in the *Observer*. 'Beyoncé's mom was there to hold my hand because I didn't know what was going on.'

Predictably, though, Michelle faced hostility in the beginning for being the new kid in an already established band. 'When I joined I heard all the talking and negativity. People saying, "Who does she think she is?"' she said. 'But, really, it was a very smooth transition, thanks to Beyoncé and Kelly. To them it wasn't a big issue . . . We went on with the shows and didn't cancel any appearances, and that's a good thing.' Pleased with the band's new arrangement, Beyoncé told *Teen*: 'Vocally, it's the best Destiny's Child has ever been. Even forget vocally. As a group we have so much peace and so much support and so much talent.'

After a traumatic few months, there was much work for the trio to do, and they all knew it was vital to claw back some stability. But, however much she put on a brave face and beamed for the cameras, it remained difficult for Beyoncé to move on because she had become the victim of a widespread blame game. Cruelly targeted on blogs and in the media, she was held responsible for the band's recent fall-out and all the chopping and changing. It was clear that the criticism affected her profoundly and she told *Vibe* bitterly: 'Sometimes I wish my father wasn't the manager, so people would just stop attacking me. Whenever something goes wrong in the group, it's my fault. Blame Beyoncé. Somebody left the group, it's Beyoncé's fault. Kelly broke her toes, it's Beyoncé's fault.'

She also told the *Guardian*: 'I had hate websites, and a lot of pressure, and people blaming everything on me. I was seventeen, eighteen years old, just an innocent person, a kid. That was a hard time for me. My father is my manager and my mother is the stylist, so I felt it was my whole life, and when people were saying all these horrible things I felt that my life was being crushed.'

Not surprisingly, she later called those days the darkest of her career and said she suffered from depression for two years. 'I didn't eat. I stayed in my room,' she told *Parade*. 'I was in a really bad place in life, going through that lonely period: "Who am I? Who are my friends?" My life changed.'

Beyoncé also felt that, for the first time, her life had been opened up to the public, taking her fame to a whole different level. 'It was tough. Before that the media didn't pay attention to me personally. It was just our music. After that, I felt attacked. The way people reacted was different. My privacy was over.'

Making matters worse, her romance with childhood sweetheart Lyndall also came to an end after seven years. Though she never revealed why it finished, Lyndall confessed some years later to cheating on her, because he didn't think he was good enough for her. 'One night, when she was out of town, I went to a bar with friends and ended up sleeping with another woman . . . Beyoncé was the love of my life. Losing her is still my biggest regret,' he lamented in the *Sun*. 'Who cheats on a woman as beautiful as Beyoncé? Well, I am that man and it's something that'll always haunt me.'

Though she hardly needed to worry, the split left her feeling anxious: 'It was hard for me to let go of him,' she said, in the *Parade* interview. 'Now that I was famous, I was afraid I'd never find somebody again to love me for me. I was afraid of making new friends.'

Thankfully, Tina drilled some sense into her young daughter, telling her that with her beauty, talent and temperament she would have no trouble in finding love. Despite her words of encouragement, Tina said that witnessing Beyoncé's pain was devastating. 'That was probably one of the worst experiences of my life,' she confided to CBS. 'Because it was so untrue and she took all the heat for everything.'

With her family's love and bottomless support, Beyoncé was able to pull herself through that bleak period and get her mojo back. It helped that Destiny's Child began notching up some big wins in 2000 – including Artist of the Year at the prestigious

Billboard awards in Las Vegas and a further two gongs at the Soul Train Lady of Soul Awards. Beyoncé's emerging talent as a songwriter was also being recognised, and a company called Hitco Music Publishing signed her up to protect and promote those skills. Hitco was based in Atlanta and had been founded by the highly influential music executive L. A. Reid – who was later a judge on the US *X Factor* alongside Simon Cowell. He was always a huge fan of Beyoncé and called her 'the most talented performer alive'.

In October the same year the band unveiled a new single, 'Independent Women Part I', which was selected to open the soundtrack for the major new *Charlie's Angels* movie, starring Cameron Diaz, Drew Barrymore and Lucy Liu. It went stratospheric, shooting straight to number one on the *Billboard* Hot 100 chart, where it remained lodged for eleven consecutive weeks – earning it an entry in *The Guinness Book of World Records*. The song also debuted at number one in the UK and hit the top of the charts in Canada and New Zealand. With its ballsy lyrics about women not relying on men to buy all their worldly goods, Beyoncé explained that she had written the song in direct response to people misunderstanding 'Bills, Bills, Bills'. 'A lot of people got the wrong idea from the song,' she told *Teen* magazine. 'They thought we were being gold-diggers and Destiny's Child is definitely not about that. We're independent women, and we take care of ourselves.'

Early 2001 saw another raft of milestone achievements, with the girls performing at George W. Bush's inaugural celebrations in Washington. With a perfectly choreographed rendition of 'Independent Women Part 1' and 'Jumpin', Jumpin'', they worked the crowd into a frenzy, with Beyoncé screaming to the Republican faithful: 'I wanna hear you say Bush!' When questioned about her own political motivations, she kept noticeably quiet, but later said: 'I played at the inauguration because there were a lot of kids in the audience that I wanted to reach, that's all. Maybe one day I will speak of my political beliefs, but only when I know what I'm talking about.'

When quizzed further, she seemed to feel awkward about being associated with the Bush administration, telling *Interview* magazine: 'They really, really wanted us to do it, and he's our president. He told us that we have a bigger influence on kids than he does a lot of the time, and he appreciates that we're positive role models.'

Tina was also keen for the girls not to be seen as pro-Republican, adding: 'It wasn't political. The agreement was that the organisers would take down all the signs and everything that was politically connected and that [the girls] would just perform for the kids.' In hindsight, the performance was certainly ironic, given that Beyoncé would later reveal herself to be a staunch Democrat and one of Barack Obama's most vocal supporters.

In February, they got to sing at their first ever Grammy Awards show. 'We were terrified,' Beyoncé recalled in *Faze* magazine. 'Madonna was sitting in the front row and we had to walk down these stairs in stilettos and we were, like, "Oh, God, I hope we don't fall. I hope we sing the right notes!" We were so nervous. We all just looked at each other, held hands, took a deep breath in, exhaled and prayed, right there on the stage thirty seconds before the song started and we killed the performance.' Wearing blue hot pants and bra tops that showed off three surfboard stomachs, they did indeed 'kill it' with a slick medley of 'Independent Women Part 1' and 'Say My Name'.

The ceremony also saw them receive their first ever Grammy gongs, with 'Say My Name' winning Best R&B Song and Best Group R&B Performance. During their acceptance speech, an emotional Beyoncé held Kelly and Michelle's hands on stage and said breathlessly: 'Thank you so much. We are so excited . . . Oh, gosh, I can't believe we're winning a Grammy, ladies!'

The same month, they released the title track from their third album, which proved one of their biggest successes. Called 'Survivor', the song dealt with the unsettling changes the band had recently been through, and they admitted that making it had been an emotional roller-coaster. 'There was so much power in the studio – we knew once we'd recorded it that it was a powerful song. It made you feel like a warrior,' Beyoncé said, in a TV interview. And Michelle told *Billboard* magazine: 'We prayed before that session, and the energy in that session was so high – the room was heated.' She added: 'Words can't describe how we felt. Some of us were crying, others were jumping up and down.'

While it was a huge hit across the world, the song went on to spark yet more controversy for the group because its lyrics referred to the band's earlier bust-up with LaTavia and LeToya. The words read:

> *You thought that I'd be weak without you*
> *But I'm stronger*
> *You thought that I'd be broke without you*
> *But I'm richer*
> *You thought that I'd be sad without you*
> *I laugh harder*
> *You thought I wouldn't grow without you*

> *Now I'm wiser*
> *Thought that I'd be helpless without you*
> *But I'm smarter*
> *You thought that I'd be stressed without you*
> *But I'm chillin'*
> *You thought I wouldn't sell without you*
> *Sold nine million.*

Although for most the track was merely a wry dig at the group's recent dramas, LeToya and LaTavia claimed the lyrics were disparaging and contravened their previous settlement with the band. In February 2002, they filed a federal lawsuit, in which they sought unspecified damages. Acting for Destiny's Child, attorney Tom Fulkerson branded their claims 'ridiculous', and told the *Houston Chronicle*: 'It's unfortunate that the plaintiffs have nothing better to do with their time than to dream up new lawsuits to file. We made a settlement agreement that we knew put things to bed, yet here we are again.'

The news opened up old wounds for Beyoncé, who told *W* magazine: 'It's just sad. I don't want no drama, I don't want no enemies. All I want to do is go into the studio, write my music, do my movies and perform. I'm not trying to hurt nobody, offend nobody. I'm just happy to be here, and it's sad that all this other stuff comes along with it.'

But arguing the case for LeToya and LaTavia, attorney Warren M. Fitzgerald Jr insisted: 'We would like a restraining order and an injunction to prevent further comment that would violate the agreement and any further performance of that song.' Eventually, the case was settled out of court in July 2002, and a statement issued by all parties read: 'The former members of Destiny's Child, LeToya Luckett and LaTavia Roberson, along with Music World Entertainment, Mathew Knowles, Beyoncé Knowles, Kelendria Rowland and T. Michelle Williams . . . have amicably resolved all of their outstanding differences . . . LeToya and LaTavia are satisfied that justice has been served.'

Aside from leading to a lawsuit, the 'Survivor' single won the group their second consecutive Grammy for Best Group R&B Performance, while its video thrust Tina's skills as stylist firmly into the spotlight. The girls had flown to Mexico for the shoot, but somewhere along the way their outfits had been lost in transit. The ever-resourceful Tina did not panic and merely headed to an army store where she snapped up military print vests, crop tops, shorts and bandannas. With these she fashioned a unique, sexy look for the girls, which suited the video's punchy theme and jungle backdrop perfectly. Their rapper friend Wyclef Jean later asked Beyoncé who had styled them in the promo and when she replied, 'My mom', he advised: 'She needs to style you all the time.'

Although in the beginning Tina dressed the girls purely to save money, she had now proved herself more than worthy of doing it to a professional level, and nobody would hear of them hiring a more experienced stylist to take over. On another occasion in South Africa, two years later, Beyoncé was asked to perform at an AIDS awareness concert. Tina realised at the last minute that her daughter's outfit for the Cape Town show was unsuitable, and dashed to a local fabric market. She cut out a dress 'free-hand', which Beyoncé teamed with a vibrant headscarf. 'It turned out beautifully,' Tina told *Ebony*. 'We kept the dress as a souvenir; we have a picture of Beyoncé wearing it with Mr Mandela. That time I surprised myself.'

As an album, *Survivor* proved a worldwide smash, peaking at number one in America, Britain, Holland, Belgium, Germany and Canada. In the US alone it went quadruple platinum, selling four million copies. It also broke records for having bigger first-week sales than those of any other female group in history. In the UK, Destiny's Child had become the first American female group to have a number-one album since Diana Ross and the Supremes twenty-four years previously. Comparisons to Diana Ross, one of her childhood idols, inevitably followed but that had its down-side. 'That sounds cool, because she's wonderful and glamorous,' Beyoncé told *COSMOgirl*. 'But people don't mean it in the nice way. They call me that because I'm the lead singer, so they think I'm a diva and go around kicking people out of the group.'

Somewhat comically, it was said that the album title had been inspired by a DJ comparing the band to contestants on the TV show *Survivor*, as they seemed to be voting each other out one by one. Working together in the studio as a trio for the first time, the girls had been anxious about getting the new sound right, with Kelly confessing: 'We went in and we prayed, and we put our best foot forward and got *Survivor*.' Showcasing her gift for songwriting, Beyoncé wrote and produced almost every track on the CD – although she admitted that was not the origi-nal brief. 'I only wanted to do, like, three songs,' she told MTV. 'The label kept saying "Do another song, do another song, do another song." It wasn't planned. It wasn't like I said, "OK, I'm going to take charge."'

Overall, the fifteen-track album showed a great maturing. It tackled subjects such as domestic violence and abuse, taking the band's pro-women theme to a higher level. Mathew stressed that this was all part of his grand scheme. 'When we put the group together, we had a plan,' he told *Texas Monthly*. 'We figured out our demographic, our customers, our imaging, what type of songs we're going to sing. It's not by accident that we write songs like "Independent Women" and "Survivor" – female-based empowerment songs. That's our customer base.'

The next single release from *Survivor* in May 2001 was another epic: the catchily named 'Bootylicious', which Beyoncé had written on a plane. Explaining to MTV how it had come to be, she said: 'We were bored [on] this long flight to London, and I was, like, "You know what? I gotta do something." I'd listened to this Stevie Nicks track and I'm, like, "This is hot!" and the word "Bootylicious" just popped in my head. I was ashamed to tell Kelly and Michelle 'cause I didn't know what they were going to think.'

But the others loved what she had come up with. In the studio, they added a guitar riff from the song that had provided the inspiration, Stevie's 'Edge Of Seventeen', and the rocker even appeared in the video for 'Bootylicious' – along with Beyoncé's sister Solange in a cameo role. The raunchy promo was built around three minutes of the scantily clad band 'booty shaking' – which was to become Beyoncé's signature move in the coming years. But in an age where the bounds of female sexuality were being pushed further and further back, the song and its underlying message provoked much debate. Beyoncé herself maintained that there was no hidden agenda: 'The meaning of the song is just confidence. "Bootylicious" doesn't necessarily mean you have to have a big booty. It's all about attitude and feeling good about yourself and not looking like everybody on TV. You do not have to be small – you can have some junk in your trunk.'

Elaborating further, she revealed that the song was also a response to people saying she had put on weight, which she decided to both celebrate and mock in the track. Regardless of what anyone thought of 'Bootylicious', there was no denying the song's cultural significance: the word gradually became so commonly used that in 2008 it entered the *Oxford English Dictionary*. Its description read: 'sexually attractive, sexy; shapely'. However, the word began to grate on Beyoncé, and some time later she said: 'It's really silly . . . To be honest, I hate the word.' She also admitted: 'Everywhere I go, everybody is saying, "booty-this" and "booty-that" and it's really irritating.'

Chapter Five

She might have been working harder than ever, but Beyoncé still headed back to Houston as often as she could, aiming to spend a couple of days a month at home. While in the city, she cherished the opportunity to do 'normal' things, even if that meant just going downtown to buy toothpaste or candy bars. As she revealed in *Elle*: 'I go to Walmart with no makeup, in jeans and a T-shirt, and walk around my mom's shop with no shoes on.' For her, coming home meant the chance to reconnect with her lost youth. 'I still like roller-coasters, talking on the phone and being silly. I like when people are silly because then I can be silly,' she told *Film Monthly*.

For all her fame and new-found wealth, she'd missed out on a conventional childhood, which evidently still bothered her at times. 'I had a tutor, which is very serious and boring, nor was I ever a cheerleader or went to games or any of those things,' she said. 'So when I'm able to, I want to do stuff that is fun. I've had the responsibility since I was fifteen of someone who is twenty-five or thirty, so now I have a lot of pressure. I employ a lot of people, I make a lot of adult decisions, and that has forced me to grow up a little faster.'

When 'chilling' in Houston, she loved getting stuck into Tina's home cooking. 'My mother is the best cook in the world,' she often stated. 'She makes the best Creole food – gumbo, jambalaya, soul food . . . When I go home I want to be babied, I want my mum to cook.' Another treat was to join her old friends for dinner at her favourite restaurant, This Is It. Frequently chiding herself for being hopeless in the kitchen, she would allow herself an occasional 'pig out' on specialities such as cornbread, mac'n'cheese and fried chicken. In spite of her spiralling wealth, Beyoncé's passion for fast-food chicken was so notorious that she was rewarded for her regular custom at the Popeyes chain. Admitting her guilty pleasure on Oprah Winfrey's show, she once said: 'At one point everywhere I went people would buy me Popeyes. They heard and gave me lifetime membership . . . I can pull out the card and get as much as I want. But I've never used it because I'm too embarrassed.' But such was her love for Popeyes' chicken that she even served it at her wedding in years to come.

Beyoncé was fiercely proud of her Texan roots, and Houston was always where she felt most comfortable to kick back and be herself. 'When I get the chance I usually just chill out at home. It's nice just to not have to dial nine before I call out,' she said. During visits home, she and Kelly would take great pleasure in reliving their childhood excursions to the Galleria, a local shopping mall with more than three hundred stores and huge branches of Macy's and Saks Fifth Avenue: 'Sometimes it can get a little crazy, because people recognise you, but usually they just leave us alone,' Kelly told Texas Music. 'But I would rather be recognised than not.'

Every homecoming was vitally important for Destiny's Child because it gave them a chance to reconnect with their beloved church, St John's. Occasionally, the girls were known to fly into Houston late on a Saturday night just so they could attend Sunday's service, flying out again straight afterwards. 'St John's is my home,' Kelly once said. 'I love St John's. I know I can't make my own path, so I leave it to God.' Beyoncé, too, would always squeeze in a service at the church when she had any downtime, insisting it 'keeps me sane'. The girls' pastor at the time, Rudy Rasmus, told the *Observer*: 'It's a real special place. We started with nine folk, nine years ago; now it's four thousand six hundred. Even though it's a large community, it's really like a small town.' He added: 'The girls grew up here . . . There's no spotlight on them. Folks leave them alone.'

When one interviewer from *Vibe* magazine met Beyoncé at the church in 2001, he witnessed her sobbing quietly in one of the pews, with Kelly also weeping a few rows in front. Speaking afterwards, Beyoncé said their tears were not due to being upset, but because they all felt so blessed. Such was the importance of church in her life that she has reportedly donated half a million dollars to St John's over the years.

Weeks away from home, living out of a suitcase, played havoc with the girls' love lives. Even on the rare nights they went out, they claimed they had little luck with the opposite sex. 'What do we do but sit there and look depressed the whole time,' Beyoncé said wryly, in *W* magazine. 'We look so unhappy and bored, no one is ever going to come up to us. And because of security, nobody can get to us anyway.'

Though she made light of it overall, there was just never any room in her itinerary for much socialising. 'I'm in one city for one day, I work there, and then I go to the next city, so I can't really meet people,' she relayed to the *Telegraph Magazine*. As she prepared to leave her teenage years behind, it should have been exactly the right time for her to embark on a steady adult relationship, but there was no chance of that. 'I'd love to have a boyfriend,' she said. 'If I could find a boyfriend who could put up with this life, that would be great, but right now, this is my first priority.' She also revealed that guys' attempts to woo her were usually hopeless and involved cringeworthy chat-up lines. 'I'm very picky. A lot of guys, their conversation sucks. A lot of people come to us and say stuff like, "You can say my name. I'll pay your bills, bills, bills. I won't be a bugaboo." It's so wack.' Asked what she would like in a potential boyfriend, she told *COSMOgirl*: 'I'm looking for someone who has his own career. He doesn't have to have a lot of money – someone in college is cool.'

Perhaps those words tempted Fate. Beyoncé was about to experience a sudden and very significant change in her romantic fortunes. It all began unexpectedly, at a shoot for *Vanity Fair*'s special 'music issue' in the late summer of 2001. Joining her on the shoot were stars including David Bowie, Gwen Stefani, Stevie Wonder and Joni Mitchell – plus a hip-hop artist and producer called Jay-Z. The New York-born rapper was called Shawn Corey Carter at birth, but few knew him by that name. Beyoncé had first met Jay-Z the previous summer, when she collaborated with a rap act called Amil, who was signed to his Roc-A-Fella record label. Beyoncé, then eighteen, featured on Amil's single, 'I Got That', which Jay-Z co-wrote and for which he directed the video.

On meeting again at the *Vanity Fair* shoot, sparks flew between

Beyoncé and Jay-Z; there was a connection between them that she had not seen coming. She was happy to exchange numbers but knew deep down that a relationship was unlikely, thanks to their relentlessly busy schedules. Also, Jay-Z lived in Fort Lee, New Jersey, some 1,500 miles away from her Houston base. Still, she felt genuinely excited about meeting a man who finally seemed to 'get' her and they began talking on the phone when they could. Before long, they were speaking every day.

In the beginning, their entire relationship was conducted by long-distance communication. Years later Beyoncé told Oprah Winfrey: 'We were friends first, for a year and a half, before we went on any date. [We were] on the phone for a year and a half. That foundation is so important in a relationship.' She also told *Glamour* magazine: 'I was eighteen when we first met, nineteen when we started dating. There was no rush. No one expected me to run off and get married.'

Eventually Beyoncé and Jay-Z began to meet up as often as their diaries would allow. They enjoyed quiet dinners, trips to the cinema or just hung out at Jay-Z's apartment, playing music. It was fairly innocent as courtships go, and Jay-Z admitted that he worked very hard to woo her. 'Well, you know, you've got to try,' he told *Vanity Fair* many years later. 'You got to dazzle . . . wine and dine.'

It was also suggested that Beyoncé was still a virgin when she got together with Jay-Z: she let slip in a 2008 interview with the *Daily Telegraph* that her one and only previous relationship with Lyndall had not been intimate in that way. 'I was too young for it to really be a boyfriend – we didn't live together, we didn't, you know . . .' she said. 'That was my only experience with a guy, and since then I've only had one other boyfriend in my life – Jay.' Appearing to back this up, Lyndall also claimed he and Beyoncé had never slept together, telling the *Sun* he never wanted to put pressure on her, due to her strong religious background. 'It was hard as the chemistry between us was electric, but I respected Beyoncé and knew it was important for her to wait,' he said.

Fortunately, Jay-Z's attempts at chivalry paid off: Beyoncé had fallen for him hook, line and sinker. But the pair still chose to keep the fledgling romance secret and were determined never to be photographed together. Beyoncé had learned, in her darkest Destiny's Child days, just how destructive endless press speculation could be and refused to offer up her private life for public consumption. She had also been badly burned when her previous comments about being single and looking for love had become tabloid fodder, saying in MTV show *Genuinely In Love*: 'They wanted to make me the most desperate thing in the world. It was, like, on the cover everywhere: "Beyoncé is lonely. We need to find her a boyfriend." So I [decided] I shouldn't talk about my personal life, because it just makes it a lot easier. And I know people speculate, and I know people wonder, and I respect that and understand that because I've always wondered about people.' She added: 'I just like to feel that I have something to myself.'

Jay-Z was equally wary of creating a media circus, perhaps because he knew his own rocky past would make him an easy target. Hailing from the Marcy Projects, a tough housing estate in the deprived Bedford-Stuyvesant district of Brooklyn where violent crime was rife, he was born in December 1969 – making him twelve years older than Beyoncé. One of four children, he lived with his mother, Gloria Carter, after his father, Adnes

Reeves, abandoned the family when Jay-Z was eleven. Times were horribly tight, but Gloria worked hard to keep the family afloat. 'My mother managed. She juggled,' he told *Vanity Fair*. 'Sometimes we'd pay the lighting bill, sometimes we paid the phone, sometimes the gas went off. We weren't starving – we were eating, we were okay. But it was things like you didn't want to be embarrassed when you went to school. You didn't want to have dirty sneakers or wear the same clothes over again.'

His father's having walked out appeared to take a serious toll on Jay-Z and, in a moving interview in Oprah Winfrey's O magazine in 2009, he said: 'When you're growing up, your dad is your superhero. Once you've let yourself fall that in love with someone, once you've put him on such a high pedestal and he lets you down, you never want to experience that pain again.'

As a result of the separation, he fell badly off the rails and even shot his brother Eric in the shoulder, believing he'd stolen his ring. Writing about the shock moment when he pulled the trigger in 'You Must Love Me', he rapped: 'Saw the devil in your eyes, high off more than weed, confused, I just closed my young eyes and squeezed.'

Though his brother survived, it was almost thirty years before Jay-Z felt ready to speak publicly about the experience. Explaining his actions to Oprah, he said: 'He was doing a lot of drugs. He was taking stuff from our family. I was the youngest, but I felt like I needed to protect everybody.'

But he knew he had done wrong and told the *Guardian*: 'It was terrible. I was a boy, a child. I was terrified.' Believing he would go to prison, he added: 'I thought my life was over. I thought I'd go to jail for ever.' In the same interview, he gave a stark insight on what life on the estate was like. 'Guns were everywhere. [They] were around every day. There were shootouts.' He even got shot at himself three times, but walked away unharmed. 'It's like there was some rogue angel watching over us.'

After his introduction to guns and violence, Jay-Z soon got caught up in the equally murky world of hard drugs. 'I was a drug dealer. Crack was everywhere – it was inescapable,' he confessed in *Vanity Fair*. 'There wasn't any place you could go for isolation or a break. You go in the hallway; [there are] crackheads in the hallway. You look out in the puddles on the kerbs – crack vials are littered in the side of the kerbs. You could smell it in the hallways, that putrid smell. I can't explain it, but it's still in my mind when I think about it.'

While he admitted selling crack as a thirteen-year-old, he insisted he never used it himself – but revealed that Gloria knew he was dealing. 'All the mothers knew. It sounds like "How could you let your son . . ." but I'm telling you, it was normal.'

With Gloria's encouragement, he reconciled with his father in 2003 and bought him an apartment, which he furnished. 'I got to tell him everything I wanted to say,' Jay-Z said in *Rolling Stone*. 'I just said what I felt. It wasn't yelling and crying and drastic and dramatic. It was very adult, and grown men, but it was tough. I didn't let him off the hook. I was real tough with him.' Father and son managed to build bridges, but not long afterwards Adnes drank himself to death, passing away the same night as Jay-Z opened a New York nightclub called 40/40. 'He was gone,' he said in *GQ*. 'He was not himself.' Though they had not had an easy relationship, his death still hurt. 'To have that connection and then have it ripped away was, like, the worst.'

With his difficult start in life, Jay-Z fortunately found the will to pull himself out of the mire and get back on track. His salvation lay in hip-hop – a passion that was ignited when Gloria bought him a portable boom box because she was fed up with him playing music in the house late at night and banging out beats on the kitchen table. After teaching himself a form of improvisational rap called freestyle, where the lyrics are often made up spontaneously, he began writing fully formed tracks. Before long, he became known in his neighbourhood as Jazzy – after his mentor, a renowned rapper called Jaz-O – which later translated into Jay-Z, a name that stuck firm. He is also nicknamed Hova, after Jehovah, which came about when he was referred to as a 'god of rap'.

As enterprising as he was talented, Jay-Z took the first steps to creating his business empire by selling CDs from the back of his car. In 1995 he established his record label, Roc-A-Fella, alongside Damon Dash and Kareem Burke. After releasing his first album *Reasonable Doubt*, he worked with rap stars such as his former Brooklyn school friend the Notorious B.I.G. – who was tragically shot dead in Los Angeles in 1997. Jay-Z was devastated at the death, saying in *Vibe* magazine: 'I can't even describe what that loss was like for me. It was worse than losing someone in the drug game, because you know that's the risk you take when you get into the streets – death or jail. This was supposed to be music.'

Although the unsolved murder made him consider retiring from the rap scene, he decided doing so would be 'selfish' and that he would stay in the game out of respect for B.I.G. After he'd been plugging away for several years, the recording that propelled Jay-Z to superstardom was the album *Vol 2 . . . Hard*

Knock Life and its lead single 'Hard Knock Life (Ghetto Theme)', which sampled the Broadway musical *Annie*. The song, released in 1998, was his first hit outside America and reached number two in the UK charts. Meanwhile, the Carter coffers were given a substantial boost in 1999 when he and Damon Dash launched their clothing line, Rocawear, which soon began racking up annual sales of $700 million.

Jay-Z's musical masterpiece was widely believed to be *The Blueprint* in 2001, which his friend Kanye West helped produce. Released on the same day as the 9/11 terror attacks, the album still sold half a million copies in its first week and was a number-one hit in the US. But it came at a difficult time: Jay-Z was awaiting two criminal trials – one for gun possession and another for assault. He always maintained his innocence of the gun crime, and the charge was later dropped, but the following October he was sentenced to three years' probation after pleading guilty to the stabbing of music executive Lance Rivera at a party. Describing what happened in his 2010 book *Decoded*, he said he had been angry because a bootleg copy of his latest work had been leaked a month before its release date. Believing Lance Rivera to be responsible, he approached him at the party at New York's Kit Kat Klub and there was a big confrontation. '[Rivera] got real loud with me right there in the middle of the club,' Jay-Z wrote. 'It was strange. We separated and I went over to the bar . . . I was . . . in a state of shock . . . I headed back over to him, but this time I was blacking out with anger.' He added that he decided to plead guilty to assault after watching his friend Puff Daddy's trial on weapons violations the same year, at which he was acquitted. Ending the tale on a curiously upbeat anecdote, Jay-Z said: 'The hilarious thing, if any of this can be considered funny, is that the Rocawear bubble coat I was wearing when they paraded me in front of the cameras started flying off the shelves the last three weeks before Christmas.'

Like Beyoncé's, Jay-Z's love life had not been entirely fruitful. He had casually dated a succession of women over the years, apparently including actress Rosario Dawson and singers Missy Elliott, Lil' Kim and the late Aaliyah, as well as R&B star Blu Cantrell. He once admitted to *Rolling Stone* that his father leaving his mother had affected his own relationships with women: 'Even when I was with women I wasn't really with them. In the back of my mind I'd always feel, like, when this sh*t breaks up, you know, whatever. So I never really just let myself go. I was always guarded, always guarded. And always suspicious. I never let myself just go.' Consequently, he said he had never felt heartbroken over a woman: 'Never, ever. Never. Never.'

But patience rewarded him: soon after meeting Beyoncé, he knew she was the woman of his dreams. When they first got together, only her family and closest friends knew about it. In the public eye, she was single and living an extremely sheltered life with her parents, which led to claims that they had expressly forbidden her to date anyone. But Tina refuted such accusations. 'What mother wouldn't want her daughter to have a boyfriend?' she said scornfully in *Ebony*. 'I'm no different from any other mother. I want my kids to be happy. I don't want them to be lonely.' She added: 'It's dumb for somebody to think that Beyoncé's dad has so much control that she can't have a boyfriend.'

Similarly, she and Mathew felt aggrieved by years of comments about them being 'slave-drivers' who worked Destiny's Child too hard and denied them a social life. 'Now that they are nineteen and twenty, we can't stop them from going to a party,' said Tina. 'They can go anywhere and do anything they want to. We can't "slave-drive" them. So why are they working so hard? Because they understand what goes into being successful.'

Those words were certainly true, because September 2001 also saw Destiny's Child invited to guest star at a special concert for Michael Jackson, their greatest idol. The gala event held in New York, to mark his thirtieth anniversary as King of Pop, was his first performance in the US in more than a decade, and featured slots from Whitney Houston, Britney Spears, Liza Minnelli and Ray Charles. Beyoncé said of the moment she met her hero: 'I looked to my right, he was standing right there, on the side of the stage. I had to put the mic down and start screaming and the audience was totally confused! We got so star-struck, we hugged him on stage.' Just as overwhelmed, Kelly added: 'And we didn't want to let go!'

Chapter Six

Just weeks later, the band set off to headline their first tour, taking in forty-two dates across America and Canada in conjunction with MTV. Before the shows kicked off, Beyoncé was interviewed by the music channel. 'It's our first headlining tour, and we're spending a lot of money on the set,' she said. 'We're gonna get pyro and fire and [have] a bunch of dance numbers. Of course, costume changes we always do, stages coming up out of the floor, all of that stuff. We're gonna have a really elaborate set for the first time.'

Living on a tour bus was like a holiday for the girls and all three rather touchingly raved about its 'really hot' shower and that 'you can completely sit up in the bunks'. After their gigs, and on nights off, they ate pizza and endless bags of Doritos on the bus and curled up to watch films – *Forrest Gump* was a favourite. Their time away from home meant they often had to skip Sunday church services, but they would convert the back of the bus into a make-shift church, reciting prayers and reading their Bibles together.

Like any band on an extended tour, the girls had their own personal dressing-room requests and at one time the media obtained a copy of their 'rider'. In it, the girls' team had asked for six bottles of Snapple Iced Tea, an assortment of sodas, chips and salsa, plus a fresh fruit platter and deli tray, no pork. They also asked for lemons, honey and fresh ginger – described as 'very important' – to treat their strained voices, as well as spring water, fresh flowers, lots of soap and towels, fruit teas, strawberry candles, two full-length mirrors and, crucially, real china and cutlery rather than Styrofoam or plastic.

There were never any requests for alcohol: the girls steered well clear of booze during that period. Responding to reports of them knocking back Cristal champagne at a party, Beyoncé told the *Observer*, 'I don't drink,' and Kelly added, 'We're role models, so we watch ourselves. And not just when we go to parties.' Many often forgot how young they still were, and Michelle said, by way of reminder: 'We're underage still.'

After all the fun and technical razzmatazz of the tour, October saw a far more sombre performance in New York at a charity event held in the wake of the 9/11 terrorist attacks. Organised by Sir Paul McCartney to honour the city's brave fire and police crews, the Concert for New York took place in Madison Square Gardens. The band performed a Bee Gees-penned track called 'Emotion' from the *Survivor* album, as well as a heartrending gospel medley, 'Walk With Me'.

With 9/11 sending shockwaves around the world, Destiny's Child felt there was no choice but to cancel their scheduled European tour that autumn. Due to begin in Stockholm in late October, the tour would have ended in London in November but, like many other American artists, including Janet Jackson, they felt the terror threat made overseas travel too dangerous. In a statement, Beyoncé said: 'We're always excited when we perform for our fans in Europe and the UK. Postponing these shows was the hardest thing for us, because we truly enjoy the fans. We made that decision at the very last second after taking a hard look at the state of the world right now. We look forward to rescheduling the original shows, adding additional shows, and we pray for a quick end to the fighting and a return to peaceful times.'

The sudden unfortunate gap in her diary meant she was free to take up an entirely new project: acting. First up came a part in an MTV television film, *Carmen: A Hip Hopera*, an African-American adaptation of the opera *Carmen*, alongside her pal Wyclef Jean, as well as rappers Mos Def and Jermaine Dupri. Beyoncé played the lead role and said: 'This girl is a manipulative, sexy, scandalous female that kinda ruins this guy's life. I had a lot of fun playing it – it's really the opposite of me so I had a great time.' Her role in *Carmen* made her grow up, she felt. 'I matured the most [on that],' she explained to *Essence* magazine. 'I was away from home, away from everything. Besides a new job, I had to make friends in a new city. I call it my college.'

With acting a new string to add to her bow, she said proudly, in an interview with NBC: 'I've been born to do this. I want to be a triple threat, you know? I'm able to dance, sing, act, and I also write and produce. And that's very rare. They want to say it's because of the sexy clothes or it's because of whatever else. No, it's because I'm talented. And I just want to be acknowledged for that.'

There was no shortage of acknowledgement: she was recognised for her musical talents and acting ability. Such was her marketability that everyone wanted a piece of her. '"It girl" is overused,' said *Essence*. 'But she has it: vocal talent, a gifted song-writer and performer, sexy and sassy, plus a humble spirit.' Scores of endorsement deals were flooding in thick and fast – including campaigns for the likes of AT&T and L'Oréal Paris. And there was a more unusual offer which she could not resist: the official Destiny's Child dolls. Toy firm Hasbro manufactured three minia-ture figurines of the girls, wearing matching blue spangly outfits. Giving the dolls her seal of approval, Beyoncé said: 'Growing up, most girls dream of having their own doll, so today, one of our dreams came true.'

Another dream came true when she accepted her debut movie role in the Austin Powers film *Goldmember* alongside Mike Myers. She confessed in *W* magazine that her first audition was like being summoned to the principal's office, and reflected: 'I never thought I'd get the part, not in a million years. I was so nervous. They asked me if I wanted to go into comedy, and I was, like, "Well, I don't know if I'd be good." Afterwards I'm like, "You dummy, what did you just say? Oh, God!"'

Beyoncé played Foxxy Cleopatra who, she said, 'shoots her guns, kicks people's butts and is very funny'. In the film she has an enormous Afro, and laughed about her 'crazy' hair during a cast interview: 'Getting ready every morning was a dramatic thing. I had big Afros, small Afros, hats, scarves, anything you could think of.' In keeping with her off-the-wall character, she caused a stir at the première by teaming a giant Afro with a thigh-skimming gold dress by designer Roberto Cavalli. She looked sensational, but she was not so happy that she'd had to diet hard for the film, telling *W*: 'I love eating, and I have a problem with being skinny. I think when you are twenty you should not have to think about what you eat. Like, you are twenty years old! But I realise that's a sacrifice I have to make for movies.'

Working alongside another of the film's co-stars, Sir Michael Caine, was an eye-opener for her and she told the *Telegraph Magazine*: 'He's so big he doesn't have to be nice . . . but he helped me with all these tips, even though I never even asked him to, and so I was like, wow!' Beyoncé was also impressed with how polite he was. 'He was nice to everybody and, you know, lots of celebrities are nice to other celebrities, but the ones who are genuinely nice are nice to all the extras and the staff, like he was . . . I want to be like him!'

But taking the part in *Goldmember* did not come without risks: she feared it might damage her credibility. 'I was scared because some singers who become actors get a lot of criticism,' she told *Film Monthly*. 'I didn't want to be one of those singers who said: "Okay, we sold records, so now I'm going to act." They approached me and I got the part, so it was great. I just wanted to make sure I delivered the right performance.'

Beyoncé need not have worried: the film was released in 2002 to a favourable reception from the critics, with the *New York Times* declaring: 'Ms Knowles knows how to strut that strut.' Impressively, her first film led to a nomination in the Teen Choice Awards for Breakout Female Movie Star, although she lost out to Hilary Duff on the night. She also went down a storm on the film's set, with co-star Mike saying afterwards: 'Everybody fell in love with her. On her last day, everyone was sad to see her go because she's so nice and funny and silly . . . and bootylicious.'

Firmly bitten by the acting bug, she shot a second movie soon after, *The Fighting Temptations*, co-starring Cuba Gooding Jr. She played Lilly, a single mother and nightclub singer recruited to help a church choir win a gospel competition. The role saw her swap her usual glossy, groomed image for a much more natural look. 'I told my agent that in my next film I wanted to seem natural,' she told *USA Today*. 'For this new movie, I tried to find the most unglamorous clothes, the most unglamorous hairstyle. I didn't wear my hair straightened. I wanted to show myself in a different light.' Drawing on the plot's vague similarity to her own background, she said: 'My mother owns a hair salon, and I grew up there, sweeping the floor and listening to the stories told by all these women who came there. Some were single mothers, some weren't, but they were positive, strong women. I loved being around that. I think that's where songs I've written, like "Independent Women", come from, and it was nice to be able to bring that to the movie.'

In the film, Beyoncé shared her first on-screen kiss with Cuba, who joked: 'We worked all night on it. Sure, she was probably a little nervous before kissing me, but she's kissed guys before.' He added: 'She's young, she'll get over it. When you are married [like me], you look forward to that kind of thing. Lord. She was wonderful.' For Beyoncé, though, the scene was not quite so relaxed. 'When I do a kissing scene, I feel so uncomfortable,' she told Associated Press. Asked if she would cope with acting out anything more *risqué* on camera, she seemed appalled: 'I know right now I definitely couldn't because I'm literally embarrassed by the kissing scene.'

During the making of the movie, it became obvious that Beyoncé had been working herself too hard over the past few months. She was suffering from a clear case of exhaustion, and briefly seemed on the verge of collapse. She was quoted as saying: 'I am so tired. Sometimes I sleep in my makeup because I don't want to spend time having it done the next day. I have a decision to make about the film. I don't want a breakdown – and that's possible.' Later, though, she played down her comments, telling *Entertainment Weekly*: 'The press exaggerated. I said I was tired. But it worked out great. I got to meet some great people.'

Still, her workload was a problem – mostly because she could not bear to say 'No' to many of the offers that came her way. 'The reason it's hard is that I decide, "OK I wanna do L'Oréal", "I wanna do a movie", "I wanna do another Destiny's Child record", and I make these commitments and then I have to do them,' she conceded in the *Telegraph Magazine*. 'That's why I haven't had time off, because I want to do so many things.'

While appearing on Ellen DeGeneres's chat show, she revealed that she found it very hard to stop and unwind. 'I don't know how to relax,' she said. 'I don't like to get a massage. The only time I can really relax is on a boat because then I have no excuse. I'm stuck. I have to take care of myself.'

With her daughter showing signs of burn-out, Tina was becoming concerned for her welfare: 'I worry about Beyoncé all the time. There are so many people asking so many things of her every day, and I'm always praying that it won't be too much for her. She loves what she does, loves entertaining. But it can wear you out. I've seen people get burned out and tired or just overwhelmed.'

With *The Fighting Temptations* filmed on location in Atlanta, Beyoncé celebrated her twenty-first birthday there, and her publishing company Hitco threw her a big Austin Powers-themed party. The bash was held at the Cascade roller-skating rink and she even had a cake made in the shape of a giant roller boot. Guests who flew in to party with her included bandmates Kelly and Michelle, as well as Jay-Z and her family. The evening was inspired by skating scenes in *Goldmember* and Beyoncé said: 'I knew I didn't want to do anything traditional and I was a little jealous when they got to do the skating thing in the film because I wasn't part of it. I'm not a great skater but I love it. It was a great party. I just went round and round all night.'

Once filming wrapped, dozens more movie offers came in, but after her recent health scare she knew she needed to tread cautiously with this side of her career and keep music as her focus. 'I had scripts where I could have had the starring role. But I didn't want to do that because I want to know exactly what I'm doing before all that pressure,' she said.

Back in her comfort zone with the band, there was a third Grammy win for Destiny's Child that February – this time for the single 'Survivor'. Though it was an immense achievement, one of the evening's talking points concerned a rare fashion *faux pas*. Beyoncé was in another of Tina's flamboyant creations and wore a sheer purple top, with an ill-judged cream bra that showed through, and a billowing purple skirt. She was unkindly compared to a character in *Aladdin* – hardly the effect she had aimed for.

Having postponed their European tour the previous autumn, the spring of 2002 saw Destiny's Child take to the road for a major world tour. After dancing with them for eighteen months, Solange got a key role, acting as compère before each show. 'I just got the audience to sing "Bootylicious" with me,' she recalled.

Sampling some of the world's most exotic cultures, Beyoncé was particularly struck by the serenity of Thailand. 'There was something about Phuket that I loved, where people rode on bikes or out on the elephant in the water,' she raved, to *Film Monthly*.

'It was humid and I walked around barefooted and nobody knew or cared who I was.' Australia also got a big thumbs-up: 'We went on the beach and people didn't bother us. I fell in love with Brisbane – it's a cute place and the people are wild.'

With a five-piece band, ten dancers and plenty of fireworks, the spectacle included all of their biggest hits and a moving gospel number, while they each wore a single sequined glove when 'Bootylicious' morphed into Michael Jackson's 'Beat It'. Naturally, 'Survivor' was left until the encore, ensuring crowds all over the globe went home happy.

The end of the tour signalled a major change for the girls. Though on paper still committed to the group, they had all begun working on their own solo music, with Beyoncé's first effort a single called 'Work It Out' from the *Goldmember* soundtrack. Kelly featured on a single with rapper Nelly called 'Dilemma' in 2002, and released her debut album *Simply Deep* soon after, while Michelle's first album, *Heart To Yours*, came out that summer too. However, she denied reports that the band was to break up to allow the trio to spread their wings. 'We won't depart from Destiny's Child,' she pledged in *Texas Music*. 'All the talk about Beyoncé going solo, Beyoncé is not going solo. No one is leaving anyone.'

But with the band announcing they were taking a three-year hiatus, their future seemed up in the air – especially when Beyoncé hit the studio in Miami to begin recording her own epic debut album, to be called *Dangerously In Love*. As she threw her heart and soul into making the record, her skills as an artist in her own right were highlighted when she won the 2002 award for Songwriter of the Year, bestowed on her by the American Society of Composers, Authors and Publishers Pop Music Awards (ASCAP).

The award was given in recognition of the tracks 'Independent Women Part I', 'Jumpin' Jumpin'' and 'Survivor' and she was the first African-American woman to receive the honour. 'It was a huge accomplishment for me,' she said, in a British TV interview at the time. 'I was the second woman ever to win that out of all of the ASCAP writers, which is ridiculous because there are so many women that are great. It's definitely harder being a woman but I'm very grateful that I got that opportunity and I'm happy that I'm opening the doors for other female artists.'

With Beyoncé's ascent to the realms of pop royalty, it was no coincidence that one of the world's biggest brands signed her up in 2002. Replacing Britney Spears, she was unveiled as the new face of Pepsi in a campaign that included two TV ads as well as large-scale radio and internet promotion. 'I'm thrilled to be joining so many talented entertainers who have created memorable Pepsi moments over the years,' she said. Her union with Pepsi was to be long-lasting and extremely lucrative, although it did provoke criticism in later years, due to the growing obesity epidemic in America.

She continued to see Jay-Z in private, but rumours that they were dating surfaced in 2002, when she collaborated with him on his hit single '03 Bonnie & Clyde', which they recorded together that August. The song opens with Jay-Z asking her, 'Are you ready, B? Let's go get 'em', and in the video they played a pair of lovers on the run. In the refrain Jay-Z raps, 'All I need in this life of sin/Is me and my girlfriend,' while she sings back, 'Down to ride 'til the very end/It's me and my boyfriend.' Showbiz columns were sent further into apoplexy by lyrics in which they referred to themselves as 'the new Bobby and Whitney', referring to Bobby Brown and his then wife Whitney Houston.

Reporters summoned up the courage to question them about their supposed romance, to no avail. 'Oh, gosh. I don't like to talk about that,' Beyoncé told *Entertainment Tonight* that November. 'But I appreciate your interest. It's personal.' When Jay-Z was given the third degree on Howard Stern's radio show, he flatly denied they were an item. And put on the spot by *Playboy* magazine, he said: 'We're just cool. We're just friends. We don't really, ah, know each other like that yet.' Asked by the interviewer if he would like to date her, he conceded: 'She's beautiful. Who wouldn't wish she was their girlfriend? Maybe one day.'

For months on end they let the tide of speculation wash over them, but then came reports that they had broken up. This was quite some feat for a couple who had never confirmed they were together, but there were clear signs of tension when they guest-starred on an American hip-hop show called *106 & Park*. As Beyoncé walked on set with Solange, who was launching her own music career, she and Jay-Z blanked one another, although he greeted Solange warmly with a kiss on the cheek. Then came claims in April 2003 that Beyoncé's friendship with another rapper, 50 Cent, had caused her and Jay-Z to go their separate ways. According to the *Sun*, she was now dating the former crack dealer, whose real name was Curtis Jackson. Apparently this never happened.

But the plot thickened over her and Jay-Z's situation when she purported to be single in an interview with *Elle* magazine the same month. What was more, she stressed that only a man like Mathew would tick all the boxes when it came to dating. 'My dad is very gentle but also tough when he needs to be,' she mused. 'It's not going to be easy to find a man in my life – it's going to be hard to live up to my father. Because of him, I have standards.' The magazine pressed her gently on the topic of Jay-Z, but she replied firmly: 'I'm not opening that door.' Admitting they did hang out together, she added: 'If someone sees us, they see us. Whatever interpretation you want to put on it, that's fine.' When the magazine asked a somewhat old-fashioned question about when she had last been kissed, she refused to respond.

With so many contradictions in the media, her fans were understandably baffled. It was even more confusing when reports flooded the internet in mid-2003 that she and Jay-Z were now engaged. Predictably, there was no official confirmation or denial and the gossip seemed to amuse and frustrate the pair in equal measure. When asked directly if she would be walking down the aisle any time soon, she said cryptically: 'Beyoncé doesn't quite have a fiancé. Not yet.' But it would not be the last time that such a rumour would do the rounds.

In May 2003, one of Beyoncé's lifelong wishes came true: she got to sing with her childhood idol Whitney Houston. They were performing in a live concert organised by music channel VH1 called Diva Duets, which aired live from the MGM Grand in Las Vegas. During the show, Beyoncé sang 'Dangerously In Love 2' and Whitney performed with her then husband Bobby Brown, but for the finale the two women joined a host of other R&B stars in a soulful tribute to Stevie Wonder. They sang his classic track 'Higher Ground', with the other divas, who included Chaka Khan, Mary J. Blige, Queen Latifah, Ashanti and Jewel. It was undoubtedly a career highlight for Beyoncé. Years later she would be devastated by Whitney's death – but there were already signs of trouble in the soul singer's life. During her and rapper Bobby's stay in Vegas, Whitney was reportedly seen visiting a doctor with a bloodied nose and, according to Fox News, she and Bobby were also seen having 'a terrible fight' at the Bellagio Hotel.

The following month, Beyoncé's debut album *Dangerously In Love* was finally released after months of fine-tuning and tinkering. To celebrate, Columbia threw her a lavish launch party at the Mondrian Hotel's Sky Bar in West Hollywood, which doubled as a seventeenth-birthday party for Solange. Some forty-three songs had been recorded for the album, with fifteen making the final cut. Incredibly, the Columbia executives had initially been far from convinced about the album's potential and almost chose not to release it. 'When I played it through for my record label, they told me I didn't have one hit on my album,' Beyoncé said, before joking: 'I guess they were kinda right. I had five.' The album went on to shift eleven million copies worldwide, with the *New York Daily News* calling her a 'sultry solo star', who had 'blossomed from a girly group'. The album was certified platinum just three weeks after its release and topped the charts in the UK, Canada, the Netherlands, Germany, Greece and the Philippines.

Describing the record's meaning in a 'making-of' video, Beyoncé appeared to allude to her relationship with Jay-Z when she said: 'Sometimes when you fall in love it's a little dangerous. Because I'm a young lady basically evolving into a young woman now, I thought that was a great title because there are so many steps in relationships and love – that's what the album is about.' And addressing her fans directly, she cheekily added: 'I did it for y'all and hopefully y'all can fall in love while listening to it – and maybe make some babies.' She also stressed that she wanted a softer side of herself to shine through this album. 'All of the songs I wrote for Destiny's Child were usually so strong – and that's a good thing – but sometimes people lose touch with you being a human,' she told Associated Press. 'I wanted people to know that I'm strong, but I can fall in love, I can get hurt, I can feel like I need someone, and everything every other woman goes through.'

As expected, Mathew oversaw the album's songs – except one: a hidden track at the end she had secretly penned called 'Daddy'. 'I actually didn't write it for the album,' she told MTV. 'I didn't want to put it on it. I just kind of did it for him. And he was speechless. He didn't know what to say or how to react, because it is really a heavy song.' In 'Daddy', the lyrics tell of her desire to be with a man who can offer similar qualities to Mathew:

> *I want my unborn son to be like my daddy*
> *I want my husband to be like my daddy*
> *There is no one else like my daddy*
> *And I thank you for loving me*

Her parents' marriage had inspired the song: 'My mother and father have been together for twenty-three, twenty-four years,' she said, 'and I've seen them go through a lot. And he has always supported his wife and supported his family and supported me and my sister and Kelly. That loyalty and that strength that he has, those certain qualities I just want in all the people around me.'

Beyoncé's cousin, Angie Beyincé, had been heavily involved with both the songwriting and production of *Dangerously In Love*, as had Jay-Z, who had co-written five of its tracks. What was more, the lyrics in one of the songs, 'Signs', seemed to refer directly to Beyoncé's feelings for the rapper:

> *In December every sign has its own mode*
> *I was in love with a Sagittarius . . .*
> *The affection of a Virgo*
> *Which sign matches good with mine.*

Eagle-eyed fans were quick to point out that Jay-Z – whose birthday is on 4 December – was indeed a Sagittarius, while Beyoncé's star sign was, of course, Virgo. When asked about the track, Beyoncé said coyly: 'People can come to whatever conclusion they like. That's the beauty of music.'

But Jay-Z's involvement in her work did not come without its complications. It was no secret that he did not get on with Mathew, and their strained relationship put Beyoncé in an extremely difficult position. In fact, Mathew said of Jay-Z the following year: 'I don't care for him at all. No, I'm not close to him. He is not somebody I like to spend time with.' And on another occasion, when asked by US radio organisation NPR what he really thought of his potential future son-in-law, he said curtly: 'Next question.'

It was claimed that Mathew feared he would 'steal' his daughter from him and begin managing her career in his place – especially because Jay-Z announced in 2003 that he was retiring as a recording artist to focus on the business side of the industry. Now worth nearly $300 million, his shock decision to step down came at the same time as he released his eighth work, *The Black Album* – he even threw a 'farewell' party at Madison Square Gardens in New

York. However, it was a fleeting move and, after selling Roc-A-Fella to Universal Music Group and being appointed president and CEO of the Def Jam label in 2004, he had a major change of heart. Later, he spoke of his regret over the premature 'retirement', saying it left him 'cringing' and 'embarrassed': 'I think I pulled the retirement ripcord too many times. People [were] looking at me, like, "Please shut up."' He also vowed he would let Fate determine the rest of his career.

Crucially, as president of Def Jam, Jay-Z made one of his biggest ever signings – in the form of a very young Rihanna. He invited the teenager from Barbados to audition for him in New York, and she recalled: 'I was in the lobby shaking! I saw just a little bit of Jay's face down the hall and I was just, like, "Oh, my God!" I had never met a celebrity, and to meet a celebrity who's also the president of the label, that was crazy!' Jay-Z and his colleague L. A. Reid were so impressed they gave her a record contract on the spot. 'We were there until four thirty in the morning closing the deal,' she said. 'Every time I signed my name I was just smiling.' It did not happen to him very often, but Jay-Z was blown away by her potential. 'I signed her in one day,' he remembered. 'It took me two minutes to see she was a star.' Her success did not happen overnight, however, and initially Rihanna was dismissed as a less-talented Caribbean copy of Beyoncé. After struggling to make an impact on the charts for two years, she eventually got lucky with the song 'Umbrella', which became a huge R&B anthem.

Jay-Z's relationship with Rihanna was an important one, and she always considered him to be a close friend as well as her mentor. And, though she had her troubles, his support would later prove to be invaluable.

Chapter Seven

Given how powerful he was becoming in his Def Jam capacity, Jay-Z's vital role on *Dangerously In Love* was hard for Mathew to stomach. But even he could not deny that his collaboration on the album's intoxicating first single took his daughter's solo venture to a whole new stratosphere. He provided the rap element on 'Crazy In Love', and the song was universally praised by critics, who described it as a 'deliriously catchy' summer anthem. *Rolling Stone* magazine hailed it 'a cauldron of energy', while *NME* called it a slice of 'funk-soul genius'. Reflecting on how the rap came about in the first place, Beyoncé said Jay-Z had been in the studio only a matter of minutes when he blurted it out: 'He just sits there and his mouth starts moving silently, and all of a sudden he does this rap,' she revealed in *Vanity Fair*. 'This was, like, three in the morning. He had to be exhausted, I was exhausted, I don't know how he did this.'

Amid speculation that the song was inspired by her feelings for Jay-Z, she said: 'I guess you would say it's the first step of a relationship – it's right before you let go and you're still conscious of the things that you're doing. You're, like, "God, I'm looking crazy . . ." but you kind of don't care because you've fallen in love with him. His love just got you buzzing.' She still refused to confirm their relationship, telling *Rolling Stone* pointedly: 'I don't say I'm single. People are, like, "Why does she say that they're just friends?" I don't say that. I just don't talk about it. I just wanna protect my private life.'

And Jay-Z was no more illuminating about their suggestive collaborations either: 'I'm not saying yes, I'm not saying no. Listen to the record. Maybe it's entertainment, maybe it's not.'

In a double whammy for Beyoncé, 'Crazy In Love' hit number one on the *Billboard* Hot 100 the same week as *Dangerously In Love* debuted at number one in the *Billboard* album chart, making her the first woman to top both charts simultaneously in both the US and the UK. The song had opened up a whole new fan base to her: while Destiny's Child had been booed at a hip-hop concert called Summer Jam, she now had genuine appeal to the R&B crowd. Realising Jay-Z's involvement had allowed this to happen, she told MTV: 'I'm very grateful. He's helped me a lot on my album. He helped me write some of the songs and . . . actually, before the hip-hop was in ['Crazy In Love'], some people didn't even accept it as such. He gave the song exactly what it needed.'

It was an arrangement that worked both ways, though, as Jay-Z fairly acknowledged. 'We exchanged audiences,' he surmised in *Vanity Fair*. 'Her records are huge Top Forty records, and she helped "03 Bonnie & Clyde" go to number one. What I gave her was a street credibility, a different edge.'

As the accolades poured in, 'Crazy In Love' remained at the top of the American singles chart for eight consecutive weeks and went on to win three awards at the MTV Video Music Awards at New York's Radio City Music Hall in 2003. That year's ceremony went down in history after singers Madonna and Britney Spears shared a lingering on-stage kiss – a stunt for which Beyoncé found herself in hot water. After allegedly claiming she would never kiss another girl and that she had 'standards', she insisted she had been wildly misquoted and that she had nothing but pure respect for her gay following. 'I have never judged anyone based on his or her sexual orientation and have no intention of starting now,' she wrote on her website. 'I have a lot of gay and lesbian fans and I love them no differently than my straight fans.'

She was so upset by the slur on her character that she addressed it again in a separate interview with *HX* magazine: 'It hurt. "I have standards" was a quote from an interview I did for *Elle* about relationships; I was talking about guys.' Beyoncé also revealed that she had personally been affected by AIDS because her gay uncle had recently died of the disease. 'He was my mother's best friend,' she later reminisced in *Instinct* magazine. 'He brought me to school every day . . . He made my clothes with my mother. He was like my nanny.'

During a live performance of 'Crazy In Love' with Jay-Z at the same MTV awards show, Beyoncé drew gasps as she strutted around the stage in a pair of tiny gold hot pants. The song's video also saw her writhing seductively in microscopic denim shorts, and it seemed that her solo career trajectory went hand in hand with this super-sexy new image. Clearly a lot of hard work and dedication had gone into honing her body, and she revealed that she had ditched her favourite foods and started running six miles a day to get herself into optimum shape. 'I gave up on burgers, fries and stuff like that,' she told the *Sun*. 'Thankfully my taste buds have changed and I enjoy experimenting with different foods. Now I only eat grilled things and I try to eat five small meals a day, rather than big, heavy ones.'

But, with her strongly religious background, the racy new direction was, for some, a juxtaposition too far. Dismissing opinion that the video was overly provocative, she said: 'The movements to "Crazy In Love" were inspired by a traditional African dance – I don't think there's anything too sexy about it. It's entertainment and I believe God is OK with that.' Defending herself further, she insisted that she would never do anything she felt would offend God and added that she would never dream of wearing hot pants to church.

There were clear limits to just how raunchy Beyoncé wanted to be and she was reported to have walked angrily out of a shoot with acclaimed photographer David LaChapelle that summer when he asked her to pose naked, covered with honey. 'Every photographer wants to be the first one who talks Beyoncé out of her clothes,' she was quoted as saying by *Sky News*. 'It's prestigious for him if I expose a nipple. People test you to see how far they can go . . . Man, if I had a dollar for every time that kind of guy says, "You'll only get the cover if you take off your pants", I'd be a rich woman.'

With 'Crazy In Love' fever still burning strongly, Beyoncé wowed a crowd of a hundred thousand as she sang at London's annual Party in the Park concert in July 2003. Held every year in Hyde Park to raise money for the Prince's Trust charity, she chatted excitedly to Prince Charles in the VIP box. He told her that Princes William and Harry were big fans of her work. 'Both of my sons have your album – and I think Wills quite fancies you,' he was rumoured to have told her. William was a year younger than Beyoncé at twenty-one and had recently begun dating his future wife, Kate Middleton. But the surprise revelation left the normally unflappable Beyoncé squirming with embarrassment and she joked afterwards: 'I went red in the face and couldn't believe it. I'm sure William can't believe that his father said that and I'm sure Charles will be in trouble when he gets home. I'm thrilled, though – Wills is very good-looking.' As a result of Charles's apparent comment, the media went into overdrive and it was later claimed that Beyoncé personally invited William to one of her upcoming London gigs that autumn.

Still, William had tough competition on his hands in the form of Jay-Z, who added more fuel to the 'are they/aren't they?' fire when he whisked Beyoncé to the French Riviera that August. An onlooker at the Eden Roc Hotel in Cannes, where they were staying, said: 'They made no secret of the fact they were together.' Eyebrows were also raised when they took front-row seats during New York Fashion Week in September. As usual, no clarification about their dating status came from either side, but Beyoncé had extra reason to keep her man close when Jay-Z's rumoured ex-girlfriend Blu Cantrell spoke of her soft spot for him. 'He's such a honey,' the singer said, in a DVD to promote her second album, *Bittersweet*. 'He's just a doll, baby. I don't care who he is dating – I've always had a crush on him.' And when asked what she would do if he propositioned her, Blu admitted: 'I wouldn't turn it down, let's just put it that way!' Although Beyoncé kept a dignified silence over her comments, it was said that she refused to go to that year's MOBO awards in London because Blu was hosting the ceremony.

The animosity between the two women stepped up a gear when Blu later attacked Beyoncé over her second single from *Dangerously In Love*, a number called 'Baby Boy', which featured Sean Paul. Blu insisted the song sounded like her own track 'Breathe', telling the Glasgow *Daily Record*: 'Beyoncé is talented and beautiful and I'm a fan, but she has a song out which is very similar to mine. She uses words which are in the hook of my song, and if she is that talented, she shouldn't have to copy someone else.' Blu added: 'She's ripping me off, but there is no animosity because I'm a very positive person. However, I'm a little disappointed because she is established and didn't have to do that.' Again, Beyoncé chose not to retaliate. Quietly dignified in the face of such criticism, she hardly needed to respond: the difference in their record sales and overall success spoke volumes.

Celebrating her twenty-second birthday in September, Jay-Z treated Beyoncé to a *Pretty Woman* party at his 40/40 club in New York. Basing the night on the hit movie starring Julia Roberts, which Beyoncé loved, he had chosen several new outfits for her to wear, from which she picked out a long, deep pink dress with a plunging neckline. When the couple arrived at the club, their closest friends and family – including Kelly, Michelle, Solange and Tina – were hiding in a private room and screamed 'Surprise!' at the top of their lungs as she walked in.

Shaking off any sign of a hangover the next day, the pair were seen watching a tennis match at the US Open, but straight afterwards it was back to work for Beyoncé. She jetted off to Europe and shot a multi-million-dollar Pepsi ad in Rome. A three-minute commercial, it also featured Britney Spears, whom she had replaced as the face of the drink, as well as singers Pink and

Enrique Iglesias. Set in a Roman amphitheatre, the 'Dare for More' campaign saw the three female rivals go head to head as scantily clad gladiators, singing 'We Will Rock You' before the Emperor Caesar, played by Enrique. 'It's great to be in the presence of such great artists and entertainers, and I've been having the time of my life,' Beyoncé said. 'I got to fly all the way to Rome, which is one of the most beautiful places in the world.' The ad was such a big investment for Pepsi that the company later threw it a glitzy world premiére at London's National Gallery in Trafalgar Square. But when Beyoncé wrapped up in a fur coat to guard against the British chill, Pink was not impressed, sniping: 'It's not something I would wear but each to their own. I've not said anything but I think everybody knows my views – I won't ever touch fur. It's wrong.' It was not the only time that Pink would hit out at Beyoncé over fur. Three years later, she told the *News of the World*: 'I only hope she gets bit on the a**e by whatever animal she wears. Some of the practices are so cruel and as a celebrity you have a responsibility to think about the message you're sending out by wearing fur. People will think it's OK or cool, but it's not.'

Next up for frantically busy Beyoncé was her very first solo tour. She put on six budget-busting shows in England in November 2003, then played in Ireland, Northern Ireland and Holland. Things did not get off to a great start when her road manager tumbled off stage on the first night, severely damaging his back, but by the third show, the tour was running like a well-oiled machine, and Beyoncé had perfected a daring opening sequence in which she was lowered head first on to the stage in a harness. 'It's just unexpected and crazy,' she said, of the risky manoeuvre, in the *Guardian*. 'It was actually my idea – I saw it in a Broadway show and it looked really cool. I do it every night, and now I'm upset because it's not fun. I'm scared to eat too close to the time. It was OK the first time, but when you have to do it thirty times . . .'

To keep the Destiny's Child faithful happy, her set included a mash-up of some of their biggest hits, including 'No, No, No Part 2', 'Independent Women Part 1', 'Survivor' and 'Bootylicious'. But it was the energetic dance routines that most impressed – not least because she spent eight hours a day rehearsing in the run-up to the shows. 'I like to do dances that are unique to each song so that takes a lot of work,' she said. In this sense, the tour gave the first hint of her increasing desire for the Beyoncé concert experience to be a world-beating masterclass in live entertainment. Within a few years, she would be known as the industry's most committed performer and an ardent perfectionist, and she explained why it was so vitally important to her in an interview with ABC News: 'People in the audience want to see a show – they want to live out their fantasies. For that two hours, they think they're me. They don't want to see something boring, so I give them a show and I'm able to be what I'm not on the stage.'

It later emerged that one of her biggest supporters on the tour was Jay-Z, who had secretly cleared his diary so he could join her on the road. According to *Ebony* magazine, the pair would spend hours in her dressing room, playing cards before each show. It seemed they had settled into a comfortable routine and they no longer cared who knew.

Following the sell-out tour, Beyoncé took a well-deserved break. She and Jay-Z headed to St Kitts in the Caribbean for some New Year sunshine. While soaking up the rays on the paradise island, she was pictured jumping into the water from a three-storey yacht while Jay-Z filmed her with a video camera. 'I don't know what's wrong with me,' she joked, in *Rolling Stone*, after the trip. 'I looked at the picture and said, "That's really dumb." I do it every year. That's my jump. It's a ritual . . . I have to jump off something so I can let go of everything that happened before the last vacation and start over. It's like being baptised.'

Back on home soil after their relaxing holiday, the pair were snapped looking distinctly loved-up at a New York Knicks basketball game, and at the end of January 2004, there was finally confirmation of the world's worst-kept secret. During a speech at a music-industry party held in a New York club, Jay-Z spoke publicly about his feelings for Beyoncé. Taking the mic at record boss Lyon Cohen's leaving bash, he said to Lyon: 'You've been one of the best friends I could have had . . . apart from this woman beside me, who I love and who I will marry very soon.'

Guests at the party were stunned by this sudden, uncharacteristic declaration and a witness was reported as saying: 'It was really unexpected. As soon as he said it everyone in the place starting whooping and cheering. Beyoncé was standing next to him cooing and looking totally in love. It was a beautiful moment.'

Jay-Z had clearly been a little hasty in speaking of their intention to marry, though, because it would be another four years before they got round to it. But now the barriers were down, they appeared more relaxed about being seen together and she helped him settle into his new $6.85 million penthouse in New York's trendy Tribeca district. After his New Jersey bachelor flat, the seventh-floor apartment was the ultimate in luxury living. Housed in a 1929 brick warehouse, its living space measured 8,000 square feet; there was a separate outdoor terrace of 3,000 square feet, which made it the perfect party pad. A few months later, Beyoncé snapped up her own bit of Big Apple real estate, purchasing not one but two apartments in a new development called One Beacon Court. Part of the fifty-five-storey Bloomberg Tower in Manhattan's posh Upper East Side, one of the four-bedroom condos was for herself, while the other was for Tina and her family. With floor-to-ceiling windows, granite and marble floors and lofty terraces with breathtaking city views, the apartments also came with twenty-four-hour butler service. Regardless of her new 'crib', she still chose to spend much of her time at Jay-Z's place and the lovebirds would often be seen out for coffee in Tribeca or lunching al fresco at one of the dozens of restaurants.

The downside of fame was that she was now recognised every-where she went – even in the ladies' toilets. 'I can't go into public bathrooms any more,' she divulged to *Glamour*. 'I feel trapped. All these people are looking, and I'm just trying to wash my hands, thinking, God, I can't wait to get out of here.'

As far as possible, she and Jay-Z tried to live entourage-free, preferring to wander the streets on their own rather than be tailed by bodyguards. But if Beyoncé was going out alone she was always accompanied by her trusty minder, a colossal twenty-eight-stone hulk called Big Shorty. He worked for her for eight years and she grew fond of him, telling the *Sun*: 'The attention can be a bit scary but I have my security guard, Big Shorty, to look after me.' Amusingly, there were false reports in 2004 that he broke one of her toes after treading heavily on her foot. She was so aggrieved that she spoke out in his defence: 'It's all over the news that he broke my toe,' she said. 'They had skits, they had parodies . . . They had anti-Shorty websites, because they made up this story that he broke my toe. I don't even know where they got it from.' Another time, he made headlines after reportedly getting stuck in a lift, but this, too, was denied, with Beyoncé's bandmate Kelly, saying: 'It's like, "Dang, Shorty, we don't make these stories up!"' Sadly for Shorty, Mathew eventually let him go in 2007 – apparently because he was 'too old and obese' to protect his daughter any longer.

Chapter Eight

2004 was turning into another frantic year for Beyoncé, and on 1 February she had one of the most important nights of her career, belting out the American national anthem to open the Super Bowl, held that year at Houston's Reliant Stadium. Her stellar rendition of 'The Star Spangled Banner' kicked off the evening's entertainment, which saw the New England Patriots do battle with the Carolina Panthers. One of the most talked-about Super Bowls in years, thanks to Janet Jackson's infamous 'wardrobe malfunction' during her performance with Justin Timberlake, it was estimated that the show was watched by up to 130 million viewers in the US – and a mind-boggling billion people worldwide. Beyoncé told *The Early Show* on CBS: 'I was so nervous before I sang the song. My heart, I could see it beating out of my chest, because this has been a dream. And I have been telling my mother since I was, I don't know eight, nine, "I'm going to do that." Every year I saw someone singing, "I'm going to do that." And she was, like, "OK, baby. All right."'

Beyoncé also revealed that Whitney Houston's 1991 Super Bowl performance of the same song had inspired her. 'I just thought that was so cool. She did such a great job. You could feel her emotions and it was just so huge.' Beyoncé even decided to don a white suit for the occasion after seeing Whitney wear one. Ditching the raunchy regalia of late, she revealed: 'I wanted to be a little more glamorous. My mom said, "Let's do a suit." She designed it. I wanted to do something sophisticated and elegant. I loved it. It turned out great.'

The Super Bowl achievement would have been enough to satisfy most pop stars for an entire lifetime, but Beyoncé now had to prepare for the forty-sixth Grammy Awards – for which she had six nominations – taking place the following week. 'This month has been really crazy. Crazy! I never expected that I would be nominated for six Grammys for my first solo album,' she said, in the CBS interview. 'I'm really proud of myself, because I worked so hard on my album and I worked for eight months on it, writing and producing it . . . I hope my performance is unbelievable. I'm going to work on it.'

And work on it she certainly did because the big night saw her and veteran rocker Prince open the show with a breathtaking duet. Wowing the audience at Los Angeles' Staples Center, Beyoncé wore a vibrant pink dress by Roberto Cavalli and they belted out a medley of their combined hits, including 'Purple Rain', 'Crazy In Love' and 'Let's Go Crazy'. 'I still can't believe it,' she said. 'We rehearsed for four days so we could get comfortable with each other.'

Later, she changed into a turquoise and silver Dolce & Gabbana dress and sang a mesmerising version of 'Dangerously In Love 2', during which she positioned herself inside a giant picture frame as if she were a living painting. She was joined on stage by seventeen backing singers and dancers, and the song ended with a dove landing gracefully in her outstretched palm. But it was the haul of awards she collected that would make the night most memorable for her. Picking up a staggering five, she won Best Female R&B Vocal Performance for 'Dangerously In Love 2', Best Contemporary R&B Album and Best R&B Performance by a Duo for a recent duet with soul singer Luther Vandross, 'The Closer I Get To You'. She and Jay-Z also won Best R&B song for 'Crazy In Love', as well as Best Collaboration for the same song. The clutch of five gongs equalled the record set by Lauryn Hill in 1999, Alicia Keys in 2002 and Norah Jones in 2003. On accepting the fifth award, she looked overcome with emotion. 'Wow. This is unbelievable.' She beamed. 'Performing was enough for me . . . I'm so honoured.' Celebrating backstage, she said: '[After] I won I went to my dressing room and all my family was there. You should have heard it. We just yelled and screamed.' To top off what she dubbed her 'wonderful night', she changed her outfit yet again and headed to the Sony Music after party at a Beverly Hills restaurant in a striking gold Armani number that complemented the five shining Grammys in her arms.

Just like when she was a little girl, the trophies were now stacking up – albeit these were more prestigious than those dished out on the local talent circuit. That February, in what was one of her most successful months ever, Beyoncé also won a coveted Brit Award for International Female Solo Artist. Receiving the statuette from rapper LL Cool J, she thanked her British fans, saying: 'Y'all are so beautiful. I love coming here. I feel like this is my second home.' But she appeared to suffer a temporary memory lapse, forgetting which members of her enormous team to single out. 'Thank you . . . So many people and I'm terrible at this . . . Right now I can't think of anyone's name.' During the show at London's Earls Court, she also took to the stage and delivered another impassioned working of 'Crazy In Love' between two upturned Cadillacs.

There was no let-up in her schedule, and in March Beyoncé began her first tour of North America, a co-headlining event with soul singer Alicia Keys and rapper Missy Elliott. 'Touring is my favourite thing to do in the world,' she said, during the final preparations for the five-week Ladies First Tour. 'I love writing songs, but until you see the artist perform it live, you don't really get the full interpretation of the song.' With costumes designed by Dolce & Gabbana, the three singers planned seven outfit changes and Beyoncé said excitedly: '[There's] a lot of old Hollywood glamour. I get a lot of my inspiration from old musicals, old films. I like to put [in] a little bit of ballet, jazz, and expose my fans to a lot of different things, but still mix it in with hip-hop.' She added that having two others on the billing with her eased the pressure of singing live. 'I'm a little nervous by myself, because whenever you make any kind of mistake, it's just you on the stage.' Typically, though, it was Beyoncé who stole the show every evening, especially when she played at New York's Madison Square Gardens and Jay-Z stormed on stage for a pulsating version of 'Crazy In Love'. Reports of a rift on the tour were played down, with Alicia insisting: 'Whenever there's two women involved in anything, people automatically say they have problems with each other. But we do not have problems with each other – we never have problems with each other.'

After the tour wrapped in April, Beyoncé and Jay-Z headed back to London where they were the star attraction at the Prince's Trust Urban Music Festival. After spending time with Prince Charles at the rehearsal, Jay-Z branded him 'cool, very cool', but the prince was not quite so complimentary, letting slip that the urban vibe was not his scene although he 'liked some of the music'. His less than effusive stance did not stop Jay-Z hanging a framed print of himself with Prince Charles on the wall of his plush New York office. It was reported that the prince had invited Jay-Z and Beyoncé to dine with him at Buckingham Palace, although it seems their schedule did not allow for such a diversion.

While still in the capital, a DJ at radio station Kiss FM, who had heard about Jay-Z's declaration of love earlier in the year, tried to get the lowdown on their much-discussed marriage plans, asking him live on air if he had any special announcements to make. 'Oh, no special announcements, no. Cut that out!' an unamused Jay-Z replied.

The summer of 2004 was an exciting time for Destiny's Child fans: the band's three-year break was officially over and Kelly revealed that they were back in the studio, working on their fourth album, *Destiny Fulfilled*. Announcing the news in July, she hoped it would quieten those who had said it would never happen. 'You guys aren't going to go back in the studio,' Kelly sneered, imitating a doubter. 'Well, I just want to say to everybody who comes up to me . . . We're back in the studio, we're putting out a record. Shut up!'

Some may have doubted Beyoncé's commitment to returning to the group that had set her career in motion, but she showed no flicker of hesitation. 'For me it was an easy decision,' she told the

New York Times. 'This is having fun with my best friends. There is nothing sweeter than three-part harmony.' There was added excitement because Mathew had previously hinted to the *Los Angeles Times* that Solange would join the re-formed group as a fourth member when the time came. He even told *MTV News*: 'Judging by what I've heard, it seems like a good idea.' Solange certainly had plenty of experience, having filled in for Kelly when she broke her toes and also frequently opening for the band as a solo act.

But, in a statement that suggested Mathew's hold on the band was weakening, Beyoncé flatly ruled out her little sister joining. 'The Solange rumour is definitely a rumour,' she said. 'She's not going to be a member of Destiny's Child.' She added: 'She's working on her album. I'm so proud of her.' Although not as successful as her big sister, Solange had forged her own career and was pursuing both acting and music projects. Her debut album *Solo Star*, released at the end of 2002, had under-performed in the charts, but plans were afoot for a follow-up.

The Destiny's Child revival was clearly going to be challenging, since so much had happened since they had gone their separate ways. In an honest chat with CBS, Beyoncé reflected on the girls' differences: 'We've all grown so much. We were nineteen and now we're twenty-two, twenty-three. We're adults. So a lot of our opinions are different. So it's going to be interesting to see what's going to happen.' She added: 'It's exciting because sometimes it's lonely being by yourself. We're looking forward to reuniting.'

Kelly agreed with her best friend: 'All of us have been in three different places, so there's a lot to talk about, a lot that's gone on personally. I think it's important to talk about that on this new record, to put what we've been going through separately into the new record . . . I cannot wait until this record is done and we can go out and we can tour, and it's gonna feel so good again. I can't even describe to you what it is. It's love, it's hard work, it's hunger.'

Almost as soon as the new album was confirmed, rumours were circulating that they would split up once it came out. They batted away such claims, but when MTV asked what the girls would do after making *Destiny Fulfilled*, Beyoncé opted for the truthful approach. 'We don't know. It's important for all of us to maintain our friendship, and it's important for all of us to be happy.'

With question marks hanging over the group's future, many industry experts felt it would be impossible for the trio to recapture their past glories on the new recording. As an example, they cited singer Justin Timberlake's bombshell that he 'could not go back to 'N-Sync after tasting solo success'. Even Rodney Jerkins, one of the producers the girls had signed to help with the album, was initially unconvinced. 'How is this going to work?' he pondered, in an interview with MTV. ''Cause Beyoncé, she blew up solo, so how's it going to work in a group together?' But Beyoncé, Kelly and Michelle brushed aside the naysayers, believing they owed it to their fans to give them what they had promised at the beginning of their hiatus.

In between their recording sessions in New York, Beyoncé managed to find time to get back into the acting zone, this time shooting a remake of *The Pink Panther* opposite comic Steve Martin. 'I'm in the studio by night with Destiny's Child, and in the day I'm here on the set,' she told an MTV reporter. Playing a pop star called Xania, who became a suspect in his murder, she was also the object of affection to Steve's Inspector Jacques Clouseau. The actor was thrilled to have Beyoncé on board, joking that she was 'lovely to look at, delightful to hold'. But he commented on her apparent lack of confidence: 'She was a little shy. But you'll find a lot of people with enormous talent are really shy and that's how they got the enormous talent . . . And she had a very simple operation going. There wasn't eighty-four members of an entourage or something. She was totally professional and a sweetheart.'

Speaking from her trailer on the New York set, Beyoncé admitted that acting did not come as easily to her as singing, but that she rose to the challenge. 'I do get nervous. It's always a learning experience. That's what life is about.' She was also keen to increase her film quota in future months: 'I'm trying to surround myself with great actors so I can keep growing and doing more movies. Hopefully, I'll do a movie a year.'

Taking a breather from work, Beyoncé headed home to Texas in August for a special family event: Solange's baby shower. Aged just seventeen, she had married her high-school sweetheart, a Houston football player called Daniel Smith, in March at an exotic ceremony in the Bahamas. Beyoncé was maid of honour and, during her speech, caused the guests to giggle when she referred to herself being single still. A source told *People* magazine: 'She made a joke about her baby sister beating her to the altar. Everyone laughed, including Jay-Z. Beyoncé's mother patted him on the arm. It was like she was saying, "Your time will come soon."'

At the wedding, she and Jay-Z were said to have slept in separate villas, but were seen looking blissfully happy as they held hands on a beachside stroll. Later, Beyoncé admitted that seeing Solange tie the knot had influenced her own feelings on marriage. 'After my sister's wedding, I did start thinking about what kind of wedding I'd want,' she told *Cosmopolitan*.

The baby shower in August saw three hundred friends and family gather to celebrate Solange and Daniel's impending arrival, who was born a few weeks later. Daniel 'Julez' Smith – a first nephew for Beyoncé and first grandchild for Mathew and Tina – was described as 'fat and healthy' by Solange's spokesman when he dropped into the world. Beyoncé was at Solange's side for the birth, which was not an experience she savoured. In fact, she had begged her sister not to make her attend, fearing it would 'traumatise' her. 'But she talked me into it – and I was right! I'm scared of that,' she told the *Daily Telegraph*.

Still, 'Aunty Bey' and 'Uncle Jay' were instantly smitten with little Julez and have both had a very close relationship with him ever since, taking him to regular Knicks basketball games as soon as he was old enough to sit still. Seeing Solange become a mother made a real impact on the elder sister and she told *Harper's Bazaar*: 'I saw her in a very different light . . . I learned patience and honesty watching her relationship with her son. She added a beautiful human being to our family. My nephew is an unbelievable child. He is smart, inventive and strong. All the things my sister is.' As a regular babysitter for Julez, Beyoncé might have become agonisingly broody but, as she told *Vanity Fair* the following year, the thought of having a baby still seemed a little too challenging. 'He's a good baby, and he's the cutest thing I've ever seen in my life – I love him to death. But yesterday I got up at four in the morning . . . the time I should have been asleep, I was watching him. I played, I had the stroller . . . and I was, like, "I don't know how my sister does it."'

Sadly, Solange's marriage did not last and she and Daniel divorced when she was just nineteen. Looking back on the failed relationship in an interview with the *Evening Standard* magazine, she explained: 'We were crazy, impulsive teenagers and I was obviously craving some sort of stability. [My family] were alarmed and frightened that their seventeen-year-old daughter wanted to get married and have a kid, but I'd been working since I was thirteen.'

August was highly symbolic for another reason too. Though Beyoncé and Jay-Z were both still reticent on matters of the heart, insisting, 'We don't play with our relationship', they dropped their guard at that month's MTV Video Music Awards. With an unexpected display of affection, they walked their first red carpet as a proper couple and it was later dubbed their 'coming-out' event. With their arms wrapped around each other and dressed in matching shades of gold and white, they whispered and giggled throughout the ceremony and seemed glad of the chance to be so natural with one another in the glare of the cameras. Interestingly, some seven years later, they would also choose the MTV VMAs to unveil the news that Beyoncé was expecting their first child.

As usual, Jay-Z went to great lengths to spoil Beyoncé on her birthday in September – but this time, her $300,000 white-themed party was marred by chaotic scenes. As she celebrated turning twenty-three on the rooftop terrace of New York's Soho House, it was reported that police stormed in and shut down the raucous bash, owing to complaints from local residents. Around a hundred guests, including Kelly, Michelle, Solange and supermodel Naomi Campbell, were apparently stunned when the event was brought to an end. Not to be deterred, everyone moved on to a club to dance until the small hours. For Beyoncé, the evening was especially memorable because it was the first birthday she had spent as Jay-Z's bona-fide girlfriend. The delight this brought her was clear to all who knew her.

Chapter Nine

In September 2004, Beyoncé and Tina announced the launch of their own clothing label, House of Deréon. Named after Tina's mother, Agnèz Deréon, the brand's slogan was 'Couture. Kick. Soul', which reflected the three generations of women. Agnèz was said to be the soul, Tina the couture and Beyoncé the kick. The venture made perfect sense because Tina's stylistic capabilities had progressed and evolved so much since she had made Destiny's Child their outfits from cheap scraps. 'All of my life I've been transferring people, always fixing them up – their makeup, their hair, their clothes,' she told the *Houston Chronicle*. 'Now, this is a dream come true, and we want to do it right.'

A keen fashionista herself, Beyoncé was just as excited and told *Ebony*: 'I love the clothes from the seventies, my mother's clothes. I love clothes from the forties, my grandmother's style, so elegant. We wanted to take elements from my grandmother's legacy – the beaded lace, lush colours, fine fabrics and mix them with clothes from my mother's generation and my generation.'

House of Deréon was also a response to the constant questions

Beyoncé was asked about her style and she told CNN: 'After so many years my fans said, "We want to buy these clothes somewhere," so it was a natural thing for us to do this line. And it's so great for us to be able to do it together, number one because we get to spend time together, and two because we have such respect for each other's taste.'

Agnèz, who had been a seamstress in Louisiana, was known for her innovative tailoring and would embellish the fabrics she used with embroidery, appliqué, lace, beads and jewelled buttons. Tina had often imitated this style with her Destiny's Child creations and the same principle lay at the heart of House of Deréon.

They began with Beyoncé wearing some samples from the range, then rolled it out in stores the following year. Describing it as a mix of vintage and contemporary, she said, 'It'll be fur with denim, classic with street.' The first collection included jeans, T-shirts, party dresses, sweaters and tailored jackets, and she added: 'I have pretty broad taste. I've been all over the world – thank God I've had the chance to do that.'

Asked what made the label special, Tina replied: 'The fit. It's the fit . . . Beyoncé is curvy and our denim helps accent and create a nice curvy fit.'

With items from the label flying off the shelves, Beyoncé later teamed up with Solange to launch a less expensive junior range, Deréon. Sales proved less successful and the pair quietly discontinued the line in 2012. Clearly, it was extremely unusual for Beyoncé not to prosper in any area of her business and the fact that she chose not to address the closure publicly hinted at her acute disappointment. Increasingly, the tight control exercised over every aspect of her life meant that negative news could often be swept neatly under the Knowles family carpet. This was one such case in which she did not have to answer to anyone, or face any grilling over Deréon's shortcomings. That was Beyoncé's prerogative.

She complemented her initial foray into the fashion arena with the release of her first fragrance, called True Star. Reportedly receiving $250,000 for the deal with Tommy Hilfiger, she shot a sultry black-and-white ad in which she rolled around singing – apparently telling the *New York Post*: 'It's the easiest job I've ever had. I spent the day lying on a couch.' The launch was accompanied by a limited-edition EP on which she sang a cover of Rose Royce's 'Wishing On A Star'. Yet there was irony in her launching a fragrance, because she was famously allergic to a chemical found in most perfumes. As with all of her future scents, she worked with experts to have the offending substance removed from True Star to ensure she did not suffer any adverse reaction. Though many celebrities might never have worn their own scents, and half-heartedly committed to such projects purely to boost their bank accounts, Beyoncé did things differently, giving her own brand a stamp of integrity as well as desirability. She was genuinely passionate about the fragrance and did not want to give anyone even the tiniest chance to knock her. 'I'm so thrilled, it's so exciting to be a part of this, it's historical for me,' she told *People*. 'There's not many women in the world who can say they have their own fragrance, and not many black women, so this is wonderful. It's so classy and so timeless and so beautiful.'

By the end of 2004, the focus was firmly back on her music as the fourth and final Destiny's Child's album was ready. In spite of a few misgivings outside the band, the recording process had turned out to be a joy and their once-sceptical producer Rodney Jerkins said: 'When I got there, just seeing the excitement of them being back in the studio together, it was just natural. Those girls are sisters and it's not just a group. They have a bond.' Mathew also spoke of how easily the group had picked up again. 'Kelly lived with us from nine years old until she moved out at twenty-one, so they really are like sisters,' he enthused to MTV. 'And Michelle has been a godsend. They really, truly love each other, and that's what makes them such a unique group. When I see Michelle, Beyoncé and Kelly together, it's pure magic. It's a beautiful thing to see.'

Beyoncé was equally complimentary of her bandmates. 'We're friends. We enjoy each other. We sound good together. We grew up together and hopefully we can set an example for other groups, and other female groups . . . It's OK to do solo projects and to grow up and get a life,' she said. 'It doesn't always have to be what the media tries to make it out to be. Women can get along and be businesswomen and be smart and not be catty all the time.'

The girls declared that the overriding theme of *Destiny Fulfilled* was a group of women seeking more mature, committed relationships – partly because Kelly had recently got engaged to Dallas Cowboys footballer Roy Williams. The final track on the album, simply called 'Love', happened to be Kelly's favourite – 'Because love is so beautiful,' she said.

The girls had gone for a more even share of the lead vocals, to dispel claims that the band was now just 'The Beyoncé Show', and the *Guardian* declared it a 'democratic album'. *Vibe* magazine remarked that it showcased 'advanced production values' and 'impressive' songwriting and also that it offered 'divine satisfaction', as if the girls were singing to God. Naturally, they were delighted with its reception, but ultimately the album was conceived more as a goodbye gift to each other than a furious assault on the charts. As Beyoncé said, 'We did this record for ourselves, not to sell a million the first week out . . . That doesn't mean as much to us as just the fact that three friends got back together to do another record. That was our destiny.'

The album performed well in the charts and shot straight to number two on the *Billboard* 200, while in total it sold eight million copies worldwide. Lead single 'Lose My Breath' was a universal hit, charting at number one in much of Europe, number two in the UK and number three in America. Three further singles followed – 'Soldier', 'Girl' and 'Cater 2 U'. However, the latter was cancelled in the UK because of minimal radio airplay. It was the fourth single from the album, which appeared to have tarnished the song for the British market. Still, it fared better in the band's heartland of America, peaking at number fourteen on the *Billboard* chart and receiving two Grammy nominations. But the single was marred by allegations from Chicago-based singer Rickey Allen that 'Cater 2 U' had been his song originally and that Destiny's Child had 'copied it'. In the end, the case was settled behind closed doors before it came to court.

Though their fans did not know it, 'Cater 2 U' would be the girls' final offering before splitting up. Even prior to recording the album, they had already decided that the time was right to move on. 'It's not a coincidence that the album is called *Destiny Fulfilled*,' Beyoncé acknowledged later. 'We knew before this last album and we embraced it,' Kelly added. 'We were, like, "You know what, we're getting older and we want to end on a high note." We want to give our fans a great final record and we want to have a great tour and, above everything, we're still going to be here [for each other]. We even make jokes about having our babies on the same day.'

In February 2005, Beyoncé had the huge but somewhat daunting honour of performing three songs from Oscar-nominated films at the seventy-seventh Academy Awards show. She sang 'Believe' from *Polar Express*, 'Look To Your Path' from *The Chorus* and 'Learn To Be Lonely' from *The Phantom of the Opera*. It was an enormously important night for her and, speaking on the red carpet outside Hollywood's Kodak Theatre, she said: 'I'm so blessed. I can't believe I'm here . . . It's so surreal to me – I know it's never been done, to perform three times. For it to be me, I'm not worthy. I will be terrified right before I get on the stage but that just makes the show better.' It turned out that she had every reason to be terrified: as she was preparing to go up and perform 'Learn To Be Lonely' with Andrew Lloyd Webber, she suffered a wardrobe crisis: one of her strappy stilettos was not clasped properly and was in severe danger of falling off. 'When I walked down those stairs, not only was my shoe not on, my ear monitor wasn't on,' she grimaced as she spoke to *Vanity Fair*. 'So, the song started, and I'm thinking, Oh, my God, my shoe's not done, my monitor's not on, and this is going to be embarrassing . . . I'm going to fall down the stairs.' With a two-second delay, she had no idea if she was singing in time or not, and when she reached the bottom of the stairs, catastrophe struck: 'My shoe is off, and it's stuck in the tulle at the bottom of the dress. I'm singing on one tiptoe, and I'm trying to balance it . . . It was a mess.'

Millions of viewers watching at home failed to notice the débâcle, which pointed to her brilliance as a live performer. And this skill was so in demand that it was reported that that spring she and the Destiny's Child girls were paid $7.4 million to play at a bar mitzvah in the South of France. British retail billionaire Philip

Green hired them to play at a three-day celebration for his son, attended by two hundred guests flown in on private jets. But Beyoncé scoffed at the sum they were said to have received. 'We didn't get seven million dollars for it,' she said, and added that it was inappropriate to discuss money.

That April heralded a key event in the annals of Destiny's Child – their last tour. The five-month Destiny Fulfilled . . . And Lovin' It tour kicked off in April in Hiroshima, Japan. Taking in more than seventy cities throughout Australia, Asia, Europe and North America, it became one of the highest-grossing tours of all time by a female group. The operation was colossal and they were supported by a small army of backing dancers, caterers and support staff who filled thirteen tour buses. Sponsored by McDonald's, the girls came under fire for openly backing the fast-food giant, but Beyoncé was unfazed: 'The great thing about McDonald's is that they have a lot of different things on the menu. I love their salads.'

Each show was a blend of the band's big-hitting songs, punctuated with a scattering of their solo numbers, most notably Beyoncé's. Shaking their booty around a pioneering 360-degree set, the girls showed off a vast array of glittering costumes. In a new departure for them, the tour was considered to be an extended fashion show, with many couture items lifted straight from the House of Deréon production line. Other top-end designers clamoured for the girls to don their sexiest garb too – the makeshift, homemade look was definitely a thing of the past. Renowned fashion guru Phillip Bloch – who styled Beyoncé in her Pepsi ads – told *People* magazine: 'When they first started, nobody would give them clothes or wardrobe budgets.' Now the likes of Elie Saab and Roberto Cavalli were fully at their disposal.

Tina, of course, remained the girls' stylist, with Michelle vowing: 'We trust her. I know that with Miss Tina I'll have continuity and I'll be comfortable.' But as Beyoncé told *Glamour*: 'We've outgrown having to dress exactly alike. We want things that reflect our person-alities but that still have some harmony.' The bold new look included a set of outfits modelled on the Broadway musical *Dreamgirls*, which was being remade for the Hollywood big screen. What was more, her biggest role yet, Beyoncé was to play Deena Jones – a character based on Motown legend Diana Ross.

But at the start of the tour in Japan, there was a major disaster with one of Beyoncé's outfits. Tina was recovering from recent knee surgery but had flown out to join them, and was horrified to discover that one of her daughter's dresses needed to be remade from scratch. After driving around Tokyo for two hours to find suitable fabric, she stayed up sewing for two days and nights to complete the new garment. But the end result was a mess. 'Beyoncé put it on, and I just hated it!' Tina told *Essence* magazine. With the show about to start, Tina burst into tears. 'I never break down like that, but I was just so upset and exhausted. Beyoncé looked at me and said, "Mom, I know you're sad, but you gotta pull it together. We have a show to do." She's always like that. Just calm.'

Tina says her elder daughter was similarly placid at a show in Dubai when she threw a sweat-soaked towel into the audience and it sparked a brawl, girls fighting to get their hands on it. 'Listen!' she appealed to the fans. 'We came here to have a good time, and we do not like people to fight.'

Despite Tina being a permanent fixture on the Destiny's Child tour, Mathew was nowhere to be seen. There had recently been reports in the *National Enquirer* that he and Beyoncé had fallen out and she was preparing to fire him. It had become the hot topic in showbiz. But when asked about the rumours, Beyoncé told *Essence*: 'My father is still our manager. He hasn't toured with us since we were seventeen.' But when her relationship with Mathew later broke down irrevocably, it seems highly likely that tension was rife during this period too.

Midway into the tour, on a sultry evening in Barcelona, the girls dropped their big bombshell. It was 11 June and the final night of the European leg of Destiny Fulfilled . . . And Lovin' It. After fretting about it for days, they plucked up the courage to tell the audience that they were disbanding after the last gig in Vancouver that September. Making the announcement, Kelly told the crowd: 'This is the last time you [will] see us on stage as Destiny's Child. We have been working together as Destiny's Child since we were nine, and touring together since we were fourteen.

'After a lot of discussion and some deep soul-searching, we realised that our current tour has given us the opportunity to leave Destiny's Child on a high note, united in our friendship and filled with an over-whelming gratitude for our music, our fans and each other. After all these wonderful years working together, we realised that now is the time to pursue our personal goals and solo efforts in earnest.'

As the sixteen-thousand-strong crowd listened in disbelief, she continued: 'No matter what happens, we will always love each other as friends and sisters, and will always support each other as artists. We want to thank all of our fans for their incredible love and support and hope to see you all again as we continue fulfilling our destinies.'

Bizarrely, the UK arm of their record company, Sony BMG,

denied they were to split, saying in a statement: 'It's not true. But it could be some years before they release another album.' Any false hope given to fans was short-lived, though, as the girls reiterated their intent to disband in just a few short weeks. And Beyoncé, for one, could not believe the level of furore surrounding their decision. 'I didn't think it was breaking news,' she told *Vanity Fair*. 'I was on vacation right after we said it, and when I got back Kelly and Michelle said, "Oh, my God, it was on CNN."'

With some thirty dates remaining on the tour, the girls knew their final show would be a gruelling one. 'We're going to need a lot of Kleenex on that day,' Kelly said. 'It's going to be hard.' Evidently, the decision to pull the plug on Destiny's Child after fourteen years had not been taken lightly and all three floated the possibility of reforming further down the line. 'I mean, we might want to do something else,' Kelly insisted. 'You never know, I might wake up one morning and call one of the girls and say, "Hey, you all sure you don't want to do another album?" You never know what can happen.'

Beyoncé ruled out claims there had been a mass falling-out: 'It's not our last record because one of us wants to go solo, or because we don't get along or because we don't like each other any more, or because of cattiness,' she said. 'It's because it's the end of this chapter in our lives. We've been doing this for fourteen years now, and our destinies have been fulfilled.' She also told the press: 'We don't like the word "break-up". We'd like to say that it's the end of a chapter in our lives.'

But having been on tour together for months, the girls knew they would find life strange post-Destiny's Child. 'I think the hardest thing [will be] being alone,' Beyoncé predicted, in *Faze* magazine. 'When you're on tour, you're in the hotel rooms, and you're tired, you're exhausted or you're lonely, you can't just call the room next door and say, "Girl, what you doing, what you watching? Can I come over there?"'

In their final few shows, the band paid tribute to the victims of Hurricane Katrina, which had obliterated New Orleans at the end of August. Michelle dedicated a powerful gospel number to the 1,833 people who lost their lives, and the tragedy affected them so much that Beyoncé and Kelly – along with Mathew, Tina and Solange – set up the Survivor Foundation, a charity to provide transitional housing in New Orleans and for storm evacuees in Texas. With Beyoncé personally donating $250,000 to the cause, Jay-Z then gave a million dollars to the Red Cross, showing a philanthropic side to their nature that would become more prominent over the years.

Destiny's Child played their last ever show on 10 September at Vancouver's General Motors Place. A highly charged affair from the very first chord, tears were shed right across the arena and Kelly was the first of the three girls to break down, during her solo in 'Bad Habit'. 'Seeing the fans all lined up in the front row, it was very emotional,' she said afterwards. Normally ice-cool on stage, Beyoncé crumpled while singing 'Dangerously In Love 2'. Changing the words to fit the sombre occasion, she sang 'Kelly, I love you' and 'Michelle, I love you', and as the song ended, her voice cracked while she held her hands over her eyes. Then, at the very end, the girls' backing dancers brought out flowers for the trio and they all shared a long embrace.

Taking their bows, Kelly wept as she told them: 'I love you. You are my angels. I love y'all so much.' Composing herself, Beyoncé looked out at the audience and said: 'We don't wanna get too mushy, ya'll . . . Destiny's Child started when we were nine years old. This isn't something somebody put together. This is love.'

The month after the split, the group released a greatest-hits album as a farewell gesture. Called *#1's*, it featured all of their best-known songs, as well as three new tracks, including 'Stand Up For Love', which was released as a single. Sadly for the group, it failed to chart on the *Billboard* 100 and it was the second single in succession to be axed in Britain. It seemed that many of their fans had moved on in the wake of the break-up and there was no longer an appetite for new music. The album compilation fared much better, debuting at number one on the *Billboard* 200 and reaching number six in the UK. After it went on to sell 3.5 million copies worldwide, the girls were later reunited briefly to accept a star on the Hollywood Walk of Fame, dodging the raindrops as they accepted the honour. It was a fitting legacy from their incredible reign.

While representing an ending, *#1's* cannily paved the way for Beyoncé's next career move. Another new song on the album called 'Check On It' featured in *The Pink Panther* – which hit the big screen in February 2006 after months of delay. It was a box-office success, but the critics were not bowled over and it was nominated for two Golden Raspberry Awards that year, including the Worst Remake category. Branded 'lousy' and 'laughless' by the *Observer*, 'dead-eyed' and 'joyless' by the *Daily Telegraph*, you might imagine that Beyoncé was put off the acting game. But she seemed nonplussed and reiterated that she had loved working with co-stars Steve Martin and Kevin Kline: 'It didn't feel like work. I laughed the whole time on the set and I'm happy I'm in it.'

She was also shooting scenes for the *Dreamgirls* movie, in

which her role promised to be bigger, better and far meatier than any of the others she had played. 'I've been dreaming about this role,' she told MTV. 'I can't even talk about it, I'm so excited. Finally, I have a role that has so many layers – it's dramatic, it's funny, I play her young, I play her older. You see the journey of her growing up, and it's really emotional. It's perfect. It's a real part. I get to act, and I don't think I've ever really done that yet.'

Having first heard about the original *Dreamgirls* musical on Broadway when she was fifteen, she had come to know a lot about the character of Deena Jones – especially because her choreographer and dancers were 'obsessed with her'. On being told that the part had come up for audition, she said, 'Oh, my God, I have to have this movie,' and turned up in costume with a series of dance steps she had learned. Despite reportedly being up against Whitney Houston for the role, she won over the producers and filming was soon under way in Los Angeles, New York, Detroit and Miami. She quickly got into character and told ABC News: 'I had a shrine of Diana Ross. She was on my fridge in my trailer, all around the walls, in the dressing room, the makeup trailer . . . all plastered with Diana Ross.' She even watched one film starring Diana fifteen times to get into the zone – and it worked: 'When I watch [*Dreamgirls*] I don't see myself at all,' she said later.

The film also starred former *American Idol* singer Jennifer Hudson as Effie White, as well as Eddie Murphy and Jamie Foxx – who turned it down several times until he discovered that Beyoncé and Eddie had been cast. Incredibly, with a production budget of $80 million, it was the most expensive film to feature an all African-American cast in US movie history.

As Deena, Beyoncé's character was a shy young woman who

became a huge star after being made lead singer of the Dreams, in place of Jennifer Hudson's put-upon Effie, who was denounced too overweight for the job. With the issue of body size being at the heart of the film, Jennifer had to gain twenty pounds while Beyoncé had to slim down. This was not easy: to get fast results she crash-dieted on a concoction of water mixed with cayenne pepper and maple syrup. 'It was tough,' she told reporters. 'The drink gave me all the vitamins I needed, but I felt weak.' Later, when she could stop fasting, she went a little over the top. 'At the wrap party, I ate so many cupcakes, I was sick. Then I ate everything fried I could find. That was the best time of my life.'

Because of their intense rivalry in the film, it was perceived that Beyoncé did not get along with Jennifer when the cameras stopped rolling – and that she was deeply envious of her bigger role. But talking to the press on the promotion trail, Beyoncé said: 'It's really unfortunate that everyone is saying I'm jealous of Jennifer. It hurts my heart because it's so clichéd . . .They just automatically assume that I'm not humble enough to sit down and take a back seat, which I am.' She continued: 'I knew that the character I played wasn't the star. She wasn't the underdog. She didn't have the struggle and the pain and the dramatic scenes that Effie had, and I was fine with that.'

Clearly feeling bruised about the constant comparisons, she added: 'I'm already a big star. I didn't do the movie to become a bigger star. The thought of being bigger is actually scary. I already have nine Grammy Awards. Everyone knows I can sing. I didn't do it for the money, either – I did it for a quarter of the money I usually make. I did it because I wanted people to know that I can act and that I can play someone so different from myself.'

Rather cruelly, the *New York Post* had said that Beyoncé's co-star had made her look like 'a pretty extra', but Jennifer slapped down reports of hostility on US chat show *Watch What Happens Live*. 'There was never any rifts at all,' she insisted. 'That is still my girl to this day. I love her and we've always been good. Always.'

As Deena, Beyoncé had to kiss heart-throb Jamie's character, record executive Curtis Taylor Jr, passionately, and he joked about the prospect of being beaten up by Jay-Z over it. Compared to her awkward screen kiss with Cuba Gooding Jr in *The Fighting Temptations*, she was now more at ease with shooting steamy scenes: 'I can tell you there was no awkwardness at all,' she said. 'It was strange but it's part of acting. You've got to do it. I treated it as any other scene. Afterwards we moved on.'

But with Deena facing emotional abuse at the hands of Curtis, Beyoncé found some of the scenes draining and during the press junkets for the film she openly admitted suffering 'a lot of dark days' on set. 'It was like therapy for me. To get to those places and for them to be true, I had to go back to the most painful things that have happened to me. I was very emotional. And when I got home I'd start crying and crying. Every day I would be walking around with swollen eyes.' Not only was it an emotionally exhausting experience, but *Dreamgirls* was also extremely demanding of her time. 'This whole movie was a sacrifice for me. I put six months aside. I've never spent six months on recording an album, on doing a tour, on doing a movie, on doing anything, because I'm usually doing too many things, so that was a big sacrifice. Financially I only made a fourth of what I made on my last movie . . . [But] I would have done it for free.'

Chapter Ten

Just days after finishing her scenes on the *Dreamgirls* set, Beyoncé jumped straight back into her music and began working on her second solo album, *B'Day*. Heading into the studio in New York, she recorded all ten new tracks in just three weeks, saying she wanted to complete it 'while I still have Deena inside me'. The film had affected her deeply and themes of female empowerment seeped into her new work. 'I used making this record as a vehicle to find myself again,' she told ABC News. 'I let out a lot of emotions that Deena was feeling.' In a bonus spoken recording on *B'Day* called 'Encore For The Fans', she made direct reference to her character's plight: 'Because I was so inspired by Deena, I wrote songs that were saying all the things I wish she would have said in the film.'

Controversially, she refrained from telling Mathew that she was starting work on the album: she now seemed ready to admit that father and daughter were having problems. 'It took a while for me and my dad to have an understanding,' she cautiously let slip in *Giant* magazine. 'When I turned eighteen and started handling my business more, he went into shock. And we had our issues. I'd say, "No," to something, and he'd book it anyway.' Admitting they would 'fight sometimes', she added that it 'took about two years, to when I was twenty, for him to realise, "Oh, she is an adult now, and if she doesn't wanna do something, I can't make her do it."' In a separate interview, she also revealed that working alongside Mathew was always challenging and that they would regularly 'bump heads' and argue.'

Questioned further about why she had not involved him, she told *Blender*: 'It wasn't without telling him – it was without telling anyone. My dad and Columbia Records would have given me a deadline, and I didn't want a deadline.'

Their relationship seems to have been further strained by her acting success: Mathew admitted that that aspect of her career troubled him. 'It's hard for me still, seeing her on the big screen,' he told NPR radio in the US. Asked by the interviewer to explain why, he said: 'I don't know. I just don't know . . . It's just that I'm so used to her singing that to see her on the big screen is just, is different for me. I'm so focused in the music side of it.'

Mathew and her record label may have been left out of the *B'Day* loop, but it was not strictly true that nobody knew about the album she was hatching. Inevitably, she needed the help of her favoured musicians, while her cousin Angie was in on it too, helping to write and produce the album, just as she had on *Dangerously In Love*. As expected, Jay-Z collaborated on several tracks. 'If you've got Jay-Z's phone number, why would you get anyone else?' Beyoncé said in *Blender*. 'He's the best. My ear for beats has changed. I used to pick beats for big pop records, but that's not what I want now. My taste is more interesting since Jay.'

Debuting at number one on the *Billboard* 200, when it was released on her twenty-fifth birthday in September, *B'Day* sold half a million copies within seven days, dwarfing the 317,000 copies that *Dangerously In Love* had garnered in its first week. It was still well short of the 663,000 opening-week sales of Destiny's Child-era *Survivor*, or the million sales that her 2013 album would notch up in just five days, but *B'Day* was rightly still considered a huge success.

Beyoncé's birthday was made even more memorable when Jay-Z left her 'speechless' with the ultimate surprise gift: a 1959 Rolls-Royce convertible, said to be worth a million dollars. That evening, Tina cooked up a batch of her famed seafood gumbo in the kitchens of Jay-Z's 40/40 club, which she served to all their friends and family.

B'Day was also a smash hit outside America, reaching number three in Britain and zooming into the Top Ten right across Europe. The first single to come off the album was 'Déjà Vu', featuring Jay-Z's rapping expertise. Released prior to the album, it was her second solo number one in the UK, while peaking at number four in the US. A planned trip to Britain to promote the single was axed by Columbia, though, after police foiled a shock new terror plot to blow up American planes.

A second single in the US, 'Ring The Alarm', featured a blaring siren in its intro and an aggressive tone throughout, as Beyoncé yelled: 'I'll be damned if I see another chick on your arm!' It explored the theme of wild jealousy, and many wondered if a new facet of Beyoncé's personality was finding its way into her music. She had never let slip any trace of irrational behaviour before, but it was alleged that the ballsy track might have been sending a coded message to Jay-Z's protégée Rihanna. There had been a string of unfounded, scurrilous whispers on the internet linking the two, so gossip fiends interpreted the song as a warning to the Barbadian star to steer clear of him. Its lyrics said: 'She's sold half a million – Gold/She don't love [you] – that sh*t I know.' Both of Rihanna's albums had been certified gold, although this might, of course, have been sheer coincidence. When asked directly about the Rihanna/Jay-Z rumours, Beyoncé was dismissive and told *Seventeen* magazine: 'When things are not true, you don't really think about it. You're not scared of it, because it's not true.' And defending her young rival, she added: 'It's amazing – when you're a new artist [like Rihanna], people are curious. That just comes with being a beautiful girl and a celebrity. People just try to link you up with everybody.'

Regardless of any hidden meaning, 'Ring The Alarm' was a belter of a song, which *Rolling Stone* said had 'enough frantic, quavering intensity to make you believe she really is crazy in love'. Canadian website Jam! called the single a 'shrill tantrum of green-eyed monsterdom'.

The song's video was partly inspired by Sharon Stone's infamous role in *Basic Instinct*: Beyoncé wore a sleeveless white top and a revealing white skirt similar to that worn by the actress. Echoing the film's notorious 'knickerless' scene, the video saw Beyoncé crossing and uncrossing her legs, but to protect her modesty she wore a pair of flesh-coloured cycling shorts under the skirt. Between endless takes of the punchy promo shoot, she admitted that she found it tough going on set and that acting so deranged was mentally exhausting.

As much a talking point as the video was the single's artwork, which showed her posing in a swimsuit with two alligators on leashes. Prompting a furious response from animal-rights group PETA, which had already confronted Beyoncé because she had used fur in her fashion line, the charity teamed up with a biologist who wrote her an open letter: 'As a specialist in reptile biology and welfare, I'm concerned about your posing with a terrified baby alligator for your new album cover. Humans and alligators are not natural bedfellows, and the two should not mix at events such as photo shoots. In my view, doing so is arguably abusive to an animal.' Though Beyoncé did not comment on the letter, her relationship with PETA has always been difficult, to say the least. In 2006, two activists ambushed her at Nobu restaurant in New York after winning an eBay auction to have dinner with her. Secretly filmed footage of the awkward encounter was posted online and showed them accosting Beyoncé as she ate. Asked why she felt the need to wear fur and include it in her fashion designs, Beyoncé merely said she felt 'uncomfortable' to be put on the spot and met the rest of their questioning with stony silence. Eventually Tina, sitting next to her daughter, as always, angrily told the pair, 'You need to leave,' and they were escorted out of the restaurant. But even this incident prompted no response from Beyoncé: hitting back at her critics has never been her style. By refusing to add fuel to the fire, she is apparently able to stem the flames. So while PETA has waged a long-running campaign against her, she prefers to keep silent about their opinion of her, and chooses not to air her views on them.

The angry stance of 'Ring The Alarm' led to questions about Beyoncé and Jay-Z's current status, especially as his own material suggested they were on thin ice. Hinting that she might have been prioritising her work over their relationship, one of his new songs, 'Lost One', contained the lyrics:

> I don't think it's meant to be, B
> For she loves her work more than she does me
> And honestly, at twenty-three
> I would probably love my work more than I did she
> So we ain't we, it's me and her.

The rap continued:

> 'Cause what she prefers over me is work
> And that's where we differ
> So I have to give her
> Free time, even if it hurts . . .
> In time she'll mature
> And maybe we can be we again like we were.

Though it was unclear if this was aimed directly at Beyoncé, the debate seemed to be resolved in Jay-Z's 2010 memoir, *Decoded*. 'These lines are about trying to have a real, serious relationship with another ambitious professional,' he wrote. 'This is about how difficult it is to respect a lover as an autonomous human being, with separate needs and goals and timelines than yours. It's one of the hardest things about a real relationship of equals. But it's worth it.'

Conversely, Beyoncé seemed keen to show all was well between them and, in a rare moment of candour about her love life, told

Giant magazine: 'It's very easy . . . We respect each other. If I have any suggestion, he respects it. If he has any suggestion, I respect it. It's just, I don't know, easy. And fun.' She also assured MTV that the aggression in 'Ring The Alarm' did not reflect her personal circumstances. 'I'm very happy and calm and in a good place in my life.'

Jay-Z's 'Lost One' had been taken from his new album, *Kingdom Come* – widely considered to be his great comeback in the wake of his earlier 'retirement'. Significantly, the album featured a collaboration with British musician Chris Martin – the curly-haired lead singer of Coldplay and A-lister Gwyneth Paltrow's husband. Jay-Z's union with Chris proved to be hugely important, and Beyoncé hit it off with Gwyneth immediately upon meeting her. Before long the press labelled them new 'BFFs' – Best Friends Forever – and they enjoyed shopping trips and leisurely lunch sessions as they became better acquainted. Chris and Gwyneth also sang with Jay-Z during a gig at London's Royal Albert Hall that autumn, with the rapper instructing the audience to wish the *Shakespeare In Love* actress a happy birthday. After the show, the foursome dined at swish Knightsbridge eatery Zuma, then hit a party at Movida nightclub to celebrate the end of Jay-Z's tour. The *Daily Mirror* reported that the group got tipsy on Dom Pérignon, with Gwyneth ditching her strict macrobiotic diet to eat a slice of strawberry birthday cake.

As Chris and Gwyneth also had a base in New York, the couples grew close quickly but, as they recognised, they were an unusual match. 'Yes, it is hilarious,' Chris said, of his friendship with Jay-Z in *Q* magazine. 'What's the common denominator? Well, underneath he probably feels a bit like me and I probably feel a bit like him.' Gwyneth stressed that they 'balanced' each other, saying: 'Chris and I are like Jay and Beyoncé: two paranoid ironists and two calm, grounded people.' Though she did not expand on whom she was referring to in each case, it was taken as read that she envisaged the two men as the 'ironists' and her and Beyoncé as the calming influence.

Lifting the lid on their connection in a later interview with *Harper's Bazaar*, Gwyneth could not have spoken more generously of her friend. 'Beyoncé is the most talented human being on the planet,' she stated. 'She has so much mastery over what she does. It's not even confidence – it's on a whole other level. It's mind-blowing. I watched her [perform] a lot to see how she did it, and I was like "Sh*t! I can't do that!"' But, shattering any illusion of grandeur, she added: 'Our best times have been when we're just sitting around in sweatpants, having a glass of wine, chatting about life . . . B is wise beyond her years. She has taught me the value of speaking your mind.'

Not long after she had met Gwyneth, *Blender* magazine asked Beyoncé which celebrity couple she thought best handled the paparazzi. 'I guess Gwyneth and Chris Martin,' she answered. And when the interviewer mentioned an earlier fracas in which Chris had scuffled with a photographer, Beyoncé shrugged. 'Well, I can relate with that. It must be really scary to have your children in front of all these people. That's your kids. That's when Mama Knowles is gonna be punching some photographers!'

Aside from their blossoming social circle, all eyes were on Beyoncé and Jay-Z at the *Dreamgirls* première in New York in December. Many noted that they arrived separately – albeit in colour-coordinated outfits – but this was not a night for trivial gossip: it was Beyoncé's chance to show the critics what she was made of. The screening at the imposing Ziegfeld Theatre was one of her proudest moments to date, especially as the audience jumped to its feet to give the cast a standing ovation while the final credits rolled. *Variety* applauded its 'tremendously exciting musical sequences', while the *Guardian* praised Beyoncé's 'entrancing presence' and *Empire* simply said: 'Bravo.' After TV host Oprah Winfrey had seen the film at a press screening, she called Jennifer Hudson during a live episode of her show the next day, likening her performance to 'a religious experience'. Upon its release, the film took a whopping $154 million at the international box office and later received eight Oscar nominations, covering six categories – more than any film for the year. Incredibly for a singer who had had no formal stage training, Beyoncé had now pulled off the rare feat of making the successful leap from singer to serious actress. Though some, doubtless, were watching, waiting and willing her to fail, her acting pedigree was set in stone. Creaky bit parts and cameo roles were a thing of the past, and this meant more to Beyoncé than most would ever realise.

After the *Dreamgirls* première, which happened to fall on Jay-Z's thirty-seventh birthday, the pair made their excuses and they dashed from the theatre, skipping the official after party at Gotham Hall. Instead of hobnobbing with the cast and industry bigwigs, they had a flight to catch. Almost as if in response to Jay-Z's cutting lyrics in 'Lost One', she reportedly splashed out three million dollars on a three-day birthday party for him. She chartered two private jets to fly twenty of their closest friends and relatives to the Caribbean island of St Barts where, according to the *New York Daily News*, they boarded a 270-foot yacht laden with fresh lobster and champagne. As details of their trip emerged, the whispers about them being on the rocks vanished into thin air and the *New York Post*'s Page Six gossip column reported that they had fled to the Caribbean to get married. This scenario highlighted the contradictory nature of such fevered media speculation – something Beyoncé struggled to comprehend. 'It's so crazy that in the same tabloid we've broken up and we're married – at the same time,' she told ABC News. 'But that's a part of tabloids so it's part of my job.' She also joked about the *Post*'s wedding story in an edition of *InStyle* magazine published shortly afterwards: 'It looks like a nice wedding – and very expensive. Unfortunately it's not true.'

The marriage rumours refused to abate. On another occasion it was said that a wedding at Martha's Vineyard in Massachusetts was imminent. Locals fuelled the gossip by saying they'd seen an enormous marquee being erected on Chappaquiddick, a small island accessible only by ferry, but, again, there was no truth to the report.

Regardless of all the nonsensical stories, the prospect of walking down the aisle was becoming more of a reality in both of their minds. Beyoncé told *Parade* magazine in December: 'My parents have been married for twenty-seven years, and they're still in love. That's a great example for me. I know it's possible.' Jay-Z signalled his intent at the opening of his new 40/40 club in Las Vegas too, saying it would happen 'one day soon'. As if to give her blessing to her daughter's future husband, Tina publicly said: 'Jay is just such a gentleman, and he is so smart. I was so happy they got together. They're two smart people, and it's great for both of them – it's such a great match.' However, it seemed that Mathew was still far from convinced about Jay-Z's credentials as a husband for his daughter. Though he did not publicly denounce any wedding plans, it became clear many years later that there was still no love lost between the two men. Interviewed by the *Sun* in 2013, he reportedly said: 'I always did my best for Beyoncé . . . Fans can decide if she's better off now with Jay-Z.'

No doubt her father's frosty relationship with Jay-Z contributed to Beyoncé's major fall-out with Mathew later, but she knew in her own heart and mind that Jay-Z was 'The One'. It seemed that Beyoncé was merely waiting for him to pick the right moment to request her hand, as she told the *Daily Mirror* she would never be the one to do the asking: 'I'm old school, the kind of girl who'll wait for a guy to get down on one knee. It's not something I'm going to be doing but I admire any girl who's got the confidence, independence and strength to ask. Anyone who wants my hand has gotta have the courage to act.' Of course, this deeply traditional view seemed at odds with the strong, confident woman she had positioned herself to be, but in romantic matters Beyoncé was surprisingly old-fashioned. As she acknowledged in *InStyle*, though, she believed a proposal from Jay-Z could still be some time off. 'You can't rush a man into anything – whether it's a relationship, marriage or having children. When he's ready, he'll let you know.'

With their relationship strengthening all the time, one compelling illustration of their closeness came after that year's BET Awards in Los Angeles. At the event, she and Jay-Z sang 'Déjà Vu', Beyoncé wearing a little silver crop top and matching miniskirt, showing off rippling stomach muscles and looking in better shape than ever. Jay-Z could not resist patting her bottom as she gyrated around him. Everyone inside the packed Shrine Auditorium could sense their electrifying chemistry. Some time later, an assistant who had been drafted in to help Beyoncé for that one day wrote a touching article about the couple's behaviour at the event. Published in *Chicago Now*, Jessica LaShawn revealed how Jay-Z told Beyoncé he had missed his flight to LA and would not make it on time to sing with her at the BET ceremony. Beyoncé was bitterly disappointed when she heard the news, and Jessica wrote: 'She wasn't sad about him not doing his verse but the fact that she wouldn't see him as soon as she'd planned. She couldn't help but mumble to her mother that she missed him. She forced herself not to cry.'

Then Jessica recalled that a little later a voice rang out in the arena: 'Hey, you.' It was Jay-Z, who had tricked his girlfriend and had made the flight after all. 'Beyoncé's face lit up as she buckled [to] her knees and covered her face to hide a childlike smile . . . Her adorable cheeks [were] red and wet with embarrassing tears,' Jessica added. 'He walked in calm and cool but as he got closer he couldn't help but smile and reach out to her and hold her while placing his head gently on top of hers and shaking it.' Jessica also said it was clear that the passion in Beyoncé's music was fuelled by her devotion to Jay-Z.

The beginning of 2007 brought yet another haul of trophies as *B'Day* won Best Contemporary R&B album at the Grammy Awards in February. But the overworked star was unfortunately suffering from a stomach bug on the night – and it was only the encouragement of her friend Ellen De Generes that enabled her to complete her performance of 'Listen'. 'I just thought. I can't do this,' she recalled. 'Then I looked right in the front row and saw Ellen. She was singing every word, she was doing the choreography and I got through it. So thank you, Ellen.'

Two weeks later, it was time for *Dreamgirls* to try its luck at the Oscars. Beyoncé had initially been thrilled that 'Listen' was nominated in the Best Song category. But snuffing out her hopes of victory, the Academy of Motion Picture Arts and Sciences decided not to recognise her as a writer of the track, even though she was one of a team of four who had composed it. Disappointingly, this meant her name was not included in the nominations list – a dashing blow for a woman who always said that her biggest goal in life was to receive an Oscar. In the end the rejection did not matter: 'Listen' lost out to Melissa Etheridge's 'I Need To Wake Up' from *An Inconvenient Truth*. But *Dreamgirls* bagged two other Oscars – Best Sound Mixing and Best Supporting Actress for Jennifer Hudson. Unsurprisingly, as stunned Jennifer went up on stage to collect her gong, the cameras panned straight to Beyoncé – who seemed determined not to add further ammunition to previous reports of their on-set rivalry. She openly wept with joy at her co-star's triumph. Being part of Oscar night was an unforgettable experience for Beyoncé, who looked radiant in a striking mint green Armani gown. Mingling with thespian heavyweights Nicole Kidman, Helen Mirren and Cate Blanchett on the red carpet, she said: 'It's a magical night. The energy is incredible. It's a little intimidating when you see all the people that you admire and they're right next to you.' Crowning a terrific run, *Dreamgirls* also took three Golden Globes for Best Motion Picture – Musical or Comedy, Best Supporting Actor for Eddie Murphy and another Best Supporting Actress gong for Jennifer. Summing up her experience with the movie, Beyoncé said: 'It's a wonderful year to be an African-American actor.'

As *Dreamgirls* mania died down, she stepped up her musical endeavours once more and *B'Day*'s third single, 'Irreplaceable', topped the *Billboard* chart for ten weeks straight. Penned by rapper Ne-Yo, it became the best-selling single in the US in 2007 and was also declared the twenty-fifth most successful song of the entire decade. With its bold lyrics telling a cheating man to pack his bags and that he was far from 'irreplaceable', the song brought Beyoncé's increasingly pro-female stance to the fore. Through her music, we were witnessing her burgeoning belief that women were independent beings who deserved equality with men on every level. This seemed at odds with her traditionalist behaviour in waiting for Jay-Z to propose. It was one of the paradoxes of being Beyoncé that would become increasingly prevalent.

As for the anti-male theme of 'Irreplaceable', she admitted during an interview on CNN's *Larry King Show*, 'Men don't like it. It's a little honest. Sometimes you feel you're not being appreciated and sometimes [men] forget that they can be replaced. It's important to have songs like that to remind us. I write the songs that I need to hear and that I feel other women need to hear. I'm all about empowerment and the strength that we have when we unite as women.'

Her exploration of female solidarity moved up a level with the video for 'Irreplaceable' as it introduced a new element to Beyoncé's music: her all-female band, the Suga Mamas. Keen for a fresh injection of talent on her forthcoming solo world tour, the Beyoncé Experience, she and her team auditioned thousands of session musicians for the ten-piece band. 'I love being around females,' she told MTV. 'They inspire me, make me stronger, and there's something special about us jamming.'

During three days of auditions, thousands of women, from as far afield as Japan, Chicago, New York, LA and Houston, were narrowed down. She explained that her motivation for recruiting the group stemmed from her own past. 'When I was younger I wish I'd had more females who played instruments to look up to. I played piano for, like, a second but then I stopped. I just wanted to do something which would inspire other young females to get involved in music so I put together an all-woman band.'

The line-up of the Suga Mamas – whose name was later shortened to the Mamas – included drummer Nikki Glaspie, bassist Divinity Roxx and guitarist Bibi McGill, who worked as a yoga teacher in her spare time. Her job on tour, she said, was to 'tell everyone what time they have to be there' and, through the use of connecting earpieces, make the show look 'seamless'. With backing vocalists, a saxophonist and percussionist also signed up, the Mamas were complete. And all of the women were fiercely loyal to their leader. 'Beyoncé is a hard worker and she inspired me to work hard and push myself beyond what I thought I was capable of doing,' said Divinity. 'I will for ever be indebted to her for that.'

In a highly unusual step for any musician, spring 2007 saw Beyoncé release a video anthology for *B'Day*, featuring promos to accompany all but one of the tracks of the audio release. In addition to the already completed videos for each of *B'Day*'s singles, nine extra promos for the anthology were filmed over a back-breaking two weeks. Though Columbia attempted to talk her out of it, she was determined to make it work and described the making of the DVD as an 'overwhelming but amazing experience'. In an MTV interview, she added: 'I knew we could do it, so we had the best people – the best directors, the best choreographers, the best makeup artists, the best stylists – to make that happen. Every one of the videos is incredible.'

In one of the promos for 'Upgrade U', she played a man, saying she based her actions on the most significant male in her life. 'I was pretending to be Jay, and he was there, and I told him he had to leave, because I couldn't do it with him in the room – it was way too embarrassing. I think I did a pretty good job. I had the lip curl down!' She enjoyed the experience of spoofing alpha-male behaviour, adding: 'It was exciting being a guy. It gave me an excuse to pretend that I was a little gangster. I could do whatever I wanted – I could slouch, be a little more tough, be a little more aggressive, say whatever I wanted. I didn't have to be so prissy. And it was great not wearing the heels.'

In addition to the video anthology, April 2007 saw her release a deluxe edition of *B'Day* with five new songs, including a duet with singer Shakira called 'Beautiful Liar'. She was seeking to connect with her Latin audience: the CD also featured some of her earlier hits recorded in Spanish. 'I took Spanish in school but I don't know how to speak it – I can say a couple of words,' she said. 'But I wanted to do the Spanish versions because four or five years ago, Destiny's Child did a duet with Alejandro Sanz and our Latin fans were so excited, they were like, "When are you going to do more?"'

It was not easy to sing fluently in another language and she told the Spanish edition of *People*: 'I did these songs phonetically, sentence by sentence. I spent a lot of time on it, making sure it was perfect, because I didn't want to disrespect the language because it's so beautiful. One of my best friends in the world is Cuban so she was the test. I brought her to the studio and told her, "Be honest. You have to tell me if anything is wrong." So when she approved it I knew everything was right . . . The heart and the rhythm of the music and the drums and the spiciness remind me of Creole. It reminds me of my heritage and where I come from.'

At a time when she could easily have taken her foot off the accelerator and enjoyed the fruits of *B'Day*, Beyoncé's hard work on these ambitious extra projects was intended to be a special 'b'day' present to her loyal army of fans – whom she had affectionately begun to call the 'Bey-hive'.

Chapter Eleven

Another gift to the Beyoncé faithful came in the shape of one of her most celebrated magazine covers of all time in early 2007. Wearing a yellow-and-pink bikini, she became the first non-supermodel or non-athlete to grace the front of *Sports Illustrated*, its cover line teasing: 'The Dreamgirl As You've Never Seen Her'. Posing on a beach in Florida and looking in incredible condition, she told the magazine: 'It takes a lot of guts. I'm really a shy person. But in my everyday world, as a musical performer, I'm playing a character. I had to tap that same character.'

In the run-up to the shoot, Beyoncé had to watch what she ate meticulously. 'At dinner, I kept thinking, This extra piece of pie will show up,' she said. As a 'normal' curvy woman, she was never keen on the stick insect look favoured by many celebrities. 'I grew up in Texas with good portions of really good food,' she told *People*. 'I love good food. That's something that's never gonna change. I'm not the type of woman that eats whatever she wants without gaining weight because I do, so I have to be a little conscious of everything I eat.'

In an earlier interview with the *Sun*, she had confessed that there were parts of her body she disliked: 'Like every woman, there are bits I'd change,' she said. 'I am not going to say which bit I would change because then everybody is going to be looking directly at it!' Having read stories in which it was claimed she often ate only lettuce or a few slices of cucumber for lunch, she said: 'I've never starved myself, and all these rumours about me only eating lettuce are just crazy. Anyone who knows me will tell you that.'

Repeatedly asked the secrets of her exercise regime, she attributed her toned thighs to endless squats. 'I hate them but they're the best,' she said. And she had also discovered a new way to stay trim without having to slug it out at the gym: 'I really love Wii Fit,' she said. 'I think it would be a great idea to incorporate choreography because for me my workout is way more fun when it involves dancing as opposed to running on a boring treadmill.'

On the day of the terrifying *Sports Illustrated* shoot, Beyoncé's biggest support team came out in force on the beach to root for her. 'Kelly showed up. My mom was there, my nephew,' she said in the accompanying interview. 'Dad was going to come, but he said, "Well, I'll, um, meet you in Orlando after the shoot. I'm not so sure that I want to see this. All my blessings, you're a big girl. But I'm not so sure I want to see it."'

Revealing her pride in the finished product, she said: 'These are photos I can show my kids some day. I can say, "See, Momma was beautiful. Look how good I looked!"' She also told Star Jones on CNN: 'It's amazing. It really is. It's a great honour for me. They've never had a musician on the cover – not only was I the second black woman I was also the first non-model or athlete.'

Ever the businesswoman, Beyoncé only agreed to the shoot on the condition that Tina could design her bikinis. The magazine agreed, and on the back of the top-selling issue, they launched a range of swimsuits for House of Deréon.

With so many projects on the go, there was barely time to pause for breath before her new world tour, the Beyoncé Experience, sprang to life in Tokyo in April 2007. With ninety-seven dates strung out over six months, the tour grossed $90 million and took in vast swathes of Asia, Australia and Europe, and even included a show in Ethiopia. Packing in hits from *B'Day* and *Dangerously in Love*, she began each concert rising from the centre of the stage, like a goddess, wearing an ankle-length silver gown, which she later ripped off to reveal a mini version underneath. Even that was eventually discarded, to reveal a barely there bodysuit, which a critic from the *Irish Independent* said would 'linger in my memory for years to come'. Featuring seven outfit changes in all and regular pyrotechnic explosions, the tour marked the debut of her energetic Mamas band – who rocked out with instrumental sections every time Beyoncé disappeared for a costume change. The show also included a Destiny's Child medley, while band-mates Kelly and Michelle put in a guest appearance at the LA show – with Jay-Z. Speculating on her supposed backstage rider, the *New York Post* said her wish list would regularly include turkey sandwiches, an endless supply of Pepsi and Honey Nut Cheerios, as well as a two-person 'love seat' and a room temperature of no less than 78 degrees.

The tour attracted favourable reviews wherever it landed. The *Boston Globe* remarked that her voice sounded as if it had been 'kissed by the gods', and raved: 'It was part Vegas revue, part hard-edged rock concert, part sweaty funk and soul revival, part diva concert-hall performance, and almost all fun to watch as the singer threw herself into the various settings and costumes.'

Many were astounded by Beyoncé's sheer stamina on stage as she flung heart and soul into every rigorous dance routine. Judging from the power and determination on display night after night, it was evident that Sasha Fierce – her childhood alter ego – was out in full force. As she told *Parade* magazine: 'I become someone else when I'm on stage. I call that stage persona Sasha Fierce. I keep her on stage and me, Beyoncé, off stage.' Curiously, she admitted that she did not feel any affinity to this other person: 'I wouldn't like Sasha if I met her offstage . . . [She is] too aggressive, too strong, too sassy, too sexy. I'm not like her in real life at all. I'm not flirtatious and super-confident and fearless like her. What I feel on stage I don't feel anywhere else. It's an out-of-body experience.'

As she confided in CNN's Larry King that year, Sasha compensated for her lack of body confidence, too. 'I'm definitely not perfect,' she said. 'I wake up, I get pimples, I have bad hair days. I can't cook, I mess up, I say things that are silly. I'm just like everyone else. I kind of created this character that gives me confidence when I don't really have it. Sasha is that person who is fearless.'

Evidently the Beyoncé Experience demanded so much that stepping into Sasha's shoes was the only way she could keep the momentum going. As she told *Rolling Stone*: 'I'm really very country and would rather have no shoes on and have my hair in a bun and no makeup. And when I perform, this confidence and this sexiness and whatever it is that I'm completely not just happens . . . It's a job. In real life I'm not like that.' Her trusty choreographer, creative director Frank Gatson Jr, said her stage presence was inspiring to watch: 'Something powerful takes her over, and in that time on stage she's gone.' He recalled a show in which she recklessly discarded a pair of $250,000 earrings, saying: 'She said she didn't know why she threw them. That's losing yourself.'

Illustrating another of Sasha's reckless moments, Beyoncé told *Cosmopolitan*: 'Once at the MTV awards, I had [a really expensive] bracelet on and chucked it into the audience. Angie had to go and retrieve it.'

As the prominence of her imaginary other self grew, rumours even circulated that Beyoncé would no longer answer to her birth name, going only by Sasha. Rubbishing such claims, Tina told *Elle* that she would still frequently tease her daughter about Sasha's influence during their frantic costume changes on tour. 'Me and Angie and Ty, her stylist, would work with her doing a quick change when she'd come off the stage between sets. Beyoncé would start screaming, "What's wrong with you? Where's my shoe?" "Uh-oh," we'd say, "Sasha is here." I'm, like, "This is some crazy person who's doing this quick change. She's another person up there." We don't take it personally. Sasha is her bragging side.'

Beyoncé's empathetic side was highlighted as she teamed up with her old pastor, Rudy Rasmus, to set up food banks on the US leg of the tour. Fans were urged to bring non-perishable foods to be distributed around communities in need, and she said: 'Hunger affects every community in the United States. Reaching out and touching lives is incredibly empowering. That's why I want my fans to experience more than my music this summer. I want them to experience the joy of making a difference by helping someone else.'

But while it was a runaway success, the tour was not without its problems. During a show in St Louis, Missouri, two fans in the front row were hurt due to a malfunction with the fireworks during the opening song. They were rushed to hospital after a shower of sparks landed on them. Their injuries were not too serious and the show could continue. Worried about them, Beyoncé visited them in hospital the following day, spending forty-five minutes chatting with them. One of the nurses on duty at the time, Darryl Williams, said: 'She was just very concerned . . . It was unannounced and we kept it very low-key so that she could spend time with them. I thought it was a great thing for someone of her stature to do.'

Another disaster occurred in Orlando, Florida, when Beyoncé tumbled head first down a flight of stairs during 'Ring The Alarm'. Her shoe had caught in the hem of her long red coat as she danced. She picked herself up straight away and carried on with the routine, then told the audience it 'hurt so bad' and begged: 'Don't put it on YouTube!' However, within hours, several videos of the incident had been uploaded, much to her embarrassment. Presumably at the behest of Team Beyoncé, the clips were later removed when YouTube announced that users had violated its terms of use. 'Even if [they] took the video [themselves], the performer controls the right to use his/her image in a video,' said a representative. But her efforts to block the footage backfired because it appeared on other sites such as Dailymotion. Speaking in defence of his girlfriend, Jay-Z said in a radio interview that even though she was 'a great performer who's on point ninety-nine per cent of the time, she's still human'. The peril in live performance struck again during her Toronto show when her dress flew over her head. Many speculated that she had inadvertently exposed a breast, but one of her spokespeople hit back: 'She's wearing a flesh-tone bra. Do you really think Beyoncé would go on stage like that?'

Elsewhere, her raunchy attire led to such strong protest from Malaysia's Muslim groups that the Kuala Lumpur leg of the tour was cancelled. Beyoncé felt she could not comply with a dress code that banned female performers from showing any skin from the top of the chest to the knees. Her management blamed a 'scheduling conflict', apologised to the Malaysian people and switched the concert to Jakarta in Indonesia instead. Another scheduled show in Istanbul, Turkey, was axed out of respect for twelve soldiers who were killed in a Kurdish rebel attack.

One number on the tour's set list, 'Flaws And All' from her *B'Day* album, reduced her to tears on stage every night and she would end the song wrapped in a pair of white angel wings worn by a male dancer. The track spoke of her love for a man who could see through her flaws and love her unconditionally – it seemed to be a heartfelt message directed to Jay-Z. Discussing the meaning of the song when she first recorded it, she said: 'It's time for people to see that side of me. It's not about glamour, not about celebrity, not about being a diva – it's about someone loving you for you.' *Vibe* magazine surmised that Beyoncé wanted the camera on her face throughout the song, 'showing the crowd her own flaws, allowing the crowd to connect to her'.

Life on the road for months on end left her missing Jay-Z acutely, and though he would fly out to join her whenever his schedule allowed, she struggled with their long-distance arrangement. After her tour ended in Taiwan in November they celebrated their reunion in New York with a quiet dinner at La Esquina restaurant. The mood was doubly celebratory as Jay-Z's new album *American Gangster* had just become his tenth number-one debut, equalling Elvis Presley's record for most chart-topping albums by any American artist. Interestingly, he went on to trounce that feat with his next two albums and in 2013 set the bar with an all-time high of thirteen number-ones upon the release of *Magna Carter . . . Holy Grail*. However, he is still some way behind the Beatles, who have had nineteen number-one recordings, more than any other act to date.

Meanwhile, the end of 2007 brought another big boost to Beyoncé's bank balance as she was plastered over billboards and TV ads as the face of Emporio Armani's latest fragrance, Diamonds. Speaking about the perks of working alongside Armani, she giggled: 'Now that I'm doing these appearances, they bring me racks of clothes – and I get to keep them. All of them. Even the ones I don't wear that day. I have storage here and in Houston – I have to ship a lot of the clothes. It's too many great clothes. I've got no complaints.' But when asked how many Armani frocks she owned, she was stumped. 'A hundred. A lot? It's very cool.'

After a short hop to Los Angeles, where Beyoncé was crowned Best International Artist at the American Music Awards, she and Jay-Z headed to Paris in December to celebrate his thirty-eighth birthday. After checking in at the opulent Hôtel Meurice, they spent a whole day in their luxurious suite, with views over the famous Tuileries gardens, with Beyoncé only nipping out to visit the spa. At sunset, they climbed into a waiting limo for a romantic drive around the city, then enjoyed an intimate dinner at L'Avenue restaurant. To end the evening, they went to a cabaret show at the Crazy Horse club, where they were seen sipping champagne and looking blissfully content in each other's company. Days after their Parisian jaunt, website mediatakeout.com reported that the pair had secretly got married in a small ceremony at designer Giorgio Armani's home in the French capital. Claiming to have a world exclusive, the site said the pair had decided against traditional rings and instead opted for matching tattoos on their ring fingers.

These latest claims were refuted by Jay-Z, but in the end, the website had not been so very far from the truth. In a documentary released some six years later, Beyoncé revealed that he had proposed on his birthday in Paris, getting down on bended knee in time-honoured fashion. 'The day that I got engaged was my husband's birthday and I took him to Crazy Horse,' she said in the 2013 documentary. 'I remember thinking, Damn, these girls are fly. I thought it was the ultimate sexy show I'd ever seen.'

There was no official confirmation of the engagement so their secret remained firmly intact. As Jay-Z had recently suggested in *XXL* magazine, he was fed up with the constant speculation: 'I think people are only interested in [a relationship] three times. When you get together, when you break up, and when you have a baby. They don't have good intentions. People just want to manipulate the situation to benefit them. I think relationships are broken up because of the media.'

As they continued to keep their cards close to their chest, 2007 ended on a very unstarry note – with Beyoncé playing her favourite game, Connect Four, for the whole of New Year's Eve. During an intimate gathering at Jay-Z's club, she went head-to-head with their close friend rapper Kanye West, who then blogged about the lengthy contest. 'Every now and then people would speak of this legendary Connect 4 champion . . . BEYONCÉ!!!' he wrote. 'I had 2 play her. [She] beat me 9 times in a row!'

In February 2008, still guarding her and Jay-Z's secret, Beyoncé got the chance to sing with one of her greatest idols, Tina Turner. The rock legend came out of retirement at the age of sixty-eight to perform with her at the fiftieth annual Grammy Awards and they duetted on a lively version of one of Tina's old hits, 'Proud Mary'. 'It felt good to be there,' Tina commented afterwards. 'People said, "You looked better than Beyoncé." Well, that's not possible . . . Beyoncé is elegant and is handling her career well.'

Although their performance was the highlight of the night, it sparked controversy as soul diva Aretha Franklin took major offence that Beyoncé had introduced Tina on stage as 'the queen'. In an odd statement the day after, Aretha said: 'I am not sure whose toes I may have stepped on or whose ego I may have bruised between the Grammy writers and Beyoncé. However, I dismissed it as a cheap shot for controversy.' Responding to her peculiar gripe, perplexed Grammy producer Ken Ehrlich said that Beyoncé had merely made 'an innocent remark [that] wasn't meant to disparage Aretha'. Meanwhile, Beyoncé's father, Mathew, branded Aretha's outburst 'childish' and 'unprofessional'. Tina Turner was similarly unimpressed: 'She's the queen of soul, and I'm the queen of rock 'n' roll. There were so many kings and queens there that night. Her ego must be so big to think she was the only one.'

The same month, it was announced that Beyoncé had signed

up for her next movie: she would play the formerly heroin-addicted blues singer Etta James in *Cadillac Records*. The fifties-set biopic co-starred Adrien Brody as founder of the Chicago record label that had opened doors for black musicians, including Chuck Berry, Muddy Waters and Etta herself. For the role, Beyoncé had to gain twenty pounds and dot her arms with needle marks to illustrate Etta's past drug problems. She additionally spent weeks visiting Phoenix House, a tough rehabilitation centre in New York, to learn more about the issue. 'I'd never tried drugs in my life, so I didn't know about it,' she told the *Daily Mirror*. 'It was hard to go there, but people at the rehab centre were so honest and helpful. I learned a lot about life and myself, and I understood Etta's need and her addiction.' She added: 'It was important for me to be raw and honest, and not be a glamorous version of Etta James. I wanted to have the swollen eyes and the veins in my face – I wanted to make it real.'

In her role as Etta, she was thrilled to sing the legendary jazz number 'At Last', but the song came back to haunt her a year later. The part required her to swear a lot. 'My mom had to leave the set,' she told *Elle*. 'I don't normally curse. Maybe twice a year. I have to be really livid.'

Co-executive produced by Beyoncé, the film signalled her rapid progression in the acting world but, as had happened with *Dreamgirls*, the film sapped her reserves. 'It was very painful for me because I'm naturally a pretty happy person. I had to think about the most painful things in my life so I could be true to this character. I was crying for twelve hours a day and coming home very grouchy.'

Some months later, it emerged that she was donating her entire four-million-dollar *Cadillac Records* fee to Phoenix House rehab centre. Treating more than five thousand addicts a day, the unit had left a profound mark on her heart, but she refused to draw attention to the gesture – which Tina found frustrating. 'Mama, let it go!' she interrupted, when her mother raised the subject during an interview with *Elle* magazine.

'I don't want people to think she's a diva,' Tina interjected.

Two years later, Beyoncé returned to Phoenix House in Brooklyn to open a beauty school that had been built using her money. Called the Beyoncé Cosmetology Center, it provided training courses to help recovering addicts learn new skills in skincare, makeup and hairdressing, enabling them to support themselves. Attending the ribbon-cutting ceremony with Tina, she said: 'Addiction is a disease and these beautiful women I met did not choose to become addicts, but they have chosen to get better.' She added that, as a child, she had seen Tina's hair salon as a place for women to 'share stories, cry, laugh, and get advice' and now she hoped others could experience the same thing at her school. 'The first sign of recovery is caring about your appearance,' she said. Bowled over by her generosity, the Phoenix House staff said: 'We express our heartfelt gratitude to Beyoncé and Miss Tina for their tremendous gift, which will indeed change lives.'

By the time March 2008 came around, it had become widely accepted that Beyoncé and Jay-Z were engaged. She had been seen with a massive rock on her wedding finger while partying at Butter nightclub in New York – and reportedly became so conscious of prying eyes that she stashed it in her handbag. But while the sighting (and abrupt removal) of the sparkling jewel worked the gossip columns into a frenzy, she later claimed that she had never worn an engagement ring, saying: 'People put too much emphasis on that.'

Whatever her stance in public, behind closed doors Beyoncé now felt ready for such commitment. 'Before the age of twenty-five, I would never get married,' she confided in *Seventeen* magazine, aged twenty-six by now. 'I feel like you have to get to know yourself, know what you want, spend some time by yourself, and be proud of who you are before you can share that with someone else.'

Though attention rapidly turned to exactly what kind of ceremony the pair might opt for, Beyoncé had previously made clear that she would never consider a glitzy celebrity affair tailored to the pages of a glossy magazine: 'I was never one of those girls who dreamed of a big wedding,' she said. 'Maybe me and my man will go away to an island; maybe we'll go to a church. I have no idea.'

One of the more outlandish rumours over their nuptials suggested that she planned to tie the knot in a replica of the late Princess Diana's wedding gown, which Beyoncé laughed off. The same report said they would serve $300,000 worth of caviar and drink Dom Pérignon champagne at $200 a bottle, but she joked: 'I wish I could talk to whoever wrote that, because it's fabulous. Somebody is so creative that they should plan weddings, because they have a great one planned for me and Jay! It even has a menu of caviar. I don't like caviar!'

Chapter Twelve

During the making of *Cadillac Records*, Beyoncé was again stretching herself to the limit, recording her third solo album, *I Am . . . Sasha Fierce*, at the same time. At least she allowed herself a longer timeframe to get the project finished, spending eight months in the studio in New York, Atlanta, Miami, LA and Ibiza. Some seventy tracks were completed during this period, with the final eleven songs split into two separate discs. The *I Am . . .* tracks showed off a more vulnerable sound with folk, strings and acoustic influences, while the *Sasha Fierce* numbers were pulsating and mainstream. Impressively, she had writing and producing credits on almost every song, yet no fewer than thirty-two songwriters and nineteen producers were involved in the deluxe edition.

The more leisurely approach to making her music was just as well, because that spring brought with it a major event that made headline news right across the world. On 4 April 2008, she and Jay-Z finally got married, after more than six years together.

Just days before, word had got out that they had taken out a marriage licence in Scarsdale, New York, which permitted them to marry within the following sixty days. They gave no hint of their intention, however, while attending the wedding of Jay-Z's assistant, Robin Broughton, that week in Philadelphia. 'They seemed very much a couple in love,' said Robin's wedding planner, Lisa McGraw. 'They held hands and were all smiles.' The date they had chosen for their big day had special significance for the couple, as their birthdays both fell on the fourth of a month, just as Tina's did. By mid-afternoon that Friday, candelabra and flowers had been delivered and were pictured on the pavement outside Jay-Z's Tribeca home. Then Beyoncé's bandmates, Kelly and Michelle, posted a video of themselves on YouTube from their room at the Four Seasons Hotel. They teased fans that they were at an 'undisclosed location' and refused to explain why they were in New York. The event seemed to be in no doubt when Jay-Z's mother, grandmother, sister and niece were spotted at a beauty parlour called the Devachan Salon and Departure Lounge for some pre-wedding pampering. Hairstylist Marvin Bull told them, 'I know there's a wedding today,' but they just laughed at him. 'His mom was saying they wanted it very small, so not many people got invited,' Marvin said.

The ceremony, rumoured to have cost around seven hundred thousand dollars, was indeed strict on numbers, with just forty guests. As well as Kelly and Michelle, they included Gwyneth Paltrow and Chris Martin, Tina, Mathew and Solange. The nuptials were conducted by Beyoncé's former pastor, Rudy Rasmus, who later said their union was driven by 'trust, respect and love'.

Instead of commissioning a celebrity favourite, such as Vera

Wang, to design her all-important bridal gown, Beyoncé had asked her mother to make one for her: Tina knew what suited her daughter's shape better than anyone. The ivory dress was strapless, with a fitted bodice and ruched, billowing train, and clung to Beyoncé in the right places. She chose not to have a maid of honour, while Jay-Z – wearing a black tuxedo – had no best man. Beyoncé's wedding ring was a beautiful 18-carat diamond rock by Lorraine Schwartz, said to be worth five million dollars. The couple also had matching tattoos of the Roman numeral IV etched on their ring fingers as a permanent mark of their commitment. But so private was Beyoncé about her marriage that she later confessed she always took off the ring before any media interviews.

Inside Jay-Z's penthouse, a white tent had been put up in the basketball-court-size living room, which 'looked like a palace', according to florist Amy Vongpitaka. She installed up to sixty thousand white orchids, which had been flown in from Thailand, in the apartment and on the terrace and confirmed: 'It was a really pure white wedding.'

On the menu was a feast of home-cooked Creole treats, with all the family lending a hand to ensure their privacy, and Jay-Z's grandmother made her famous oxtail dish. There were also platters of appetisers, stacked with shrimp scampi and Beyoncé's favourite, Popeyes' fried chicken. As everyone got stuck into cocktails and free-flowing champagne, the evening entertainment kicked off with their first dance – not a romantic, slushy number but 'Crazy In Love'. DJ Cassidy, a favourite of Jay-Z, took to the decks, and guests danced to hip-hop and 'oldies' – such as the Jackson Five and Whitney Houston. The bride and groom decided to give their vocal cords a night off and did not sing, but the party went on until five a.m., with Jay-Z smoking 'very expensive cigars' all night.

Six years later, the pair would post surprise video footage of their big day on giant screens while on tour together. This showed the moment Jay-Z put the ring on Beyoncé's finger, as well as her punching the air in delight as they walked down the aisle. But back in 2008, it was so hush-hush that they did not confirm the marriage, even though it was glaringly obvious that they were now husband and wife.

The day after the wedding, the pair flew to North Carolina, where the rapper was due to resume his tour with Mary J. Blige. Photographed stepping out of their private jet at Greensboro airport, they attempted to hide from photographers, but a wedding band was clocked on Jay-Z's left hand. Up on stage that night, Mary J. let the cat out of the bag by declaring: 'Congratulations to my man Jay-Z and my girl B.'

Back in New York two days later, Jay-Z was seen watching a basketball game at his 40/40 club. Congratulated by a handful of revellers in the bar, he claimed he did not know what they were talking about. Solange also 'played coy' when she was quizzed over the wedding during a visit to a magazine office, saying she had 'no idea' if her sister was enjoying married life. 'Family is family, and we're [a] very tight-knit, protective family,' she said.

As private as ever, the newlyweds refrained from releasing an official wedding image to the press, with Beyoncé saying: 'Absolutely not – it's so not worth it.' Neither did the world have any idea what her dress looked like until three years later when she gave a quick glimpse of it in a video for 'I Was Here', on a concert DVD called *Live At Roseland*. 'My mother designed that dress,' she eventually said. 'I'm so proud of that dress because she did such a beautiful job. It's my favourite dress I've ever worn.'

Months passed before they formally acknowledged that they were married. Eventually a brave interviewer tackled Jay-Z in the September issue of *Vibe* magazine that year. After he casually referred to Beyoncé as his 'friend', the journalist probed, 'You said your "friend" but this is your wife. Are you still not willing to confirm?' Defensively, Jay-Z replied: 'That's ridiculous for me to confirm. I don't have . . . I'm gonna say, I think that was a ridiculous question. I just think it's really a part of your life that you gotta keep to yourself. You have to, or you'll go insane in this type of business. You have to have something that's sacred to you and the people around you.' Refusing to budge, he added: 'I shared so much of my life, my childhood and my family, the death of my nephew, with the world. I should have something to hold on to. You need something for your sanity.'

Beyoncé kept quiet for six months and only felt ready to share her news in an interview with *Essence* that October. Asked why she had not talked about the wedding, she said defiantly: 'We decide everything. My word is my word. What Jay and I have is real. It's not about interviews or getting the right photo op. It's real.'

She also said she had been determined to keep a lid on proceedings because she didn't want the drama of a big bash. 'It's been my day so many days already. We've been together a long time. We always knew it would happen.' Then, during an appearance on *Oprah* in November, she was equally measured. 'It's difficult because I had to really learn how to have boundaries, and balance,' she said. 'It was difficult and it still is because I'm so excited about it, but it's important that I keep things that are pure and real in perspective, and I keep it separate from my performance life.' As Oprah gently coaxed her, she offered just one tiny nugget about the ceremony: 'It was very private . . . Outside it was paparazzi madness and inside it was really beautiful.'

As time went by, Beyoncé opened up a little more about the nuptials and even admitted in 2010 that she and Jay-Z had signed a marriage contract. Speaking to *Neon*, she said: 'I do not deny that there is a marriage contract. I would encourage any woman getting married to put on such a treaty.' But she added: 'For details, I don't express myself. I am not here on trial.'

In the unusually candid interview, she suggested that her own financial and domestic worries were the same as those of ordinary folk. 'What separates us is perhaps the price of butter,' she pointed out. 'But in all that is essential, I feel like every hard-working woman.' She also stressed that her and Jay-Z had to deal with exactly the same relationship hurdles as everyone else, saying she wanted children eventually but that her husband was 'entirely not aware of that fact yet'. And she admitted that while she often liked to relax at home in a tracksuit, Jay-Z 'assumes and believes that women even wear high heels just to go to the bathroom'.

Squeezing in a delayed honeymoon in May, Beyoncé and Jay-Z slipped away to the $2,000-per-night Sanctuary Camelback Mountain Resort in Phoenix, Arizona. Though they only stayed a few days, because of work commitments, it provided a welcome retreat from the whirlwind of recent events, with stunning mountain views, a meditation garden, five tennis courts and even a hummingbird sanctuary.

On their return home, the showbiz website TMZ reported that the pair had bought a palatial new marital home in Scarsdale – the suburb outside New York in Westchester County where they had obtained their marriage licence. The modern colonial home was around 15,000 square feet in size and set within two acres of land. This was to add to their existing portfolio of homes in Manhattan and Miami, where they also owned a beachfront villa with seven bedrooms and eight bathrooms.

Alongside settling into their new home, a freshly inspired Beyoncé hit the recording studio in California to continue with *I Am . . . Sasha Fierce*. The first track she worked on post-wedding was, rather aptly, 'Single Ladies (Put a Ring On It)', which became her best-selling song of all time. Advising men to propose or risk losing their women for good, it urged:

> *Pull me into your arms*
> *Say I'm the one you want*
> *If you don't, you'll be alone*
> *And like a ghost I'll be gone.*

The song's producer, Christopher Stewart, revealed that it related to her secret wedding: 'It was the only public statement that they ever made about marriage. When we went into the studio she didn't have a ring on or anything, because at that point they were still really hiding it.'

During a break from recording, Beyoncé joined her new husband at one of the biggest events of his life – the Glastonbury

Festival in Somerset, where he was to perform for a crowd of seventy thousand. While hanging out with him backstage prior to his slot, Beyoncé was not the main attraction for once and she blended effortlessly into the background, wearing an unassuming parka jacket and barely there makeup.

The fact Jay-Z was down as 2008's headlining act had sparked anger, with many saying the age-old hippie festival was not the right environment for hardened hip-hop. The *Sun* felt his involvement made it 'the worst Glastonbury line-up ever', while other music commentators blasted it as 'a disaster' and 'tragic'. Even Noel Gallagher of Oasis waded into the debate: 'I'm sorry, but Jay-Z? No chance. Glastonbury has a history of guitar music.' Accusing Noel of 'ripping off the Beatles' by way of counter-argument, Jay-Z described the fall-out 'the biggest controversy I've ever been involved in'. He then opened his set with a cover of *Oasis*'s most famous song 'Wonderwall', during which he pulled on a guitar and had the crowd chanting his name. 'I knew I had an ace with "Wonderwall",' he told the *Observer*. 'I knew they'd appreciate the humour in that, so I'd at least get to the third song.'

Confounding the critics, his set was hailed a triumph, with Beyoncé giving him the biggest endorsement of all. 'I was so proud of him that night,' she told the *Daily Telegraph*. 'To come into that atmosphere and that incredible place and do what he did . . . I was dancing like crazy, dancing crazy hip-hop moves offstage. I don't know if I've ever seen him do a better show. He rocked that crowd, showed them what he's about. Jay is, well . . . he's the number one. But there was something going on that night – something more than just music.'

* * *

In August Beyoncé's ultra-lucrative contract with L'Oréal Paris was plunged into controversy, when the cosmetic giant was dramatically accused of 'whitening' her skin in a series of press ads for its Feria hair colour. In the promo shots, Beyoncé appeared to have paler skin and lighter hair than normal, although she had signed a contract pledging she would not make any 'radical changes' to her own appearance. The company vehemently denied any such retouching, saying: 'It is categorically untrue that L'Oréal Paris altered Ms Knowles's features or skin tone in the campaign for Feria hair colour.' It added: 'We highly value our relationship with Ms Knowles.'

However, some media outlets were not convinced and the *New York Post* alleged that 'digital lightening' had been used, which made Beyoncé 'virtually unrecognisable'. In addition, gossip website TMZ launched an online poll to ask if it was 'a slap to blacks'. Beyoncé and her team did not comment, but whatever the situation, Beyoncé has always been highly vocal about her pride in her skin colour. 'I feel like now, at least with my career, I've kind of broken barriers,' she once said. 'I don't think people think about my race. I think they look at me as an entertainer and a musician.'

When the furore had died down, October 2008 saw the release of 'Single Ladies', which immediately took the world by storm. Sitting at number one on the *Billboard* 100 chart for four weeks, it also topped the charts in the UK, Canada and Australia and garnered more than six million digital downloads. The black-and-white video was shot on a low budget, with no costume or set changes, using minimal camera shots and cuts. Its *Sasha Fierce*-esque aggression, with Beyoncé and her two dancers in black leotards and killer stilettos, all rippling thighs and energetic booty-shaking, attracted most attention. The glint of Beyoncé's knockout wedding ring gave the video extra bite. However, the very fact that she was wearing a ring prompted criticism from those who felt such a symbol flew in the face of what was surely meant to be a feminist shout-out to women. She was flaunting diamonds bestowed on her by a man and seemingly stooping to the idea that a woman needed 'a ring on it'. But in Beyoncé's defence, she had never claimed outright to be an ardent feminist and her spin on the F-word was certainly less rigid than the term implied. But she was only too willing to hold her hands up to this. 'I guess I am a modern-day feminist,' she cautiously told *Vogue* later. 'I do believe in equality.' For her, it was not about complex ideology or activism – it was about championing women, pure and simple. 'Why do you have to label yourself anything?' she asked. 'I'm just a woman and I love being a woman.'

Feminist debate aside, the frenetic moves seen in the 'Single Ladies' video came at a cost: during filming Beyoncé got covered with bruises. 'I fell when we ran up the wall,' she said. 'We all fell pretty badly but we got back up and kept going. I wrapped the video at two thirty in the morning and my feet were all wrapped up – but that's part of the job.'

Albeit the cheapest and quickest of all her videos to make, Beyoncé agreed that it was 'the most iconic . . . something special'. It spawned a cult dance craze and hundreds of YouTube tributes. She told MTV: 'It's beautiful to feel you touch people and bring a song to life with a video.' The promo's director, Jake Nava, was overwhelmed by the response: 'I don't think any of us predicted the amount of parodies it would attract. It's a testament to

Beyoncé's mind-boggling talent and to the fact that, sometimes, less really can be more.'

Arguably the funniest 'Single Ladies' spoof occurred on US show *Saturday Night Live*, with singer Justin Timberlake playing one of Beyoncé's backing dancers, complete with leotard, heels and grinding moves. She initially hesitated about taking part, but agreed after Justin dropped into her dressing room to persuade her. 'Justin is crazy . . . I can't believe how hilarious he is!' She laughed. 'Why are his legs more beautiful than any woman's?'

'Single Ladies' became the second most watched online video of all time, with more than 525 million views. The single was also nominated for nine MTV awards at the 2009 VMAs, but the ceremony memorably erupted into chaos when it failed to bag the Best Female Video trophy. In an incident dubbed 'Kanyegate', 'Single Ladies' was beaten in that category by pop singer Taylor Swift's video for 'You Belong With Me'. As the teenager was proudly collecting her award, rapper Kanye West stormed on stage and, interrupting her speech, blurted: 'I'm sorry, but Beyoncé had one of the best videos of all time.' As the crowd fell silent and Beyoncé looked on in horror, Taylor's golden moment had been well and truly ruined. When Beyoncé received an award for 'Single Ladies' later in the evening for overall Best Video, she reminisced about her first MTV win with Destiny's Child, calling it 'one of the most exciting moments in [her] life'. She then invited Taylor up on stage to finish her acceptance speech and 'have her moment'.

Speaking about the incident later to *Oprah* magazine, Beyoncé defended Kanye. 'I knew his intentions and I knew he was standing up for art,' she said. 'When they didn't call my name, he was completely shocked. When he walked on the stage, I was, like, "No, no, no!" He spoke and I'm, like, "Oh, no, no, no!"' But she said Kanye's actions did not spoil the event. 'It ended up being a great night.'

While a phenomenon in its own right, 'Single Ladies' was released alongside another lead single, 'If I Were A Boy', also taken from *I Am . . . Sasha Fierce*. Much slower in tempo, it was a ballad designed to show the opposite side of Sasha – 'who I am underneath all the makeup, underneath the lights and underneath all the exciting star drama'. Beyoncé called the track 'broad', different from anything else she had ever recorded, and it went on to become her biggest-selling single in the UK.

After the success of its two singles, the strongly personal *I Am . . . Sasha Fierce* was released in November and sold more than seven million copies globally. While it received mixed reviews, with some critics calling the double-disc concept a gimmick, Beyoncé seemed more concerned that the recording had given her the chance to fully express herself: 'I'm a human being. I cry. I'm very passionate and sensitive,' she said. 'My feelings get hurt. I get scared and nervous like everyone else. And I wanted to show that about myself. [The album] is about love. I'm a woman, I'm married, and this portion of my life is all in the album. It's a lot more personal. I'm very private and I don't talk about a lot of things, but there are certain songs that are on the album that are very personal. It's my diary. It's my story.'

While she was on promotional duties for both the singles and the album, it was fair to say that Beyoncé had grown a little distracted. In America, history was being made and she and Jay-Z had been playing a crucial part in it. After joining the campaign trail for presidential candidate Barack Obama early in 2008, they proved two of his most vocal celebrity supporters over the coming months and used every opportunity to drum up support for him. They developed a surprising friendship, which attracted acres of media attention. Obama first became part of their lives when one of his associates set up a meeting with Jay-Z at the start of the year. Beginning a long-standing 'bromance', the two talked 'for hours' and in Jay-Z's book, *Decoded*, he wrote: 'I wish I could remember a specific moment when it hit me that this guy was special. But it wasn't like that. It was the fact that he sought me out, then asked question after question about music, about where I'm from, about what people in my circle . . . all the way back to Marcy were thinking about politically.'

Obama was just as impressed. 'Every time I talk to Jay-Z, who is a brilliant talent and a good guy, I enjoy how he thinks,' he told *Rolling Stone* later in his campaign. 'That's somebody who is going to start branching out and can help shape attitudes in a real positive way.' At a rally in Raleigh, he roused the crowd with what appeared to be a reference to one of the rapper's biggest hits, 'Dirt Off Your Shoulders'. Responding to a sharp verbal attack from his rival Hillary Clinton, Obama made a gesture of dusting down his suit, and when his spokesman was later asked if this action was a nod to his new friend, he replied: 'He has some Jay-Z on his iPod.'

With their friendship sealed, Jay-Z began performing at electioneering events, to which he would bring along his equally enthusiastic wife – who said of the Democrat hopeful: 'I have had the pleasure of meeting Mr Obama, his wife and his children, and they are the American dream. They are so elegant, so classy, so intelligent and everything that I want to be. They make me really proud of my country.'

At one rally in Philadelphia, Jay-Z declared: 'Rosa Parks sat so that Martin Luther King could walk. Martin Luther King walked so that Obama could run. Obama's running so that we all can fly . . . I can't wait until November fifth and I'm going to say: "Hello, Brother President."'

However, at one fundraiser at the Hollywood Bowl, which took place just weeks after they got married, Beyoncé and Jay-Z were reported to have had a feisty lovers' tiff. Working the crowd on stage, Jay-Z got stuck into the principles of the Bush administration while rapping a few songs. But then, as the DJ put on Beyoncé's 'Crazy In Love', he marched over to the mic, and yelled: 'F**k that. Sorry, Bey, but f**k that – let's play something else.' Presumably intended as a joke, onlookers said Beyoncé did not see the funny side and was furious with her husband, storming away from the side of the stage. A witness at the event told the *Daily Mirror*: 'After he came off stage, she confronted him, demanding to know what the hell his comments had been about. She was gesturing wildly and not looking happy. Like any good husband would, Jay-Z grovelled and tried to get out of it with compliments . . . Later peace was restored and they were smiling and holding hands again.'

In the final run-up to election night, Beyoncé was in Japan promoting *I Am . . . Sasha Fierce*, but she cut short the trip at the last minute and flew back to the US. 'I said, "What am I doing? I'm completely making a bad decision. I have to go home, I'm gonna kill myself if I'm not home in America." I knew I needed to be here.' And when Obama swept to victory to become the very first African-American president, she could not mask her elation. Watching the results at home, while kitted out in a navy blue double-breasted suit with a red-white-and-blue-striped tie, she recalled: 'I fell asleep literally with tears in my eyes, crying and smiling at the same time. I woke up with mascara running and a smile on my face. I've never been so patriotic! I'm just beyond excited.'

Speaking of her bold new hope for the future, she said: 'My nephew, who is four, when we say, "You can do whatever, you can be whatever", it's not cliché.' She added: 'I feel like we have grown so much as a nation and we will continue to grow because of Mr Obama.' With Obama's inauguration ball to follow in January, she was keen to be a part of it from the word go. 'Whatever they want – if they need me to volunteer, they need me to sing, I'm there and I'm ready.'

Video footage taken at a celebratory concert soon afterwards showed Obama greeting Beyoncé and acting out the famed 'Single Ladies' hand dance, waving his palm forward and backward. 'I got a little something,' he said, then drew the line at donning a leotard, joking, 'I'm not like Justin.'

Destiny's Child got their first record deal in 1996, when Beyoncé was just 14. The original line-up included (L–R) LeToya Luckett, Kelly Rowland, Beyoncé and LaTavia Roberson. In their early days, the girls always wore matching outfits made by Beyoncé's thrifty mother Tina Knowles, who proved an expert with scraps of material and a sewing machine!

With new recruit Michelle Williams on board and LaTavia and LeToya out of the band, Destiny's Child went from strength to strength. In 2001, they even unveiled their own doll range in time for Christmas!

Beyoncé has always been extremely close to mum Tina, but her relationship with manager father Mathew was gradually torn apart over the years. The rift was deeply traumatic for Beyoncé and the pair are now said to seldom speak.

Beyoncé and rapper Jay-Z's feisty 2003 collaboration, *Crazy In Love*, was a worldwide hit and their chemistry on the song was electrifying. They initially got together after a photo shoot in 2001 but did not go public until much later.

Proudly showing off her prestigious *Sports Illustrated* cover in 2007, Beyoncé was the first non-supermodel or non-athlete to be picked for the honour, but she said she had to diet hard to get into her bikini.

Beyoncé's portrayal of Deena Jones in the Oscar-winning 2006 movie, *Dreamgirls,* opposite Jennifer Hudson sealed her status as a credible actress.

Over the years, Beyoncé has won 17 Grammy awards and been nominated for a staggering 46. In 2004, she could barely hold her collection of five gongs, while she went on to break records in 2010 by winning six.

After going down a storm in front of 170,000 muddy fans, Beyoncé said her 2011 headlining slot at Glastonbury was the 'highlight of my career.' Though the crowd did not know it, she was in the early stages of pregnancy and held a protective hand over her stomach while performing.

After 'putting a ring on it' when she married Jay-Z in April 2008, Beyoncé's release *Single Ladies* the same year sparked a global dance phenomenon which even President Obama took part in.

Good friends with Gwyneth Paltrow ever since the actress' husband Chris Martin first collaborated with Jay-Z, the pair were all smiles at the Grammys in 2011. Gwyneth has said that Beyoncé is 'the most talented human being on the planet'.

When the ecstatic singer revealed she was expecting daughter Blue Ivy at the MTV VMAs in 2011, all records were broken as more than 8,000 Tweets were sent per second. Her expanding baby bump could already be seen.

Millions watched as Beyoncé proudly sang the American national anthem at President Obama's second inauguration ceremony in 2013, but the event was mired by a miming controversy.

Beyoncé's 14-minute Super Bowl halftime show in February 2013 was a thrilling spectacle – especially when her former Destiny's Child bandmates Kelly Rowland and Michelle Williams joined her on stage to perform some of their old hits.

A successful singer in her own right, Solange performed at the 2014 Coachella music festival in California – and welcomed a special guest on stage in the shape of her big sister. The happy duet was the calm before a major family storm, however.

Curly-haired Blue Ivy is the apple of her parents' eye and has a strong mix of both of their looks. She was born in New York in January 2012, with Jay-Z letting slip in one of his raps that she was conceived in Paris.

In one of the most shocking showbiz stories of recent times, Beyoncé's sister Solange was secretly filmed attacking Jay-Z in a lift after the 2014 Met Gala. The event was dubbed 'Elevatorgate' and sparked a host of conspiracy theories.

Beyoncé and Jay-Z's 2014 *On The Run* tour was dogged from the word go with reports of marriage trouble – as well as rumours they would separate once it ended. But on stage, they looked as in love as ever with the rapper kissing and cuddling her during most shows.

Chapter Thirteen

Once Beyoncé's joy at Obama's victory had abated, she and Jay-Z made headlines for a more material reason: they had been named Hollywood's richest couple by *Forbes* magazine. Their combined earnings for 2008 were reported to be $162 million, and their ranking dwarfed nearest rivals Will and Jada Pinkett Smith and the Beckhams, who pulled in $85 million and $58 million respectively. On his own, Jay-Z made $82 million, largely thanks to signing a whopping new deal with concert promoter Live Nation, while Beyoncé made $80 million from her various music, film and fashion projects. Although in later years Beyoncé's earnings began to outstrip her husband's, at this stage their income was roughly even – no doubt appealing to her burning sense of female equality. Yes, they were a power couple, but with proportionate input. But just as they hated talking about their relationship, the topic of money was off-limits too, with Jay-Z attesting: 'I'm not motivated by that . . . I don't sit around with my friends and talk about money, ever.'

The end of November also brought the world première of

Cadillac Records in Los Angeles, where, excitingly for Beyoncé, her on-screen namesake Etta James was in attendance. 'Just imagine!' she squealed on the red carpet. 'I always loved her voice, but now knowing what she's been through, she's one of my heroes. I'm not sure if she thought [I would be good] as her . . . I'm very, very nervous.' But Beyoncé apparently had little to worry about: seventy-year-old Etta told her, 'I loved you from the first time you sang.' They seemed to be two kindred spirits – but, sadly, the relationship hit a sour note soon afterwards.

A few weeks after the release of *Cadillac Records*, Beyoncé had one of her greatest challenges: performing live at Obama's inauguration ball in January 2009. She opted to showcase Etta's classic song, 'At Last', which had won her acclaim in the film. She sang the track while Obama and First Lady Michelle slow-danced across a stage lit by fairy lights, an undeniably touching scene that left her fighting back tears. She told *Marie Claire*: 'I had to tell myself, "They asked you to do this. You have to do a great job. This is their history. Calm down. Calm down." I barely made it. Literally seconds before the song started, I was crying like a five-year-old.'

Jay-Z was every inch the proud husband, watching from within the audience instead of backstage so he could 'feel the energy of everyday people'. He added that sharing in such a rite of passage was 'unbelievable'.

However, one person seemed less keen on Beyoncé's standout performance: Etta herself. During a concert of her own in Seattle days later, she started off by saying: 'You know your president, right? You know the one with the big ears?' Dissing Beyoncé in the same breath, she continued: 'I tell you that woman he had singing for him, singing my song, she gonna get her ass whupped.' She went a step further: 'I can't stand Beyoncé. She had no business up there singing my song that I've been singing for ever.'

Her outburst inevitably spread like wildfire, at which point the veteran star insisted she had been joking. 'Nobody was getting mad at me in Seattle,' she said. 'They were all laughing, and it was funny.' She also maintained that the jokes were 'not from a vicious place', and told the press: 'I didn't really mean anything. Even as a little child, I've always had that comedian kind of attitude.' Taking back her snipe at Obama, she said she had always found him 'handsome' and 'cool'. Nevertheless, she did concede that she had been aggrieved not to be asked to sing for the new president, saying she felt 'left out of something that was basically mine'. She poured more salt into Beyoncé's wounds when she was asked if she could have done a better job and answered: 'I think so. That's a shame to say that.'

Though many were outraged over her barbed comments, Beyoncé remained the consummate pro and refused to retaliate. Nothing was worth the risk of letting her guard slip. It was far more important to walk away as the dignified party, so even when her life was subject to mass scrutiny and affront, she dealt with it carefully and coolly. Furthermore, when Etta passed away, suffering from leukaemia, in 2012, she wrote on her blog: 'This is a huge loss. Etta James was one of the greatest vocalists of our time. I am so fortunate to have met such a queen. Her musical contributions will last a lifetime. Playing Etta James taught me so much about myself, and singing her music inspired me to be a stronger artist.'

* * *

As February rolled in, it meant only one thing: it was time for the annual Grammy-fest. But while Beyoncé was nominated for Best R&B Vocal Performance with the song 'Me, Myself And I', on this occasion she was beaten by Alicia Keys and came away empty-handed. For once, Jay-Z was the focus, winning a trophy for 'Swagga Like Us' and performing the track with Kanye West and Lil Wayne. But this year's event was not memorable for its musical accomplishments. Instead it went down in history for sinister reasons. Following a pre-Grammys party, the rapper Chris Brown brutally assaulted his then girlfriend Rihanna, during a ferocious argument in their rented Lamborghini. In photographs that caused shockwaves across the world, she was shown with a bloodied and bruised face. Brown was later sentenced to five months' probation and 1,400 hours' community service.

The incident left Jay-Z incandescent with rage. He was still highly protective of his protégée Rihanna, who was only twenty at the time. *US Weekly* reported that he 'hit the roof' and said: 'Chris is a walking dead man. He messed with the wrong crew.' Beyoncé was naturally horrified by the attack too. She told CNN's Larry King: 'I'm here to support her . . . She's like family to me and to Jay.' The two women went back a long way, and Rihanna had told how seeing Beyoncé in concert for the first time in 2004 had left her 'very star-struck'. 'I was in tears,' she said. 'I could not believe that Beyoncé was right there . . . It was very inspiring and it motivated me so much.'

Despite Beyoncé's obvious concern at the assault, there were ongoing reports that she had a difficult relationship with Jay-Z's prodigy. Aside from the rumours of an affair, which she had already dismissed, it was said that she disapproved of the younger star's often hedonistic behaviour, especially because she had always maintained a clean image for herself. But Rihanna laughed off the idea of a feud, saying it was 'frustrating' and that Beyoncé was 'one of the sweetest women I've ever met'. When questioned on another occasion about their apparent rift, Rihanna again refuted it: 'Beyoncé is not the enemy. She is the competition but we get on fine. We're great.' But the same year it was reported that Beyoncé's team had banned a DJ from playing any of Rihanna's music at a House of Deréon launch party in Toronto.

As time went on, it was said that Beyoncé had grown 'tired of her drama' and that she had told Jay-Z to distance himself from her. When there were reports that Rihanna was planning to get back with her violent ex, Chris Brown, she was appalled – and apparently unhappy that Jay-Z did not step in. 'That's not my place,' he told hip-hop radio station Hot 97. 'I can't control the outcome of her life. I can't intervene.'

Whatever the case behind the scenes, it is clear that Jay-Z has always been like a father figure to Rihanna and, sounding just like a parent, he added: 'I can give advice, if asked, you know, and that's it. I can provide information, and then life has to play out. Life has to happen.' Meanwhile Rihanna once told *People* that she relied on Jay-Z to vet potential boyfriends for her. 'I just found out from a mutual friend that guys will talk to Jay before they try to approach me . . . If it's a good guy, I know Jay won't shut him down. But if he's not, Jay will be like, "No, no, no."'

The beginning of 2009 enabled Beyoncé to add another film to her CV: she signed up for the thriller *Obsessed*, co-starring *The Wire* actor Idris Elba. In the first role that did not involve her singing, she played a woman called Sharon whose family was being threatened by a stalker, leading her to fight back. 'It was interesting playing someone that didn't have all the makeup and hair,' she said. 'But I related to her not being a victim and being a person who takes matters into her own hands. I really think that's realistic for the modern woman. If you threaten someone's children, a woman will completely lose it.'

The plot meant there were many violent scenes, which she enjoyed filming. 'I was absolutely throwing real punches. I've taken boxing classes so I was using some of that training. I was getting myself pumped up and sweating and was really going for it. I loved doing the fight scenes because they were similar to choreography. I'm always so politically correct and so nice, it was great to let out that aggression.' Clearly, it was hard to uphold the proper and correct persona she portrayed in the public eye consistently. Unlike many other stars with more of a *laissez-faire* attitude, she worked hard to toe the line and not offend. Once the spotlight was off her in a role like this, she relished the chance to be rebellious.

Keen to let loose on set, Beyoncé demanded she do all her own stunts – bruises or no bruises. 'Literally I had to wear long sleeves for three weeks, but I'm not afraid. I like to get down and dirty,' she said. 'If someone tells me the stunt double will do something that I know I can do I'm going to always try and do it.'

The film also required her to share several screen kisses with Idris, who said locking lips with her and then meeting Jay-Z in the bar later was 'a bit weird'. But while the film fared well at the box office, the critics were generally unimpressed and had a field day. *Rolling Stone* gave it zero stars, while another reviewer said it was like *Fatal Attraction* but 'without the bunny boiling'. Even worse, the *Guardian* said Beyoncé had little to do in the movie 'except squawk in outrage', while the *Daily Telegraph* branded her 'ungainly' and 'forgettable'.

If the criticism bothered her, Beyoncé did not let it show – especially as she had already embarked on her *I Am . . .* world tour when the film opened in cinemas. The eleven-month tour, which began in late March 2009, put paid to all the suggestions that she and Jay-Z were about to start a family. 'There's never enough time in the day for everything.' She laughed as she prepared to leave. 'I eventually want to have a family, although right now I'm not ready for that.'

Her biggest series of live shows yet, she played to more than a million fans in 108 concerts in Europe, the Americas, Asia, Africa and Australia, grossing almost $120 million in total. Intense twelve-hour rehearsals began two months before opening night in Edmonton, Canada, which she revealed took place in high heels at all times. 'I have a rule that when I have my heels on, everyone has to have their heels on too,' she told *Billboard*. Sometimes the dancers are like, "Oh, God, we hope Beyoncé comes in late," because I'll go all day. And in the end I'll have blisters and my toes will have bruises. It's really hard sometimes.'

During this time, she slimmed down dramatically. 'I lost a lot of weight naturally, just from twelve-hour rehearsals,' she said. 'That's a lot of dancing. I would never work out for twelve hours, but I'm able to move around and not think about it. It's part of my job.' She also told *People* that she was eating 'really clean' as she prepared to hit the road, feasting on 'fish and, in the morning, Special K'.

With a main stage and a smaller 'B stage' in the middle of each arena, the set was designed to show the two sides of her personality, while she described the production as her most theatrical yet. 'I tried to bring jazz and hip-hop, ballet and fashion, and everything together,' she said. 'It is the best thing I've done as far as my tours go.' In one of her songs, 'Baby Boy', she soared above the crowd on a trapeze, upon which she would perform a series of acrobatic spins. 'My back and my hips are double-jointed,' she once boasted. 'I can do a lot of freaky things . . . I'm like a circus performer.'

Again she was backed by her all-female band the Mamas, while Tina handed over responsibility for the costumes to French designer Thierry Mugler, whom Beyoncé lauded as 'an icon and a legend'. Using the words 'Feminine. Free. Warrior. Fierce' as his inspiration, Thierry made her six elaborate costumes, which he called 'ferocious power-glam superheroine outfits'. They included a gold sequined leotard with a giant bow on the back and a full-length silver gown adorned with crystals. Her look also featured fishnets, mismatched gloves and power shoulders to represent 'single women, *femmes fatales* and power brokers in a hi-tech *Blade Runner* world'. After he had finished each creation, Tina adjusted them so that Beyoncé could dance freely. 'It was just amazing to work with him because he is so creative,' Tina told MTV. She added that the edgier costumes on this tour were evidence of her daughter 'constantly evolving', but stressed that the final style choices were always left to Beyoncé. 'It's her decision, it's her career.' Thierry also had the challenge of creating outfits for the backing band, singers and dancers. 'In all, seventy-one costumes,' he said.

Though the arrangement was mainly harmonious, there was one small clash of ideas when Thierry planned for Beyoncé to sing her version of 'Ave Maria' wearing a black dress. She protested, saying she thought the song would be more atmospheric if she donned a white wedding gown. She got her way and teamed the frock with a veil, which gave the performance an even more ethereal quality.

As usual, the shows were punishingly hard work, but she accepted her fate willingly. 'I'm never gonna go on stage or do a video and not work until my feet are blistered and until, basically, I can't walk any more,' she said. And as she told *Billboard*: 'I'm an all-or-nothing type of woman. Either I'm doing absolutely nothing and relaxing – reading a book, sitting by the ocean and not answering any questions – or else I'm hands-on and giving one hundred per cent, working really hard.'

As with her previous tour, Beyoncé's perfectionist streak was irrepressible. There was surely no other performer on the planet who put as much work into their shows – which was both a blessing and a curse. Every part of the production from the lighting to the dancing had to be just right, and her dedication affectionately earned her the name B-Zilla among her crew. 'I feel like I'm my competition,' she confided in *Seventeen* magazine. 'I don't try to compete with other people. I just try to better myself. I go and watch everything that I've done. I have my YouTube days, when I watch every performance, and I listen to my music, and I watch my videos to figure out what I need to do, what I need to fix, and how to become a better singer.' Though we often hear artists wheeling out old clichés about giving 110 per cent for their fans, this would be no brazen overstatement for Beyoncé. She quite literally does put every fibre of her being into her performances and stops at nothing until she knows there is nothing left to give.

During the tour, she at least allowed herself a three-week break, and welcomed the chance to explore remote spots, often uninterrupted by fans. She loved slipping unnoticed into churches and museums and delved into history all over the world. During her time off she would also go for bike rides with her assistants, saying such activities helped keep her grounded.

Determined not to spend any more time in hotel rooms than was necessary, she said: 'I visited the Pyramids in Egypt. I saw the Great Wall of China and went out in the middle of the ocean in Australia to see the whales. I actually got sprayed in the face. I made some great memories this year.'

But, as before, the time away from home and her husband took a great toll on her. In video footage later screened in a fly-on-the-wall documentary shot during the tour, she broke down in tears over the often harrowing loneliness she suffered. Filmed talking to camera without a scrap of makeup, she said: 'Why did God give me this life? Sometimes it's overwhelming. Why did God give me my talent, my gift, my family? But I know you're not supposed to question God. So I'm grateful for the life He's given me.' As she wiped away a stray tear, she added: 'I'm so grateful. I'm alive and I'm living the dream. I'm living my dreams.'

She struggled without Jay-Z: 'I'm flying home today. I miss my baby.' It seemed that life away from familiarity had also brought her maternal instincts to the surface as she revealed she was 'getting close' to wanting a baby.

The documentary, called *Beyoncé: I Am . . . World Tour*, was a genuine labour of love as she directed it herself. 'I feel like the only way I can truly tell the story is if I am a part of it,' she said, in an interview on ABC News' *Nightline*. 'There are a lot of things that I reveal about myself that I would have never given to a different director.' The DVD also saw an exhausted Beyoncé talking about having performed nine nights in a row. 'I'm just really upset that I don't have anyone that's concerned about my body and my wellbeing,' she said. 'When you work that hard, you just need someone to say, "Stop." You know? Your voice is a muscle and it needs rest, and imagine nine days. I was just delirious and feeling sorry and bad . . . And in the end, I cried because clearly I'm a human being and I bleed and I hurt and I cry and I fall just like anybody else.'

In one scene, she admitted that she would resort to conversing with her laptop in times of need. 'There was one moment I was in China and I was in this huge suite and I looked out the window and there were just thousands of people walking and I couldn't believe my life,' she said. 'I guess I was a bit lonely and I wanted to talk to someone so I opened up my computer and I just talked.'

At the première of the documentary in New York, she faced another barrage of questions about her baby plans, but admitted she was used to it. 'I mean, it's a part of it,' she said. 'At this point they said I've been pregnant, like, eight times, so I'm kind of used to it. I just hope that one day, when I decide to be pregnant that people are happy for me . . . Everyone's, like, "Oh, God, please! She's been pregnant a hundred times." One day, hopefully, I will be. So whatever. It's a part of being a celebrity, I guess.'

While on tour, Beyoncé also had to deal with the shock news about Michael Jackson's death. He passed away at his home on 29

June following an overdose of an anaesthetic drug. On hearing what had happened, she wept as if she had lost one of her own relatives. After composing herself she made a statement:

> 'This is such a tragic loss and a terrible day. The incomparable Michael Jackson has made a bigger impact on music than any other artist in the history of music. He was magic. He was what we all strive to be. He will always be the King of Pop! Life is not about how many breaths you take, but about how many moments in life that take your breath away. For anyone who has ever seen, felt or heard his art, we are all honoured to have been alive in this generation to experience the magic of Michael Jackson. I love you, Michael.'

Though their paths seldom crossed in later years, Beyoncé had a clear affinity with the tragic star and frequently insisted she would never have begun her career if he had not so mesmerised her as a young girl. On the fifth anniversary of his death in June 2014, she posted a deeply personal letter on her website:

> 'When I was just starting out, my first producer used to make me listen to Michael Jackson's live performance of "Who's Loving You". He would have me watch that for hours back to back to back. What he wanted me to learn was his soul. You could hear his soul . . . For whatever reason, he could evoke more emotion than an adult. It was so raw and so pure . . . Michael taught me that sometimes you have to forget technique, forget what you have on. If you feel silly, you have to go from the gut, just let it go. Michael Jackson changed me, and helped me to become the artist I am. Thank you, Michael. Love always, B.'

Back on the I Am . . . world tour, she had introduced a tribute section to her set, where she would show a video of herself aged five preparing to see Michael in concert. During the song 'Halo', she changed the words of the chorus to: 'Michael we can see your halo/I pray you won't fade away.' Her documentary also showed her reciting a prayer ahead of her first show after his death. 'Lord, we ask that we can feel his spirit on the stage, we dedicate this show to him and his family,' she said, with her eyes closed. 'We continue to pray for them. Lord, we ask that we're able to touch someone in the audience the way that he touched us.' But in spite of her pain, the show had to go on and she never let heartache dampen her gusto on stage.

During a break in the tour between the end of November and February, Beyoncé arranged a spectacular fortieth-birthday party in the Dominican Republic for Jay-Z. On the guest list were his rapper friends Kanye West and P. Diddy, as well as Tina, Solange and cousin Angie. The weekend bash was held at the luxurious Campo de Casa resort, with ocean-front villas boasting infinity pools overlooking white sands and crystal clear waters. Beyoncé arranged every last detail, hosting a Friday-night dinner party in which everyone was instructed to wear 1920s garb. During the meal, a video was played in which Jay-Z's friends told him how much he meant to them, then synchronised swimmers performed in the pool and there was a spectacular firework display. Guests danced all night long, and the following morning Beyoncé invited them all to their villa for a hangover-curing lobster and steak brunch.

The celebration coincided with Beyoncé and Jay-Z's decision to take on both of their respective surnames. It was reported that the pair were to be formally known as Shawn Knowles-Carter and Beyoncé Knowles-Carter. A source was quoted as saying: 'They want to keep Knowles because Beyoncé's parents didn't have any sons and they're keen to keep the name going strong.'

Jay-Z was relaxed about hitting his landmark birthday and felt there was much to celebrate as his latest album *Blueprint 3* topped the charts, breaking musical records in the process. 'I feel fantastic about turning forty,' he said. 'I'm in a great place, got a fantastic album, my eleventh number one, which beats Elvis, so I'm feeling like the king of pop.'

One person notably missing from the celebratory occasion was Beyoncé's father, Mathew. Over the previous few months, his presence at such events and his contact with Beyoncé had dwindled. It emerged that Tina had filed for divorce in November that year. The papers were lodged in Harris County, Texas, bringing about an end to almost thirty-one years of marriage. The documents said that Tina and Mathew 'ceased to live together as husband and wife on or about January 5th, 2009' – the date of their thirtieth wedding anniversary.

Beyoncé was saddened by the news, but her parents had not been functioning as a proper couple for a long time. In addition, Mathew had been hit with a paternity lawsuit that October by former *Scrubs* actress Alexsandra Wright, who claimed she was six months pregnant with his baby. When she eventually gave birth to a son, Nixon, in February 2010, Mathew at first denied being the father, but a DNA test allegedly later proved otherwise. This would not be the only time he was to face claims he had fathered another woman's child.

Tina's divorce petition asserted that the marriage was

'insupportable because of discord or conflict of personalities which prevents any reasonable expectation of reconciliation', according to TMZ. Meanwhile, in a statement, she and Mathew confirmed: 'The decision to end our marriage is an amicable one. We remain friends, parents, and business partners. If anyone is expecting an ugly messy fight, they will be sadly disappointed. We ask for your respect of our privacy as we handle this matter.' The divorce was not made final for another year, but it was an unsettling time for Beyoncé.

Chapter Fourteen

In January 2010, the world was left reeling by the deadly earth-quake that tore apart the Caribbean country of Haiti, killing more than three hundred thousand and leaving a million home-less. Beyoncé was devastated by the scenes of devastation and despair and, as with Hurricane Katrina, she was one of the first celebrities to get behind the relief effort as she pledged a sizeable donation of her own money. As the official face of a 'Fashion for Haiti' T-shirt, which raised more than a million dollars for the cause, she also performed at a quickly organised telethon in London, singing a moving acoustic version of 'Halo' with close friend Chris Martin. Fighting back emotion, she changed the words of the song once again, telling the people of Haiti she could 'see their halo'. Also deeply affected by the tragedy, Jay-Z had written and rush-released a charity single called 'Stranded (Haiti Mon Amour)' with Rihanna and U2, which they performed at the same telethon. Given her and Jay-Z's considerable dedication to supporting charitable causes, Beyoncé was somewhat stunned in 2012 when American singer and activist Harry Belafonte launched a scathing attack on the pair, accusing them of a lack of social conscience. 'I think one of the great abuses of this modern time is that we should have had such high-profile artists, powerful celebrities. But they have turned their back on social responsibility. That goes for Jay-Z and Beyoncé, for example,' he said. Although she never normally liked to draw attention to her humanitarian efforts, on this occasion she was so incensed that her team sent what they called 'an abbreviated list of the unselfish work Beyoncé has done and continues to do' to the *Wall Street Journal*.

Sometimes she felt compelled to make a stand. 'People know what kind of shoes I have on, what type of wardrobe and they ask about marriage,' she told ABC News. 'But one thing people don't know is that if you want to be like me, a part of being me is giving back.'

Harry Belafonte's comments seemed particularly unfair when it later emerged that, over the years, Beyoncé had drip-fed seven million dollars into the Houston housing development she had set up in 2007 in the wake of Hurricane Katrina. The Knowles-Temenos Place Apartments provided employment training, meals and HIV/AIDS screening for residents, with the aim that they would eventually become self-sufficient. Her old pastor Rudy let slip just how much she had donated to the cause, telling radio station KHOU 11 News: 'She's an incredible human being . . . [She] has an incredible heart and has been extremely helpful in our mission and our ministry here.'

Brushing aside the apparently unjust criticism of her commitment to humanitarian need, Beyoncé turned her attention to the release of her latest fragrance, called Heat. But, as she admitted, juggling so many balls at any one time was proving difficult. 'I love so many different things, and to have the discipline to turn certain things away and focus on one thing at a time so that I can give it one hundred per cent is really hard,' she told *You* magazine at the New York launch of the scent. 'Probably the biggest challenge in my life is time – making sure I have time to be a wife, to be a singer, to be a songwriter, to be an actor and still have time for my clothing line and now for my perfume.' To keep herself sane, she said, carving out time for herself was essential. 'I try really hard to make sure that every day I have my thirty minutes of quiet time. Mostly I just lie in bed and meditate and think what my goal is. Some days, of course, I can't manage thirty minutes, but it's really important to have those quiet moments.'

There was little peace to be found from her next musical project: a joint single with singer Lady Gaga, called 'Telephone'. This followed an earlier remix of Beyoncé's track 'Video Phone', which they collaborated on and subsequently bonded over in 2008. Recorded for the eccentric singer's *Fame Monster* album, Gaga – who had affectionately been known to call herself Gee-yoncé – was keen to get Beyoncé on board, believing they had similar values and beliefs.

Coupled with a nine-minute video, which cost at least half a million dollars, the extravagant promo saw Gaga being released from jail and met outside the prison gates by Beyoncé, who whisked her away into the desert to commit bloody murder in a diner. It was nominated for a clutch of MTV awards but *NME* said the video was 'nearly ten minutes of product placements, a *Thelma & Louise* storyline, bizarre outfits and some uniquely Gaga-esque dance moves'.

The single hit number one in the UK and number three in the

US, and evidently the pair loved working together. After Gaga announced her outlandish plans for the video, she revealed that Beyoncé asked her: 'What's in your head, girl?' But despite being two of the hottest pop stars on earth, she insisted there was no rivalry. 'We're not competitive at all,' Gaga told TV host Ryan Seacrest. 'We're so different, you know, and we respect each other so much. She's so kind. We get along . . . She trusted me because she likes my work, and she trusted me because she knew that I love her and that it's a mutual respect. It ended up being a master-piece because she was so courageous.' Speaking on Tyra Banks's chat show, Beyoncé returned the compliment. 'I am such a huge fan of hers . . . She's just so smart and she's becoming an icon in her own right.' She added: 'I'm a girl's girl, so to show that women that are successful can support each other and have a good time, I'm just so happy to bring that message across with Gaga.'

As the end of the month closed in, it was time for Beyoncé to prepare for the fifty-second Grammy Awards in LA. She had notched up ten nominations so it was always going to be a big night for her – but nobody could have predicted just how immense. Collecting a phenomenal six awards, she broke all records for the highest number of Grammys won in a single evening by a female artist – a feat only Adele has been able to match, in 2012. Beyoncé's wins were for Song of the Year, Best Female Pop Vocal Performance, Best Female R&B Vocal Performance, Best Traditional R&B Vocal Performance, Best R&B Song and Best Contemporary R&B Album.

After collecting her gongs, she told *Access Hollywood*: 'I don't know how to explain to you how I feel. It means so much to me. As I look around I know how amazing this is and what an honour it is . . . I have sixteen Grammys – are you serious?'

The normally reserved singer also stunned the audience when she dedicated her win to Jay-Z while up on stage. 'This has been such an amazing night for me. I'd like to thank my family including my husband – I love you,' she stuttered. Later, she confessed that she had been so delirious over her win that she had had no idea what she was saying. 'He was shocked,' she said. 'He was just, like, "What did you say?" I was just, like, "What did I just do? No, I didn't just say that." I was so happy, I could've said anything. That's why I ran off the stage.' But she insisted that Jay-Z was not angry with her for the rare slip. 'He said, "You have six Grammys and you smell good."'

After composing herself, she told Tyra Banks: 'It was just a genuine moment and I looked in the audience and I saw my nephew and I saw my cousin Angie and I saw him . . . and it's the first thing that came to my mouth. After I walked off the stage I just bawled because that's when I realised what just happened to me and everything I have been working for my whole life. It paid off that night.'

It was a victorious night for Jay-Z too: he took three Grammys, including one he shared with Rihanna for their joint single 'Run This Town'. The pair provided one of the Grammy highlights when they took his and Beyoncé's nephew Julez up on stage with them to collect the award. Wearing a little tuxedo and sharing the clear good looks of his mother, Solange, Julez got a rapturous reception – especially when Rihanna picked him up and asked him if he would like to say anything, to which he quietly replied into the microphone, 'No, thanks.'

The Grammys would not be complete without Beyoncé singing as well as winning – and she did not disappoint with an electrifying performance of 'If I Were A Boy', which she mashed up with Alanis Morissette's 'You Oughta Know'. Looking incredible in a studded black-leather corset dress with heeled ankle boots on stage, she later changed into a more demure dress and hit an after party at Hollywood hotspot Guys & Dolls with Jay-Z and Rihanna. Putting aside any past issues they might have had, the two women posed happily together for the paparazzi, while one partygoer said of the group: 'They went through twelve bottles of Ace of Spades champagne in ninety minutes.'

With no let-up in her I Am . . . world tour, Jay-Z revealed how their Valentine's Day date that year had taken place on Skype. But the final curtain came down on the show four days later on a humid February night in Trinidad and Tobago. As Beyoncé, dripping sweat, left the stage and shared a celebratory glass of wine with her jubilant team of musicians, dancers and singers, she knew something had changed within her. For the past year, she had been leading a double existence and her stage persona had consumed every fibre of her being. Now the tour was over, she wanted peace and calm. She wanted to go back to being her real self, the Beyoncé without the swagger and the aggression. Her decision was made: Sasha Fierce was dead.

Confirming the news in an interview with *Allure* magazine that month, she explained that she no longer felt she had to hide behind her alter ego. 'Sasha Fierce is done,' she said. 'I killed her. I don't need Sasha Fierce any more, because I've grown and now I'm able to merge the two.' With Sasha's boundless energy making her untouchable as a performer, this came as a shock to both the media and her loyal following. But she was adamant it was time for a new side of her personality to shine. 'I'm much more interested in showing people the sensitive, the passionate, the compassionate person that I am. More so than Sasha Fierce,' she reiterated in *Dazed and Confused* magazine.

She also knew that, after nearly a year on the road, her reserves had been completely obliterated. She was literally running on empty and decided to take time out for most of 2010, telling her fans: 'It's definitely time to take a break, to recharge my batteries. I need to just live life, to be inspired by things again . . . I've always worked hard, but I feel like I worked harder this past year than I have since I was starting out,' she added. 'I just had all these great opportunities.'

Highlighting how the life of a global superstar is not all it's cracked up to be, she had found herself losing sight of what was really important to her. 'My life was award shows, tour buses and hotels,' she said, in a later documentary about her year off. 'You're getting awards and people are saying how much they respect you. I couldn't even hear it any more. I'm, like, "Thank you, thank you, thank you." I'm just thinking about the next shoot, the next video, next single, the next tour.'

In the end, it was Tina who convinced Beyoncé to down tools for a while, before it destroyed her health. 'My mother was the person that preached to me and almost harassed me every day – "You really need to live your life and open your eyes,"' she said. 'I never even realised I needed a year off and I never realised that I don't know how to take a year off.' In the past, she had spent her rare days off mainly sleeping – as she once told *Cosmopolitan*: 'Sometimes I'll stay in bed all day and watch TV and eat whatever I want. I'll eat cereal and Oreos and change channels every three minutes.' But this time, she needed a more substantial rest than the odd duvet day could provide. As she prepared to retreat from the spotlight, she said her goal was to do 'random things . . . I want to go to restaurants, maybe take a class, see some movies and Broadway shows'. She also had a new hobby to explore – painting. She and Jay-Z had long been big art collectors and thought nothing of splashing thousands on a Warhol piece, but she also enjoyed using oils to paint portraits of women. It was an area of her life she was shy about, though, as she told ABC News: 'I've never shown anyone any of my paintings except my mom and my family.' Even today, Beyoncé's artwork is kept under lock and key, showing a lack of confidence we do not normally associate with her.

She also aimed to spend more time with her nephew, Julez. 'He's a wonderful kid, amazing, so smart. And I spoil him, so it's a lot of work. He's a twenty-four-hour job.' In the documentary about her break, called *Year of 4*, she revealed that simple things, like picking Julez up from school, made her feel complete again. 'It gave me time to reflect and it gave me time to really think about my life.' Another highlight was scuba-diving in the Red Sea, and footage from the documentary showed her floating serenely in the water. 'The coral was spectacular. It was unreal that something on the earth that beautiful exists and I was so close to it,' she reflected. By consciously bringing herself back down to earth in this way, she hinted that at last she felt ready to start a family: 'I can be the mother I want to be and dedicate myself to my family.' Predictably, the fact she was choosing to disappear from public life during this time led to even greater speculation about her and Jay-Z having a baby. The gossip gathered such momentum that at one point Tina tried to take the heat out of the situation by telling reporters that she was having a baby – at the age of fifty-six. 'The truth is that it's not Beyoncé that's pregnant, it's me,' Tina joked, before adding that if every so-called 'exclusive' about her daughter being pregnant had been true she would have five or six grandchildren by now.

Thanks to a constant stream of limousines and chauffeurs, Beyoncé had never needed a car before. But during their lengthy spell of R-and-R, Jay-Z taught Beyoncé to drive and she was regularly spotted behind the wheel of one of his motors during early-morning lessons around New York. They were also pictured living it up on rather more exotic yachting trips around Mediterranean hotspots, such as Cannes and Portofino. However, not all of their excursions were quite so glamorous: the couple were said to have checked into a humble Premier Inn when Jay-Z headlined the Isle of Wight festival in June. Newspaper reports said they stayed in a £29-per-night room, and dropped in for a low-key dinner at a local Pizza Hut.

During her year off, Beyoncé had some very tough decisions to make about how she wanted her future as an artist to evolve. She had not been seeing eye to eye with Mathew for some time and, once his divorce from Tina was finalised, her allegiance to her mother was even tighter. After months of agonising consideration, she came to the conclusion in late 2010 that she wanted to go it alone. It was time to cut the cord of Mathew's management.

This was a monumental step and one she knew could not be taken lightly. Mathew had overseen her career since she was a little girl and had not only been the driving force behind Destiny's

Child and her solo success but had also managed Beyoncé's former bandmates, Kelly and Michelle, until they had left his company in 2009 and 2010 respectively. But his two roles of father and manager could no longer co-exist. As he once admitted, though he continually worked to be a good dad to her, the personal side of their relationship was severely compromised by the pressures of business.

That he had always had reservations about Jay-Z heaped further strain on their relationship, and when NPR radio had asked if it was more difficult to be Beyoncé's father or her manager, he replied: 'I would say both. Sometimes I have to make very difficult decisions as a manager that's not always best for my child. When she was in Destiny's Child, I didn't make decisions based on what was best for Beyoncé. I had to make decisions that were best for the group, and sometimes that affected her personally. Those are tough decisions.

'There are some times when I have to take off the manager hat and be a father. And sometimes I have to take the father hat off and be a manager. I'm not perfect so I make mistakes with that.'

Beyoncé's decision to take control of her career was inspired by another important male figure in her life: Michael Jackson. 'It just feels like no one else can tell me how I am supposed to perform, and I think it's what separates the Michaels and the Madonnas from the artists that are great but are just not quite the Michaels and the Madonnas,' she told Reuters.

Although she and Mathew quietly parted ways in 2010, the fact was not made public until March 2011. In a statement released to the media, Beyoncé said: 'I've only parted ways with my father on a business level. He is my father for life and I love my dad dearly.

I am grateful for everything he has taught me . . . I grew up watching him and my mother manage and own their own businesses. They were hardworking entrepreneurs and I will continue to follow in their footsteps.'

Mathew also issued a statement: 'The decision for Beyoncé and Music World Entertainment to part was mutual. We did great things together, and I know that she will continue to conquer new territories in music and entertainment.'

Inevitably, the announcement made rich pickings for the music press, and the gossip pages were filled with speculation over why Beyoncé had 'fired' him. But Mathew tried to be philosophical about their split. 'Business is business and family is family,' he said. 'It should come as no surprise that at twenty-nine years old, almost thirty, she wants to have more control of her business.' He also insisted that their parting would allow him to concentrate on promoting his own record label, specialising in gospel and inspirational music, along with developing new artists.

Whether or not he was putting on a brave face is open to debate but he was keen to insist that the split was simply a business decision and had nothing to do with the break-up of his marriage to Tina, or the love-child he had supposedly fathered. However, the drama took a sharp new twist in July 2011, when it was alleged that Beyoncé had sacked Mathew because he had stolen money from her. Showbiz website TMZ said Mathew had been replaced by a representative from concert promoter Live Nation after Beyoncé's law firm conducted an audit of her finances and most recent tour. He was quick to deny the allegations, accusing Live Nation of lying to his daughter.

'We absolutely have not taken any money from Beyoncé, and

all dollars will be accounted for,' he told Associated Press. 'In no way have we stolen money. Again, this is about the people who have made these claims – they have to come into the light.'

The theft allegations prompted Mathew to file papers in a Texas court alleging that Live Nation had forced him out of managing his daughter's affairs because they wanted to run her lucrative tours. Despite resorting to legal action, Mathew continued to insist that there was no hostility between him and Beyoncé. 'The relationship with Beyoncé is extremely amicable. I want to make that clear,' he said. Mathew also said he did not believe the allegation that he stole money from his daughter was the reason he was fired, saying it was part of a more structured overhaul of her entire operation: 'She changed almost every aspect of her business.' Asked if he believed that there had been a deliberate plan to oust him, he said: 'I'll let people come to their own conclusion.'

However much both argued that things were still cordial, Mathew hinted that they did not speak on a father-daughter level throughout the whole messy affair. 'We have not had that conversation,' he added, stressing to Associated Press that dialogue through their lawyers was more likely. 'The only way we will be able to understand this is through a court of law. That's the only way either one of us will be clear if someone in our camps did something that was not correct.'

Beyoncé only opened up about the true impact the split had had on her two years later. In an HBO documentary called *Life Is but a Dream*, her sadness was visible for the first time. 'I'm feeling very empty because of my relationship with my dad,' she said. 'I'm so fragile at this point and I feel like my soul has been tarnished. Life is unpredictable but I feel like I had to move on, and not work with my dad. And I don't care if I don't sell one record. It's bigger than the record, it's bigger than my career.'

In spite of her grief over the severing of their ties, she emphasised that she could not have continued with Mathew as both father and manager. 'I needed boundaries and my dad needed boundaries,' she said. 'It's easy to get confused with this world that's your job that you live and breathe every day, all day, and you don't know when to turn it off. You need a break. I needed a break. I needed my dad.'

Taking charge of her own destiny was not without its problems and she admitted finding it hard to achieve a balance between the business and creative aspects of her career. Instead of working with her father, she had to get used to running an entirely new team – which included Live Nation – while avoiding any kind of compromise on her music. It proved quite a challenge and disturbed her sleep. 'I'm sleeping with my BlackBerry,' she said. 'And I'm having dreams that I'm answering emails.'

But, overall, the freedom of being her own boss changed Beyoncé's life for the better, and she relished nurturing and expanding her empire, Parkwood Entertainment. Though she had set up the company in 2008, it began to thrive when she branched out on her own. Anyone who was ever invited into the inner sanctum at her New York offices would be wowed by the sight of her collection of Grammy Awards, which lined an entire wall in the conference room. But it was her so-called 'archive room' that most impressed. The temperature-controlled office contained almost every photograph of her ever taken, every interview she had taken part in, videos from each of her hundreds of shows, plus all the diary entries she ever committed to her laptop. It took more than two years to file, date and label all the material in what she calls her 'crazy archive', but there could be no prouder testimony to her success.

At the forefront of Parkwood Entertainment was her cousin, Angie. In the nineties, she had started working with Beyoncé, doing everything from the Destiny's Child laundry – of which there was a lot – to booking their hotels, flight tickets and concerts. 'I'd finish the show and go to the cash office with all the promoters and I would count out the money,' she told *Out* magazine. 'I refer to myself as a lioness. I'm a bad chick. I don't play. I went in there with all male promoters, and I'd count that money out.'

In later years, however, she became a fundamental part of Team Beyoncé, as vice president of operations at Parkwood and co-writing many of her cousin's songs. Another key player was visual director Ed Burke, who had never heard of Beyoncé when he first met her in 2004. After agreeing to shoot her for a day, he ended up photographing her all over the world in the years that followed. Recalling a time when he and Beyoncé climbed an Egyptian Pyramid together, he told *Out*: 'It smelt like urine because there are no bathrooms up there. She looked like Mother Teresa, wearing this white dress and a head wrap, and when we got to the top she sang Donny Hathaway's "A Song For You".'

Also very much in the mix was Beyoncé's long-serving publicist, Yvette Noel-Schure, who assumed a maternal kind of role at Parkwood. They were together when the 9/11 attacks occurred and she remembers Beyoncé telling her: 'My mom's not here, so I guess you're our mommy today.'

One of the most important members of the 'B-Team' was her long-term stylist Ty Hunter, who had first come into the equation when he had helped Tina source Destiny's Child outfits seventeen years previously. Having started out as a humble window dresser, Ty claimed a hand in almost every single outfit worn by Beyoncé – although he still maintains that she always has the final word. 'Beyoncé is in full control of her whole process – she's not the type of artist who you can tell what to wear. She's in charge of her,' he told *Teen Vogue*. 'From the sound to the lights to the clothes to the stage, she is a part of every single thing. I think that's why she is where she is. She's not going to do anything she doesn't want to do. She's not a puppet.'

As stylist, Ty has had to bear the brunt of any wardrobe malfunctions and habitually lives in fear of them happening when his boss is on stage. 'During tours zippers pop and we safety pin them up . . . Sometimes the zipper of a boot won't go up and you have to switch the shoes out really quickly. I've even had to run on stage a few times because her zippers will just slide down. If you're ever watching a YouTube video and you see me on stage, it's because a zipper just decided it wanted to come down. She'll continue performing and I'm backstage dying.'

Surprisingly, for a woman who always looks a million dollars, Beyoncé has never been much of a shopper and once admitted she 'hated' online browsing. When she does flex her credit cards, it is often in her favourite high-street store, Topshop. 'There's one in New York but I was mad at first because I didn't want anyone else to go there,' she said. During one trip to the flagship branch in London, she racked up several thousand pounds in a matter of minutes. 'It was like that shopping scene out of the film *Pretty*

Woman,' reported the *Sun*. 'Everyone was gobsmacked by the speed she was choosing clothes. When she hit the shoe section she picked up even more speed. The woman clearly loves footwear.'

Fortunately, Ty's work with Beyoncé has always been aided by her natural eye for fashion and her penchant for making bold statements. Her stage outfits are a designer's dream, and while showrooms refused to lend their pieces to her in the old days, it's a very different story nowadays. After she had modelled for one of her biggest fans, Tom Ford, at New York Fashion Week in 2011, he raved to *Harper's Bazaar*: 'Beyoncé is a force. She radiates positive energy. That is what true stars do. You feel it when you are around her, you feel it when you see her perform, you feel it when she sings, and you feel it when she looks you in the eyes and smiles.'

Fashion legend Donatella Versace has always held a similarly high opinion of her. 'She's a style icon,' she said, as far back as 2004. 'Her sense of style is perfect.'

As for Beyoncé's own style inspirations, she had long admired Kate Moss and said: 'She's always been a trendsetter and so edgy. You never look back at her, even ten or fifteen years ago, and think, What was that?' Victoria Beckham and Gisele Bündchen are other favourites. 'Their style is modern but always classic,' she told *Harper's Bazaar*.

With so many clothes at her disposal, it was reported in 2009 that Beyoncé had to book two hotel rooms on a trip to Manchester because she had so much luggage with her. It's certainly a far cry from her childhood days, when Tina had to beg her to take a greater interest in her wardrobe choices. 'At one point, I was a tomboy and wouldn't wear dresses,' she recalled in *Cosmopolitan*.

'And when I first became a teenager, I hated purses. My mom used to say, "You're a young lady, you should have a purse." I refused. She had to beg me.' These days, she's fighting them off with a stick. 'I get sent about fifteen designer bags a month. I can only imagine how much they cost. Even I wouldn't buy some of them.'

Still, it was not all posh frocks and blinging bags. When *Flaunt* magazine asked which one piece of clothing she could not live without, she replied: 'A white T-shirt.' Preferring a simple look when she's not working, it's skinny jeans all the way. 'When I'm at home I usually wear the same thing every day. I have my straight-leg jeans and a pair of Christian Louboutins and a little jacket and a white shirt,' she told the *Daily Mirror*.

Luckily, her body shape works well for her favoured look, as she explained in *Cosmopolitan*: 'I accentuate my waist. I know things that are too loose underneath my hips are not good because I look really boxy. Plunging necks look good on me. My arms are full, and certain cuts make [them] look even fuller. My legs are really curved and look longer in straight-leg jeans. Tops either have to be really short to show off the top of my midriff, or long. I can't do in between.' Judging from the countless fashion polls she has topped over the past decade, she and her team of stylists have made an art form of dressing those famous curves.

Chapter Fifteen

She had originally vowed to steer clear of the recording studio during her year off, but that plan soon fell by the wayside. Addicted to the buzz of making music, Beyoncé went back into the studios in New York just three months into her hiatus. But this time around, it was a far more leisurely process and thirteen months elapsed from the album's conception to its eventual release.

Freed from the shackles of her father's management, she said: 'I booked the studio myself and paid for the studio myself, and I just had fun. I just did whatever I wanted to do.' On this, her fourth solo offering, she wanted to create a personal, reflective sound, blending a contemporary R&B feel with rock'n'roll influences and live instrumentation. 'This album was a labour of love,' she told Reuters. 'I felt like the emotion and live instruments and soul were missing out of the music industry. I wanted to bring it back to the music I grew up listening to.'

But while it was liberating to have Mathew out of the picture, she revealed in the album's accompanying documentary, *Year of*

4, that it felt 'very risky' to go it alone. 'I've been managed by my father for a very long time and [it was] a real change when separating from him. It was scary, but it empowered me and I wasn't going to let fear stop me.' Clearly there were new struggles, which she had not yet grasped. 'It's very difficult managing myself. Every night when I go to sleep I ask hundreds of questions but I'm learning so much. And I'm making mistakes and I'm learning from them.'

Justifying her decision to branch out on her own, she added thoughtfully: 'Sometimes we don't reach for the stars. Sometimes we are satisfied with what people tell us we're supposed to be satisfied with, and I'm just not going for it.' By showing she was no longer prepared to be controlled by any man, she was also sending out a clear feminist message. She proudly pointed out that her going it alone was proof that young women can own and run music businesses, without male invervention.

Her determination to succeed on her own has been the driving force in Beyoncé's life ever since, and even in 2013 she said: 'When I decided to manage myself, it was important to me not to sign to some big company. I wanted to follow in Madonna's footsteps and be a powerhouse. When you get to this level, you don't have to share your money or your success . . . And we did it. And it's my company.'

Beyoncé knew very early on that the album's title would simply be *4*, because her fans had long been suggesting it. 'Everywhere I look, I see them calling it *4*,' she told *Billboard*. 'I had a whole other name and concept, but I keep seeing that the fans love the name *4*, and I think it would be a really nice thing to let them name the record.' Of course, she needed little persuasion, with the number representing her, Jay-Z and Tina's birth date as well as her wedding anniversary.

Going the extra mile, as she had on her previous recordings, the production of *4* took her to ten studios right across the globe and was assisted by nearly twenty producers, including The-Dream, Kanye West and André 3000. In fact, aside from her own work, the only constant input came from her recording engineer, Jordan Young, more commonly known as DJ Swivel. 'She was looking to mess around with some ideas,' he said. 'Of course I was interested in the project right away.' Discussing the process with *Sound on Sound* magazine, he said it 'involved experimenting with horns, percussion, drums, guitars and keys ... It was very freeing, and having the ability to do whatever you want and whatever she wants was a very cool way to start. Having fun is the best way I can put it. There were no rules.'

He added: 'Ideas would come in and she'd say, "OK, that's great, but let's add live drums to this part", you know? It was her experimenting, getting her ideas out, and a great team of people around her executing those ideas.'

Some seventy tracks were recorded, with twelve making it to the final release. But while she took her time with the album, Jordan said the schedule was still tough on occasion. 'I remember one day we worked for thirty-six hours straight, and she cut six entire songs. I think she even managed to squeeze in a couple of business meetings too!' In her documentary she suggested – only half joking – that there was no need for rest during crucial phases of recording. 'I am a workaholic and I don't believe in "No",' she said. 'I don't believe in "I need to sleep." If I'm not sleeping, nobody's sleeping.'

As well as New York, they recorded at Peter Gabriel's multi-instrument studio in Wiltshire, with other sessions held in Las Vegas, Los Angeles, Atlanta and Honolulu. Combining business with pleasure, Beyoncé also worked on *4* in Sydney, where Jay-Z was touring with rock band U2 and recording his collaboration album *Watch the Throne* with Kanye. Taking advantage of the balmy Australian December, the pair were spotted relaxing at the beach and eating al fresco at harbourside restaurants. While Jay-Z celebrated his birthday Down Under, his wife's belated gift was no doubt worth the wait as she reportedly bought him a two-million-dollar Bugatti Veyron Grand Sport – the fastest car in the world. Adding to his motor collection, which already comprised a Rolls Royce Phantom, Ferrari F430 Spider, Maybach 62S and a Pagani Zonda Roadster, the supercar had a top speed of 255 m.p.h., with fellow Bugatti owners including Simon Cowell and Tom Cruise.

Though most people can only imagine such extravagance, a two-million-dollar price tag was relatively small change for Beyoncé and Jay-Z. They always refrained from talking about their finances, but had recently made headlines for being declared the year's highest-earning 'Power Couple'. According to *The Guinness Book of World Records*, the pair had raked in a combined total of $122 million over the previous twelve months, with Beyoncé ploughing $87 million into the joint kitty, and Jay-Z contributing $35 million. She appeared to be showing the world that anything he could do she could do far better. And with her career firmly in the ascendant and youth still on her side, there was evidently no limit to the realm of influence and wealth she could eventually grasp. Never mind the Spice Girls – we were witnessing Girl Power in the extreme.

Given their status as the world's richest celebrity couple, the incessant tales about their luxury lifestyle and expenditure were hardly surprising, but always fascinating. For instance, on Valentine's Day the previous year Jay-Z upgraded somewhat from a dozen red roses, presenting his wife with a platinum mobile phone worth $24,000. And on Christmas Day in 2010 she was said to have discovered $350,000-worth of Hermès Birkin bags under the tree. For her twenty-ninth birthday the same year, Jay-Z was even rumoured to have bought her a private island in the Florida Keys for a cool $20 million. Hopkins Island, a 12.5-acre property located off Little Palm Island, boasted a beautiful guest cottage in addition to the elegant main house and pool. That was on top of the Miami mansion and New York homes they already owned.

However, unlike many other public figures whose wealth seemed off the scale, Beyoncé and Jay-Z would always strive to 'keep it real'. One journalist friend of the couple, who was invited to interview them at home for *Ebony* magazine in late 2010, described them as surprisingly low-key in each other's company. 'For all their might as solo power players, their relationship is remarkably free of drama,' she said. 'They sit around in their pyjamas and watch cable and snuggle, which may, after all, be the ultimate fantasy.' And their TV show of choice? The reality series *Jersey Shore*, which Beyoncé described as 'hilarious'.

When asked about the perfect romantic evening with Jay-Z she said she liked to 'light some candles, have a good meal and watch an old movie'. She had also become slightly more adventurous in the kitchen than in the early days, telling *Cosmopolitan*: 'I don't cook much, but I'm good at spaghetti and sandwiches. I know they're easy but they're my specialty.'

For all the trappings of their wealth, the high-level security and their entourages, Beyoncé remained resolute about not giving up her freedom for her fame. 'I'm not going to live my life afraid of taking my nephew to the park or going to the grocery store or crying in church, if I feel the need, because someone is going to get a picture,' she insisted to MTV. 'I know that the paparazzi are just doing their jobs – people have their jobs, their hustles, and I respect that – and it's something I can't stop. So I live with it. I deal with it. I try to live my life . . . Sometimes it's a lot of pressure, but who doesn't have pressure? The grass is always greener. If I weren't doing this, I'd be wanting to do this, so I can't complain.'

Similarly, she often struggled with the nature of her 'celebrity' tag, telling *Parade*: 'I think I am past needing celebrity. I don't want to feel the void I see in a lot of celebrities . . . the unhappiness underneath the smile.' For a long time, she strongly resisted the 'diva' connotations too, saying: 'I do normal things, walk in the park . . . I don't want to be off on my own diva planet. I want to be on earth. I want to be normal.'

Her cast-iron will to retain her freedom meant schmoozing at every A-list nightspot and party did not appeal either. Other stars, like Britney Spears and Lindsay Lohan, saw every aspect of their lives played out in the press, making their consequent fall off the rails even more spectacular. Staying under the radar suited Beyoncé – and she would later turn down an invitation to attend the so-called celebrity wedding of the century when Kim Kardashian married Kanye West. The idea of being in photographs and TV clips she had no control over worried her. Explaining to CNN how she had managed to avoid the pitfalls that some of her contemporaries plunged into, she said: 'The media does not attack me the way it attacks them. They can't go anywhere without paparazzi . . . I still have a little bit of privacy and I think maybe it's because I don't go to too many parties.' But that was not to say she did not know how to have fun. 'I don't think I'm boring – I love what I do and I get more satisfaction out of writing a song, or maybe from painting or being on a boat in Anguilla. Just things that are a little more relaxing than going out.'

She added: 'I do party – when I'm on vacation I have my red wine, I'm with my friends, we dance. That's the time to party. There's a time and place for that. When I'm working I'm pretty focused.'

In February 2011, she was able to share some of that focus with her friend and budding singer Gwyneth Paltrow, who was performing a duet with Cee Lo Green at that month's Grammys. Following up her guest appearances on the TV show *Glee*, she was also recording her own solo album, and it was Beyoncé who helped her through her Grammy rehearsal jitters. 'This story always makes me cry,' Gwyneth half sobbed to *Elle* magazine. 'It's ten in the morning and Beyoncé schleps it all the way down to the Staples Center to watch. I mean, she's Beyoncé! Beyoncé's, like, "Okay. The singing is great. But you're not having any fun." She's, like, "Remember when we're at Jay's concert and Panjabi MC comes on and you do your crazy Indian dance? Do that. Be you!"'

Back in the studio, Beyoncé and her team had decided unanimously that the first single from *4* would be 'Run The World (Girls)', which was released in April 2011. With a pounding beat and rousing chorus – 'Who run the world? Girls!/Who run this motha? Girls!' – its strident feminist leaning was designed to give women strength in a male-dominated world. 'I try to write songs that will bring out the best in all of us and keep us close together,' Beyoncé stated on her website. 'I think about saying the things that women want to say but sometimes are not confident enough to say.' The song also celebrated hard-working females juggling a family with a career – being 'smart enough' to make money and yet 'strong enough' to have children too. It featured a heavy dose of marching drums and African percussion, and she told *Billboard*: 'It reminded me of what I love, which is mixing different cultures and eras – things that typically don't go together – to create a new sound. I can never be safe. I always try and go against the grain.'

The African element of the song proved crucial in making the video for 'Run The World (Girls)'. Desperate to come up with an innovative new style of dance, Beyoncé trawled the internet for ideas until she came across a clip of three young men from Mozambique. Calling themselves Tofo Tofo – which means 'body shaking' in the local Maputo language – they were experts in a unique system of dance called Pantsula. Beyoncé immediately knew this would be perfect for her video, but there was one big problem. When she and her troupe of dancers attempted to learn the moves, they simply could not master them. Long days spent watching Tofo Tofo clips and practising in the studio in front of floor-to-ceiling mirrors proved fruitless. Beyoncé was fed up. She hated failing at anything. Drastic action was required, as she explained in the *Year of 4* documentary: 'I said, "I have to have those young guys fly to wherever we are and they have to teach us the choreography."'

A three-month search to find them ensued, in which the US Embassy in Maputo was roped in to help. 'We searched everywhere around Mozambique, which sounds crazy, but we found these guys,' she told Australian chat show *Sunday Night*. The three baffled men were flown to LA and, amazingly, had never heard of Beyoncé. 'They had no idea who I am, which is so great.'

After teaching her and the dancers the moves, the men appeared in the video alongside them – a magical if not surreal experience for the trio. 'They had no idea of the level of production or what they were part of,' Beyoncé stressed. '[But] there's nothing that can stop them from dancing. I love to surround myself with that kind of energy.'

Beyoncé called the choreography for 'Run The World (Girls)' a 'huge part of the pie', and that video was one of the most impressive of her entire career. Filming in the Mojave desert in California, she resembled some kind of post-apocalyptic warrior, kitted out in armour, thigh-high boots and a series of elaborate couture dresses by Givenchy, Jean Paul Gaultier and Alexander McQueen. Some were plucked from her own cavernous wardrobe by her stylist, Ty, but she was also loaned a striking emerald Pucci gown, which came with strict instruction that it be returned after the shoot. Disaster struck as Beyoncé slipped into the dress and accidentally put her hand straight through one of its delicate sleeves. Ty was aghast as a gaping hole opened up all the way down the arm – then did what any enterprising stylist would do. Bravely, he grabbed a pair of scissors and snipped off the entire sleeve. 'I was, like, "OK, well, I'm going to have to return the dress, but the sleeve is somewhere else."'

As the video wrapped and Tofo Tofo said their final

goodbyes, Beyoncé broke down in tears. 'I could completely identify with the amount of love and passion that those guys felt when they were walking away from the set,' she said in *Year of 4*. 'It just reminds me of when we first started. It made me feel like I was fifteen years old again on my first video set, and I didn't want to go home . . . I remember that moment, trying to get that last look of the set and just being torn because I never wanted to leave.'

Her first live performance of 'Run The World (Girls)' took place during a commemoration of the twenty-fifth and final season of Oprah Winfrey's chat show. *The Farewell Spectacular* was filmed in Chicago, with Beyoncé vamping it up in a tuxedo-style leotard with red heels. Joined by forty female dancers and watched by celebrities including Madonna, Tom Hanks and Tom Cruise, she dedicated the song to her friend: 'Oprah Winfrey, because of you, women everywhere have graduated to a new level of understanding. Of what we are, of who we are and, most importantly, who we can be. Oprah, we can run the world!' This was a somewhat ironic dedication in many ways, given it was Beyoncé who ran this particular gauntlet and that she was the one doing the empowering. Open-mouthed and repeatedly uttering 'Unbelievable!' throughout Beyoncé's racy performance, the veteran TV star saluted her at the end of the song and shouted, 'Girls, girls, girls!'

Though ostensibly seen as a song about women for women, 'Run The World (Girls)' was one of Beyoncé's most successful tracks in the gay arena. A staunch supporter of same-sex marriage, she had long cherished her affinity with her gay fans, telling PrideSource website: 'I've always had a connection. Most of my audience is actually women and my gay fans, and I've seen a lot of the younger boys kind of grow up to my music.' She added: 'I remember my friends were telling me when the song "Run The World (Girls)" first came out in the clubs the kids were going crazy, and I thought it was so wonderful and I was so excited to know that the reception was so positive.'

The following month, the album 4 was leaked on the internet prior to its official release, sparking an influx of legal warnings and anger within Beyoncé's camp. She responded rather more serenely on Facebook: 'My music was leaked and while this is not how I wanted to present my new songs, I appreciate the positive response from my fans. When I record music I always think about my fans singing every note and dancing to every beat. I make music to make people happy and I appreciate that everyone has been so anxious to hear my new songs.'

When it was launched in the official way, its mixture of upbeat tracks and softer ballads brought her yet another number one in both the UK and America, while she became only the second female artist to have four consecutive solo albums debut in the top spot on the *Billboard* 200, after Britney Spears. Though sales were down on her previous albums overall, 4 still sold three million copies worldwide. Her label blamed the leak for the dip in sales, but pitching in from outside, her father said her management set-up had become too disparate. He and Beyoncé were said to be barely speaking, but he took a swipe at the involvement of Jay-Z's label Roc Nation, which he had set up in partnership with Live Nation in 2008. 'The team ironically appeared to be a cross-pollination of Beyoncé's team, Roc Nation's team, and Live Nation's team, who ironically have the most to gain,' Mathew said. 'I'm challenging all of these folks on integrity, professional integrity.'

But, as *Billboard* noted, the album was hardly a flop: '*4*'s bow is pretty big for 2011. It marks the third largest sales week of the year, after the number-one bows of Lady Gaga's *Born This Way* [1.1 million sales] and Adele's *21* [351,000].'

Regardless of the intricacies of sales performance, Beyoncé was deeply proud of her latest work and shared her thoughts about it on her website. 'The album is definitely an evolution,' she said. 'It's bolder than the music on my previous albums because I'm bolder. The more mature I become and the more life experiences I have, the more I have to talk about.'

The album's artwork was shot on the rooftop of the Hôtel Meurice in Paris, where she and Jay-Z had got engaged several years previously. With smoky eyes and her arms raised above her head, she wore a fur stole over her bare chest, which just about preserved her modesty. In another promo shot, her body was splayed into a wide star shape as she clung to two ropes, with her feet in stirrups. 'This was not very fun,' she told *Access Hollywood*. 'I was actually quite angry and sore and I wanted to get out of this crazy position. They kept saying, "Do the splits!" and, I'm like, "No!" I was, like, "Get the shot, get the shot!" because my heels were caught in these crazy ropes. But it makes for a very interesting picture.'

As Beyoncé's fans were to find out in the months to come, that trip to Paris turned out to be symbolic of far more than a mere glossy photo shoot. Indeed, Jay-Z would later reveal that what occurred behind closed doors there changed the entire course of their lives.

* * *

As usual, Beyoncé hit the campaign trail hard with the new album, and in June she was granted her long-held wish to replicate Jay-Z's success and pl ly her own Glastonbury set. In doing so, she was the first solo female artist to headline the Pyramid stage in more than twenty years. Speaking of her first impression of the famously rain-soaked site, she said: 'Well, it's fascinating to see everybody in the mud. It's like they're all united as one.'

Opening her ninety-minute set with the obligatory 'Crazy In Love', she rose on a hydraulic platform as fireworks showered around her, before launching into her and Destiny's Child's biggest hits – and a surprise cover of 'Sex On Fire' by the Kings of Leon. With her Etta James tribute 'At Last' also featuring, she sang 'Halo', changing the words to 'Glaston-bury, I can feel your halo.'

Wearing hot pants and a gold belted jacket with her curly hair blowing in the wind, her set was textbook perfect and she seemed stunned by the ear-splitting screams of appreciation that rang out around Worthy Farm. 'You are witnessing a dream!' she yelled back at the crowd. 'I always wanted to be a rock star!'

The press was no less awestruck by her faultless show, with the *Guardian* raving: 'Fireworks, slick choreography and all the hits – Beyoncé didn't put a foot wrong.' And a critic from the *Evening Standard* wrote: 'Entertained? I almost needed respiratory treatment.'

Naturally, Jay-Z watched proudly in the pit beneath the stage, alongside Gwyneth Paltrow, who apparently sang along to every word. Her husband Chris Martin observed the show from the side of the stage, as he had helped Beyoncé prepare for her huge moment. 'He's the master of this,' Beyoncé said of the Coldplay frontman. She and Jay-Z had watched his band perform at the same festival the previous evening, with Beyoncé wrapped in a hoodie and jeans, dancing along with Gwyneth.

She also revealed that she had consulted U2 rocker Bono about her set list, saying: 'I'm the biggest fan of U2 . . . I was, like, "OK, you guys are a little bit more familiar with the festivals." I needed to make sure they gave me their approval before I did the performance.'

After coming off stage, exhausted but exhilarated, she made it clear how much the night had meant to her. 'This is the highlight of my career. I was able to see my husband perform here a couple of years ago and it was one of the most exciting nights for me.' She added: 'I was jumping up and down and history was made that night. I was so happy to be there and witness it for myself. I remember saying one day I would love to do a festival similar, and never, ever thought I would be able to headline Glastonbury . . . I'm so happy because, you know, I don't normally do festivals and one hundred seventy-five thousand people and I was very nervous. Everyone gave me so much love and I will never, ever, ever forget this night.'

The following day, Beyoncé filmed a slot on Piers Morgan's ITV chat show and seemed elated from the previous night. 'I'm still walking on the clouds,' she said. 'I'm still kind of shocked. I can't believe what happened to me yesterday.' When Piers asked how she had felt before going on stage to face her biggest ever audience, she responded: 'I just had to tell myself, I deserve it. I'm a diva. I've worked hard. And I psyched myself up, and once you hear the crowd and you get past the first couple of minutes, then it's time to rock.'

She also spoke to Piers about her landmark thirtieth birthday, which was fast approaching. 'I can't wait, because twenty-nine is very strange. You are still in your twenties, but you feel like you are supposed to be thirty . . . I feel like thirty is the ideal age, because you are mature enough to know who you are, and to have your boundaries and your standards, and not be afraid, too polite – but you are young enough to be a young woman.'

Then came the oh-so-predictable, but entirely necessary question. 'Can we expect the patter of little Beyoncé and Jay-Zs?' Piers asked.

She took a deep breath and diplomatically replied: 'Only God knows.'

As the world was about to find out, there was rather more to the story than that . . .

Chapter Sixteen

In hindsight, Beyoncé's Glastonbury performance was all the more spectacular than it first seemed, because her high-energy routine masked one very significant fact: she was in the very early stages of pregnancy. Equally surprising was that she had also unknowingly been expecting when appearing at the *Billboard* Awards in Vegas the month before. On that occasion, she wore an ultra-revealing silver dress, shaped like a cobweb that bared most of her flesh. At the event she won the title of Millennium Artist, itself a huge achievement, but no doubt she would remember the night as the beginning of her journey into motherhood. 'I have been pregnant through every event I've done, from the *Billboard* Awards to Glastonbury,' she later said, with an understandable degree of disbelief.

According to later reports, the happy news was confirmed to her shortly before her Glastonbury performance, but she was determined not to leave fans or the organisers in the lurch by dropping out. However, the *Sun* reported that she did submit a last-minute alteration to her list of dressing-room requests. A source told the newspaper: 'Originally [Beyoncé's backstage rider] contained KFC, junk food, chocolate . . . Then all of a sudden she wanted only healthy options – fruit juices, vegetables, water, strictly no alcohol. There was a mad panic to get her what she wanted in time.'

Although some eagle-eyed fans watching her show had guessed that she was expecting from the way she seemed to clasp her stomach protectively on stage, the news remained a secret for many more weeks – until well after she had passed the three-month mark. But Gwyneth Paltrow later let slip that her friend had been suffering with terrible morning sickness at the festival. Discussing her Glastonbury endeavours with *Harper's Bazaar*, she said: 'She was absolutely incredible, especially as she was barfing in between.'

Her pregnancy might also have accounted for her and Jay-Z's decision to stay at the exclusive Babington House Hotel near the festival site rather than camp in the VIP area. The pair were heli-coptered to and from Worthy Farm, retreating to their Walled Garden Suite – accessorised with outdoor hot tub – when the crowds and the mud all got too much.

After Glastonbury, the mum-to-be filmed a one-off ITV concert in London called *A Night with Beyoncé* – but the show was plunged into chaos when she began losing her voice midway through the recording. Blaming extreme tiredness in the wake of her relentless work schedule in recent weeks, rather than let slip her big secret, she cut the set short and masked her failing vocals by enlisting the help of the audience to sing the chorus of her final song, 'Countdown'. Although she had to call it a night earlier than planned, Beyoncé remained dedicated to ensuring her fans had a good time, and earlier in the day she had given pizza to the devoted fans waiting outside the studios, some of whom had camped out overnight.

Back in the States, she continued promoting 4, completing a mini-tour in August, which sold out in just twenty-two seconds. The 4 Intimate Nights with Beyoncé shows were held at New York's Rosedale Ballroom and saw her perform the album in its entirety. Playing to just three thousand fans per night, the low-key nature of the gigs showed that her priorities were changing as an expectant mother – although, of course, the public was still in the dark. 'This is going to be a little different, y'all,' she welcomed the audience. 'It'll be more intimate.' She later admitted that she was convinced everyone would guess her news: 'The whole time I definitely was thinking, Everyone knows, everyone can see. When you're pregnant, it's a little bit harder to breathe, so it was hard doing all the choreography and singing at the same time.'

The four gigs were a marked contrast to her usual frenetic world tours, but when she was asked later if she had been disappointed that she couldn't promote 4 in such an epic manner, she simply expressed happiness that she had been able to perform at all.

Each show ended with one of the album's most contemplative songs, the ballad 'I Was Here'. The unmistakably powerful track had become known as her tribute to the victims of 9/11, and as she sang, 'I was here, I lived, I learned,' she could not stop the tears pouring down her cheeks.

Trying to keep her pregnancy out of the spotlight during this time proved stressful, especially as her work commitments were stacking up for the coming months. Her record company,

Columbia, had scheduled a hectic year ahead, with chairman Rob Stringer telling *Billboard* in June: 'The touring plan is extensive. The promo plan is extensive. We also know we are going to put out a lot of singles and . . . shoot a lot of videos from the record.' Not only that, but she was also due to start filming her lead role in a new movie, *A Star Is Born* with Clint Eastwood, in February 2012, coinciding exactly with the time she was due to give birth. This was a project she was hugely excited about because it had been one of her favourite films as a young girl.

Towards the end of August, the evidence of Baby Carter-Knowles was becoming increasingly difficult to disguise, even in loose-fitting clothing, and she knew the time had arrived to come clean. But in keeping with her and Jay-Z's tendency to do things their way, the announcement did not leak from an unnamed 'friend' or come via a carefully worded statement from publicist Yvette. Instead, the information was delivered live on TV by Beyoncé herself at that year's MTV Video Music Awards. And one simple gesture was all it took for her news to break.

As she posed on the red carpet and dutifully kept smiling for the horde of photographers and TV crews, she made a graceful half-turn to show a side view of her body silhouetted in a long orange gown by the Paris fashion house Lanvin. She then pressed her hands above and below a now clearly visible bump and exclaimed: 'I have a surprise!'

Later that evening, when she took to the stage to perform 'Love On Top', she had changed into a glittery purple jacket, white shirt and high-waisted black trousers. At the end of the song, she threw down her microphone, ripped open her jacket to display her tummy and stroked it tenderly, making big circles with her hands.

The audience erupted into a cacophony of screams and cheers as she told them: 'I want you to stand up on your feet. I want you to feel the love that's growing inside me.' The cameras then panned to Jay-Z in the crowd. He was on his feet, grinning from ear to ear and clapping wildly. His friend Kanye was jumping up and down and shook the father-to-be by the shoulders.

The announcement set the showbiz world buzzing. Incredibly, the news broke all Twitter records with more than eight thousand tweets per second. The site itself tweeted the following day: 'Last night at 10.35 p.m. ET, Beyonce's big MTV #VMA moment gave Twitter a record bump: 8,868 Tweets per second.' Her reaction was understandably one of bemusement. 'It's crazy – I don't even tweet!' she said.

The most faultless PR exercise imaginable, the moment also showed that Beyoncé was very much in control of how her life played out and was subsequently reported. 'I didn't want a crazy picture or gossip story to break the news, so I decided to say nothing and proudly show my baby bump,' she said, in an interview with *Harper's Bazaar* after the event. 'I felt it was more powerful to see the love and enthusiasm as opposed to saying anything.'

But she revealed that she had been anxious about the stunt and considered almost seventy gowns to wear before settling on the orange Lanvin number. Admitting it was the most challenging red carpet experience of her life, the mum-to-be confirmed that the whole manoeuvre was as carefully choreographed as one of her dance routines and that she put much thought into it.

To ABC, she stressed: 'Physically I was starting to show, so it was only a matter of days before someone zoomed in. So I just wanted it to be from me, and I wanted it to be something that was a celebration of something so beautiful. I figured the biggest statement was to . . . just be.'

The overriding feeling that set in after the VMAs was one of relief. 'Honestly, I just felt free. I really did, because I'd been holding the most exciting thing in for so long, and I just felt, like, "Wow, now I can enjoy and now I can just experience this the way that every woman should." I felt, like, "Oh, I can breathe and be happy." I went straight off the stage and cried. I hugged my mom, I hugged Jay and just cried. It was a beautiful day.'

While Jay-Z knew exactly what was going on, her former bandmate, Kelly, let slip she had been in on the secret for 'quite a while too', telling US Weekly: 'I think she'll be an incredible mother because she's always been motherly. She takes so many traits from her mother, and I just think it's going to be so natural for her.'

Beyoncé had made no secret of her wish to be pregnant by the age of thirty and she was therefore right on schedule. On 4 September, she celebrated her landmark birthday by jetting off to Venice with Jay-Z. In Italy, they combined a romantic break with a party on a luxury yacht attended by a select group of friends, including Gwyneth Paltrow, who had often spoken of her friend's natural affinity with children. 'With my kids she is easy and fun,' she said. 'They know that she is interested in them, and they can tell when a grown-up is faking.' It had also been revealed that her children Apple and Moses now called Beyoncé 'Aunty B' and Jay-Z 'Uncle Jay'.

The celebration could not have been happier for Beyoncé now that a baby was on the way. Seen relaxing on the sun-soaked deck of a chartered yacht called *Odessa*, the circle of friends made use of the onboard hot tub, cinema room and lounge bar, as well as its five plush suites. Beyoncé was seen chatting animatedly to Gwyneth during the trip and it seemed the actress had plenty of advice for the first-time mum. Apparently advocating the benefits of wheatgrass shots and meditation, she was also said to have recommended Beyoncé rub her belly with coconut oil and use crystals that promote peace, love, and good health. *Closer* magazine also claimed that Gwyneth sent her friend packages of herbs and vitamins.

Regardless of these good intentions, it seemed that Beyoncé had strong cravings for naughty treats and could not resist her favoured snacks of crisps and Oreo cookies – of which she admitted: 'Once I start eating them, I can't stop. I can finish a whole packet.' Her liking for tomato sauce was also heightened. 'I don't know if you'd call it weird, but I'm having ketchup with everything,' she said. 'I mean, I liked it before I was pregnant, but I now literally won't eat anything without it.'

But she quashed reports of more outlandish cravings, telling ABC: 'I was on a plane and the flight attendant came and was, like, "I have your hot sauce and pickles and bananas," and I'm, like, "That is absolutely disgusting, what are you doing?" He's, like, "I read it on the internet."' Definitely off the menu were foods with a strong odour like onions, which made her feel sick. 'I smell everything,' she said. 'If it smells bad I smell it, if it smells great – I love it.'

As the weeks went by, Beyoncé settled happily into pregnancy and was visibly glowing every time she stepped out in public. At the New York launch of her latest perfume, Beyoncé Pulse, she dazzled in an ultra-short blue sequined minidress and said: 'I am having so much fun. It has been the most fun time now that [my pregnancy] has been announced. It was really difficult to conceal.' Though others with her degree of fame and fortune might simply have put their feet up for the next six months, workaholic Beyoncé would not hear of it. 'When you are excited about something, you don't have to think about your energy,' she told reporters at the perfume launch. 'It's natural and comes from adrenalin. It is important that I don't look at this like an illness. I am not sick. I am the same woman and I have the same passions.' She also revealed: 'I've been performing the whole time and dancing and singing in the studio. I think my baby has heard lots and lots of very loud music.' Filmed talking to a camera in bed in a later TV documentary, she spoke of the momentous occasion when she sensed the little life moving inside her. 'I felt the baby kick for the first time. Kicked five times.'

Clearly, she was not planning to slow down when the new arrival made its grand entrance into the world either, and when asked if she planned to take her child everywhere with her, she replied: 'Yes, I'm sure I will. I think that it shouldn't stop you. I think of course my life is going to change, and I definitely will make sacrifices, but you know, I think I will be able to bring hopefully my little rider with me.'

Showing how determined she was not to let her baby change her or turn her into an obsessive 'Pramzilla', she said: 'I haven't been going crazy. I know that it's important that I don't lose myself.' Keeping this sense of perspective on the pregnancy was vitally important to her, and she said: 'I know it's going to be difficult at times and I know that, like my mother, I'm going to get on my child's nerves, but it's all out of love and I'm just ready. I'm ready for the next chapter.'

As a result, she did not put a stop to her international travel commitments, and in September, she and Tina dashed to London for the UK launch of their House of Deréon line at Selfridges. Walking hand in hand with her mother down the catwalk at the Oxford Street store, Beyoncé looked more radiant than ever, with a post-Italy golden glow and blonde-streaked hair. She still managed to wear a pair of skyscraper heels and was shimmering in a black sequined trouser suit. 'What I'm wearing today is part of the collection and it's not supposed to be, but it actually is really good for maternity wear.' She laughed. Evidently, choosing her pregnancy wardrobe had become a favourite new hobby. 'Now that I can be proud and excited about it, I'm having so much fun shopping. It's great,' she said.

When asked how she felt about becoming a grandmother, Tina said: 'I am so delighted. I'm over the moon.' And speaking to *Life & Style* magazine, she said Beyoncé was going to be 'an awesome mom' and that she and Jay-Z were 'very, very happy and just glowing. It's great to see.' Tina also revealed that Beyoncé had suffered badly with morning sickness in her first trimester: 'She went through it, but she's got past it now. She's craving waffles . . . The normal – just wanting to eat!'

Solange was thrilled that she was going to be an aunt, and said Beyoncé's experience of looking after her son Julez would stand her in good stead. 'She took him to Disneyland and to toy stores and carnival rides. She did the entire experience with him. She's so incredibly patient. She's going to be a phenomenal mother, there's no question about it.' Solange told instyle.com that she had been helping her sister choose baby clothes. 'I go straight to net-a-porter.com and I copy and paste URLs and send them her way,' she said. 'We also go shopping together. She's getting bigger. It's so fun when you're actually showing and you're able to show-case that.'

In September the sisters hit New York Fashion Week. Unusually, the buzz was not about the clothes or the skinny models traipsing listlessly up the runways: the front-row fashionistas were far more excited by seeing 'Babyoncé', as the media had dubbed her. With her bump neatly tucked away under a belted gold wrap dress, she almost caused a stampede at the J. Crew, Vera Wang and Rodarte shows. 'This morning I woke up and I was, like, "Really? A fash-ion show?" But I wanted to spend time with my sister,' she said.

Combining their style sense with her new-found interest in all things baby, Beyoncé and Tina were inspired to start another busi-ness venture – this time working on a maternity collection for House of Deréon. 'I think a woman's curves when she is pregnant are so beautiful,' Beyoncé said. As the ultimate 'yummy mummy', she avoided anything that looked matronly and opted for soft, flowing materials to complement her body in a feminine and funky way. She also experimented with mixing different textures, suit jackets and blazers. 'It's been so exciting for me. I love figur-ing out designs that still make me feel edgy and sexy while pregnant. Flowy fabrics are always flattering, but I still rock my stilettos,' she said.

Keeping as busy as ever, despite her advancing pregnancy, October saw Beyoncé release a new single, 'Countdown', from 4. Scenes from the sixties-themed video showed her ballooning baby bump, which director Adria Petty revealed was never part of the plan. 'When we first started shooting, she had not made the announcement and I do not believe that was the goal . . . I believe she had a number of commitments and had not anticipated her special arrival.' In a 'making of' video that accompanied the song, she said: 'Hello! It's September twenty-third . . . Right now I'm actually shooting the video for "Countdown" and I'm six months pregnant, pretending that my stomach is flat in body suits.'

As with any celebrity pregnancy, the 'bump-watch' brigade was permanently out in force to analyse Beyoncé's expanding waist-line, but nobody could have predicted the huge controversy that emanated from her appearance on Australian TV show *Sunday Night* that October. During the chat, she told the host, 'I'm very grateful that God has blessed me with the biggest gift any human can have,' adding: 'I feel free. I feel very empowered.' But what she said hardly seemed to matter, because a storm was swiftly break-ing out online. As she had sat down to talk to the host, footage had appeared to show an inexplicable squishing effect around her midriff. Viewers leaped to suggest that her stomach had 'collapsed' live on air, claiming that her bump was false, and social media swiftly erupted with the unfounded accusation that she was 'faking' her entire pregnancy. As speculation mounted that she was wearing a prosthetic belly, Beyoncé was hurt beyond words – even though one more sympathetic school of thought suggested the squishing effect was simply due to an unfortunate rolling down of her tights or Spanx underwear as she sat down. Sparking a frenzy of worldwide debate as video of the incident went viral, other wild ideas took off, including a theory that a surrogate mother had been hired to carry her child to prevent any ill-effect on Beyoncé's body. Another rumour ran that the couple instead planned to adopt a child and that she was faking her pregnancy to cover it up.

The footage of her seemingly deflating bump prompted endless discussion in newspapers and magazines and on TV. One US talk show went as far as staging a practical experiment in which two pregnant women volunteered to sit down to find out if their stomachs folded in, like Beyoncé's had. The results were inconclusive, leaving viewers just as baffled as before.

Beyoncé's publicist Yvette Noel-Schure was certainly not in any doubt as to the truth of the matter. As soon as the rumours began, she put out a fiercely worded statement that claims of a prosthetic baby belly were 'stupid, ridiculous and false'.

Daft and untrue the stories might have been, but Beyoncé admitted in a *Vogue* interview some time later that she had been stunned by the accusations. 'Like, who would make that up?' she wondered. 'You can't take it too seriously.' A long time later, she angrily blasted the story as 'a stupid rumour, the most ridiculous rumour I've ever had about me. To think that I would be that vain . . .'

Jay-Z also admitted that the cruel comments had left him feeling very upset for his wife. 'It's just so stupid,' he told *Vanity Fair*. 'You know, I felt dismissive about it, but you've got to feel for her. I mean, we've got a really charmed life, so how can we complain? But when you think about it, we're still human beings.' He added: 'Even in hip-hop, all the blogs – they had a field day with it. I'm, like, "We come from you guys, we represent you guys. Why are you perpetuating this? Why are you adding fuel to this ridiculous rumour?"' It was a torrid time for a couple who had always trodden a wary path with the media.

Beyoncé decided to start taking it easier and, in November, slowed her work schedule. Still, she refused to live like a recluse and instead went on the road with Jay-Z to support his and Kanye's Watch The Throne tour. She turned out for almost every show – and somewhat inconveniently had to take several toilet breaks at the Fort Lauderdale concert. At one show, shunning the VIP box, she was also pictured dancing in the front row, while flaunting her now huge belly in a red dress.

The same month, Jay-Z was named *GQ* magazine's 'King of the Year' and said he was determined to be a better father than his own dad had been. 'I'm just a different kind of guy,' he said. 'I'm a highly principled person.' But when the men's magazine asked him if his baby would be thoroughly spoiled, he insisted that money was irrelevant. 'Providing – that's not love. Being there – that's more important.' Promising he would be there 'one hundred per cent' for nappy-changing, he was later asked if those nappies would be made of gold. 'No,' he joked. 'Leather!'

Assuring readers that he would never leave Beyoncé and their child, Jay-Z also told *People*: 'I don't think any person, or any male, goes into a relationship thinking that they're going to leave or they wouldn't be there.'

'Babyoncé' excitement peaked when best friend Kelly accidentally let slip that Beyoncé and Jay-Z were expecting a little girl. Talking to reporters at the *Cosmopolitan* Awards in London that November, she said, 'I'm so happy for my sister and her husband. They're so happy in this moment right now, as they should be. They've made a little bundle of love. I'm so excited for them.' Stumbling onto the subject of gift ideas for the baby, she continued: 'I have no idea what I'm going to buy Beyoncé at the baby shower because Jay is going to buy that little girl every single thing possible. She won't be spoiled but she will be very well looked after.'

As the jubilant reporters realised they had a great exclusive on their hands, Kelly then made the same admission to *US Weekly*. 'I think she'll be very well behaved,' she said. 'Her parents will make sure of that.' It was then reported that Kelly had bought her friends' unborn daughter a designer bathtub to make amends for blurting the news. The baby-sized porcelain tub by Californian designer Lori Gardner was said to be covered with almost forty-five thousand imported Swarovski crystals, which had taken two months to apply by hand. ABC News claimed that Kelly had opted for the pink version, which cost $5,200.

Such luxury was obviously going to be part and parcel of the baby's life from day one. It was reported that Beyoncé and Jay-Z had hired an interior designer to create not one but three nurseries in their various homes. While the nursery in Manhattan was said to be a whopping 2,000 square feet, they opted for smaller but identical versions in their Miami and Scarsdale houses. The idea to make each room exactly the same had apparently come from Gwyneth Paltrow, who said such a measure would prevent the baby ever feeling confused about her surroundings. According to estimates, each of the three nurseries cost around a quarter of a million dollars to kit out and decorate. With a $21,000 'fantasy crib' made of solid cedar and birch said to be the focal point of their plans, a source was quoted in US tabloid magazine *Star* as saying: 'Beyoncé wants 18-carat gold trim on everything. The crib is like a mini four-poster bed with silk curtains, and they're going to town with the cashmere throws. Plus there's a top-of-the-line sound system with an iPod dock so they can play the baby nursery rhymes, and a flat-screen TV that comes down from the ceiling.'

The colour schemes had been carefully thought out, too, and

Beyoncé and Tina spent days sifting through baby catalogues and interior design books. 'They've picked a mixture of calming tones and colours, combined with some serious glamour,' said the insider. Other items they were said to have thrown serious cash at included a $16,000 high chair lined with Swarovski crystals, a $600 hand-made golden rocking horse from Japanese jeweller Ginza Tanaka, and a $290 silk 'burping' dress by Jean Paul Gaultier.

By the end of December they were as prepared for the birth as they would ever be, and Beyoncé had even traded in her prized car for a more practical Mercedes van. However, this was no standard-issue vehicle; she spent a cool million dollars getting it custom-finished for their baby. Not only did it have hand-stitched Italian leather seats, but it was also equipped with a full bathroom, a $150,000 sound system and plasma TV.

The end of the year was marked with a surge of false reports, citing that Beyoncé had given birth to a baby girl called Tiana-May. Though it was an elaborate hoax, the timing of the story was not far wrong. Just eight days later, her and Jay-Z's first child came into the world.

Chapter Seventeen

Baby Blue Ivy Carter made her grand entrance on 7 January 2012. She was born at New York's Lenox Hill Hospital and her long-awaited arrival was accompanied by an official statement from the couple, which read: 'Hello Hello Baby Blue! We are happy to announce the arrival of our beautiful daughter, Blue Ivy Carter, born on Saturday, 7 January 2012. Her birth was emotional and extremely peaceful, we are in heaven. She was delivered naturally at a healthy 7lbs and it was the best experience of both of our lives. We are thankful to everyone for all your prayers, well wishes, love and support. Beyoncé & Jay-Z.'

Unlike many celebrity mothers who choose to undergo a Caesarean section – often having a crafty nip and tuck at the same time to obliterate a 'mummy tummy' – Beyoncé was very keen to point out that she went *au naturel*. Her labour seemed to have been a breeze. 'I felt like when I was having contractions, I envisioned my child pushing through a very heavy door,' she told *Vogue*. 'I imagined this tiny infant doing all the work, so I couldn't think about my own pain. We were talking. I know it sounds crazy, but I felt a communication.

'Everything that scared me was not present in that room,' she explained. 'So for me to really let go and really appreciate every contraction . . . it was the best day of my life.'

The joyous occasion appeared to come with a hefty price tag: it was claimed that Jay-Z shelled out $1.3 million to take over an entire floor of the New York hospital for his daughter's birth. Refuting this, a hospital spokeswoman said that Beyoncé had merely occupied one sixth-floor suite. Tina, Mathew and Solange were all spotted there at various intervals, clutching flowers and pink balloons tied with silver and black ribbons. The family ordered takeaways and bottles of red wine as they awaited the baby's arrival.

There were undoubtedly extreme security measures in place at the hospital, with staff taping over CCTV cameras to prevent images leaking out. With Beyoncé apparently checking in under the false name Ingrid Jackson, armed guards were seen prowling outside the hospital that night too, and some reports stated that a bulletproof door had been installed at the entrance to her suite. Secrecy surrounding the birth was so intense that some families complained they were 'evacuated' to other parts of the hospital to guarantee the couple's privacy.

Inside her suite, there was no way Beyoncé was prepared to let her high standards drop and she worked hard to look her best. 'I tried my best to roller-set my hair, and I wore my gloss when I arrived at the hospital,' she told *People*. 'I committed myself to the end and wore my kitten heels.' Still, there came a time when her efforts to look immaculate were scuppered. 'After many hours of labour, I didn't care how I looked.'

One of the overriding emotions she felt as her newborn

daughter was placed in her arms was relief, which left her weeping uncontrollably. She had been absolutely terrified of the labour process and later told *Shape* magazine: 'Giving birth was one of my biggest fears, and having Blue forced me to face it.'

Within a few hours of announcing their happy news to the world, conspiracy theories about their baby's name were running wild. One of the more elaborate notions was that Blue Ivy written backwards spelt 'Eulb Yvi', which some claimed could be Latin for Lucifer's daughter's name. Laughable this might have been, but Twitter still went into minor meltdown as the rumour spread. Thankfully, the *Examiner* pointed out that the Bible made no mention of Lucifer having a daughter. Another more logical theory concerned the couple's love of the number four. In Roman numerals, this is written as IV so could easily represent the name 'Ivy'. It was also mooted that 'Blue' stemmed from her parents' love of the colour and that Jay-Z had released three albums with *Blueprint* in the title during a ten-year period.

In the end, Beyoncé gave the strongest hint of their possible reasoning for the name, by posting a passage from a novel on her Tumblr account. The excerpt from Rebecca Solnit's book, *A Field Guide to Getting Lost*, focused on the significance of the colour blue and said: 'The world is blue at its edges and in its depths.' The last sentence she posted read: 'The light that gets lost gives us the beauty of the world, so much of which is in the colour blue.'

There was certainly no doubting the joy Tina felt on meeting her first granddaughter. She called Blue Ivy 'beautiful' and said that she was 'doing great', while she also described her new role as 'amazing – the second best job I've ever had'. Although reports were rife that Beyoncé wanted to keep Mathew at arm's length from his new grandchild, he contradicted such claims while appearing on ITV chat show *Lorraine* a few weeks after the birth. Promoting his latest girl band in London, he said: 'I was with Blue Ivy two days ago. I had her in my arms and was singing a song I used to sing to Beyoncé and then after I finished singing the song she kind of went, "aaaah".' He added: 'You just want to love and kiss her but the great thing with grandkids is that you can give them back.'

Beyoncé's sister Solange was ecstatic about meeting her niece and tweeted that Blue Ivy was the most beautiful girl in the world, while Gwyneth said: 'Welcome to the world, Blue! We love you already.' Singer Rihanna tweeted: 'Welcome to the world, Princess Carter! Love, Aunty Rih.'

Three days after the birth, Beyoncé and Jay-Z took their precious bundle home, leaving the hospital at one forty-five a.m. in a bid to throw photographers off the scent. They were shadowed by a convoy of security cars as they made the short journey to their Tribeca penthouse. Later it emerged that one of Blue's first gifts was a stash of children's books from Oprah Winfrey, while Gwyneth was said to have bought her a Bugaboo stroller and ex-bandmate Kelly presented a Bob Marley Babygro and cashmere blankets that cost three hundred dollars each. On visiting the family at home, Kelly and Michelle apparently 'started a little singsong' with Beyoncé, which was 'just like old times'. Describing Blue as 'absolutely gorgeous', Michelle took to Twitter to ask fans to give the Carters some space. 'This is a beautiful, precious, private time between two people and excitement is to be expected but NOT disrespected!' she wrote.

Another friend who was quick to congratulate the new parents was President Obama, who revealed that he had called Jay-Z to offer some fatherly advice: 'I made sure that Jay-Z was helping Beyoncé out and not leaving it all with Beyoncé and the mother-in-law,' he told a Cleveland radio station. It seemed Beyoncé felt far from aggrieved: she reportedly presented Jay-Z with a $500,000 sapphire ring to thank him for the beautiful baby he had given her, as well as his love and support through the ups and downs of pregnancy.

Such was the fascination with the pop world's most eagerly awaited offspring that genealogy website findmypast.co.uk did some digging and discovered that Blue would bizarrely be related to the Duke and Duchess of Cambridge's first child, whenever he or she came along. More than a year in advance of Prince George's birth, the site claimed that the royal baby would be the twenty-third cousin twice removed of Blue Ivy, a connection that supposedly stemmed from their shared French heritage.

Though the strictly private couple had always been against releasing images to the press in the past, they made a rare exception and released a photo of the exhausted new mum cradling their daughter in her arms. With a shock of thick dark hair and equally dark eyes, Blue Ivy looked placidly at the camera, showing a strong resemblance to her mother and father. The photo was accompanied by a brief statement: 'We welcome you to share in our joy. Thank you for respecting our privacy during this beautiful time in our lives.' The note was signed 'The Carter Family'.

In a somewhat unusual step, the couple later attempted to trademark Blue Ivy's name, with Jay-Z explaining: 'People wanted to make products based on our child's name, and you don't want anybody trying to benefit off your baby's name.' However, the request was refused, since an events firm already existed with the same name.

The proud dad marked the new addition to the Carter clan in a unique way, posting a thoughtful track on his blog entitled 'Glory', which referred to her as B.I.C. – meaning Blue Ivy Carter. Just a week old when the song shot into the charts, Blue became the youngest person in history to feature in the *Billboard* countdown. The song was recorded just hours after the birth and featured her first heartbeat, as well as the lyrics:

> *The most amazing feeling I feel*
> *Words can't describe the feeling, for real*
> *Baby I'll paint the sky blue*
> *My most greatest creation was you.*

And though he had been unflinchingly guarded throughout the pregnancy, one of the verses described Blue dancing in Beyoncé's tummy, playfully asking: 'Did you wiggle your hands for her?' With an added comic touch, another section of the song said:

> *You're a child of destiny*
> *You're the child of my destiny*
> *You're my child of a child from Destiny's Child.*

Jay-Z amusingly called his newborn a 'smarter faster me', and rapped: 'Hard not to spoil you rotten, looking like little me.'

And with a startling honesty never seen before, 'Glory' revealed that Blue had been conceived in Paris at the Hôtel Meurice the previous spring, while Beyoncé was in the French capital shooting her album cover for 4.

> *Daddy's little girl*
> *You don't yet know what swag is*
> *But you was made in Paris*
> *And mama woke up the next day*
> *And shot her album package.*

The song also told of how he and Beyoncé had suffered utter heartbreak when they lost another baby, prior to conceiving Blue: 'Last time, the miscarriage was so tragic.' It expressed their fear, too, that history might have repeated itself when Beyoncé was expecting Blue. 'We was afraid you disappeared, but nah, dear, you magic,' Jay-Z continued. 'All the pain over the last time/I prayed so hard it was the last time . . . There you have it, sh*t happens.'

The touching lyrics of 'Glory' gave a rare insight into Jay-Z's sensitive side, and led an NPR radio critic to ask on Twitter: 'Has a rapper ever spoken about miscarriage before?'

As soon as the song was released, news of the power couple's secret miscarriage sparked headlines right across the world. They understandably did not specify when it had happened and Beyoncé remained totally silent about her husband's admission, but she eventually felt ready to talk about it a year later in a heart-rending HBO documentary called *Life Is but a Dream*, which aired in February 2013. In one of her video diaries shown in the programme, she said: 'About two years ago, I was pregnant for the first time. And I heard the heartbeat, which was the most beautiful music I ever heard in my life.' Like all expectant mothers, Beyoncé said she 'envisioned what my child would look like' and that she had 'picked out names' and was feeling 'very maternal'. Likening pregnancy to falling in love, she added: 'You are so open. You are so overjoyed. There's no words that can express having a baby growing inside of you, so of course you want to scream it out and tell everyone.'

But complications in the early stages of the pregnancy soon led to tragedy. 'I flew back to New York to get my checkup – and no heartbeat. Literally the week before I went to the doctor, everything was fine, but there was no heartbeat.' After realising she had lost the baby, Beyoncé said that her way of dealing with the pain was by capturing her emotions in music: 'I went into the studio and wrote the saddest song I've ever written in my life,' she said in the documentary. 'And it was the best form of therapy for me, because it was the saddest thing I've ever been through.' The song was called 'Heartbeat' and its lyrics were poignant:

> *I guess love just wasn't enough for us to survive*
> *I swear, I swear, I swear I tried*
> *You took the life right out of me*
> *I'm longing for your heartbeat, heartbeat.*

A later song titled 'Heaven' also appeared to allude to the miscarriage:

> *Heaven couldn't wait for you . . .*
> *I fought for you the hardest*
> *It made me the strongest*
> *So tell me your secrets*
> *I just can't stand to see you leaving.*

In an interview with Oprah Winfrey to publicise *Life Is but a Dream*, Beyoncé was asked why she had chosen to speak out about their misfortune. 'There are so many couples that go through that and it was a big part of my story,' she explained. 'It was one of the hardest things I've been through.' And 'It's one of the reasons I did not share I was pregnant the second time, because you don't know what's going to happen. And that was hard, because all of my family and my friends knew and we celebrated. It was hard.'

Of course, the miscarriage left her terrified the same thing would happen again. 'I was afraid,' she told Oprah. 'But my doctor told me that I was completely healthy, and don't be crazy and paranoid, and to live my life, and that's what I did.'

A month after Blue Ivy's birth, Jay-Z performed his revelatory song 'Glory' during a gig at New York's Carnegie Hall. 'One hand in the air for Blue,' he shouted, geeing up the crowd. As the song ended with the sound of her crying, he seemed relieved not to have broken down. 'I didn't think I was gonna make it through that one, that was tough,' he said. Beyoncé turned out for the concert, her first public appearance since giving birth. Photos began appearing all over the internet and in showbiz magazines, the world marvelling at her impossibly trim post-pregnancy body. Wearing a close-fitting orange Alice Temperley dress with towering Christian Louboutin heels, she already seemed to have shifted any trace of baby weight – despite claiming she had put on almost sixty pounds prior to giving birth.

And how did she do it? It was simple: 'I worked crazily to get my body back,' she said, with refreshing honesty. Though many celebrity mothers claim the weight 'falls off' naturally, Beyoncé did not want to paint such an unrealistic portrait of motherhood. 'I wanted to show that you can have a child and you can work hard and you can get your body back,' she later revealed. 'I was a hundred ninety-five pounds when I gave birth. I lost sixty-five pounds . . . You can have your child and you can still have fun and still be sexy and still have dreams and still live for yourself.'

Though she said breastfeeding helped, her success was attributed to trainer Marco Borges, who apparently had her doing twice daily workouts and sticking to a strict diet. This reportedly included egg-white omelettes for breakfast, protein shakes or turkey slices for lunch and yellowtail sashimi for dinner. Snacks were limited to edamame beans, berries or a green apple. She and Marco were said to wake at five a.m. for a two-hour gym session, then do it all over again at five p.m. A source was quoted in *Star* magazine, saying: 'They do a mix of cardio, Pilates, plyometrics, yoga and, of course, dance.'

While she looked fantastic, her rapid weight loss led to a second round of 'fake-pregnancy' rumours, with new allegations that she had not given birth to baby Blue. They gathered steam that March when she appeared at a fundraiser hosted by Michelle Obama for her husband's re-election campaign, which was co-hosted by her mum, Tina, and the actor Robert De Niro. Wearing a flattering navy Victoria Beckham dress that clung to her curves, her stomach seemed flat again. As pictures from the event started appearing online, so did the accusatory tweets. 'Looking skinnier than ever. Will the real surrogate please stand up!' posted one sceptic. Another said: 'Still think Beyoncé has a fake baby.' Then website TMZ poked fun at the surrogacy rumours with a video clip about Beyoncé's body that listed a host of other conspiracy theories: 'Who killed JFK? Did Beyoncé really give birth? Mysteries that may never be solved!' it said, before adding: 'She totally had that baby – though she is oddly thin already. Hmm.'

While she ignored the ludicrous comments, Beyoncé later revealed that she deeply regretted putting herself under so much pressure so soon after giving birth. In an interview with *Shape* magazine, she said: 'I didn't have a lot of time to lose the weight because I scheduled a show months after I gave birth, which I would never do again!' Stressing that she always struggled with her weight, she added: 'I'm not a person that is naturally very thin. I am a person that has to work at keeping my body in shape.' Posing in a series of skimpy swimsuits for the publication, she said her biggest sacrifice had been in cutting out refined carbs. 'I ate a very low-calorie diet. I stayed away from red meat and ate a lot of fish, replaced pasta and rice with quinoa.'

As she stressed in the *Shape* article, her motivation for losing weight was that she soon had to return to work. Though she had been due to start filming the movie remake of *A Star Is Born* in February, the film was put on ice to allow her time to adjust to motherhood. Instead, her big comeback was due a few weeks later at a series of four concerts to launch the new $2.5-billion Revel Resort & Casino in Atlantic City, New Jersey. Posting a video on her website as she prepared for the shows, she said: 'I'm enjoying being a mother, so it's like going back to my old job. It's a little strange, but it's important that you don't lose yourself . . . I'm back to work. I'm back to business.' She was also seen sitting on the floor with her dancers discussing the event. 'What I'm trying to say with the show . . . yes, I had a baby, but it just made me more grounded.'

Now she was planning her return to work, it was claimed that TV mogul Simon Cowell had spotted an opportunity and was offering her a staggering $500-million five-year deal to become an *X Factor* judge in the US. He had recently shunted Pussycat Dolls singer Nicole Scherzinger and Paula Abdul off the show so there were two vacancies, and rumour had it that he thought Beyoncé would be the dream signing. He later quashed such whispers, telling US show *Extra*: 'The budget for the show is a hundred million dollars. That would never ever happen. It's absolute nonsense. I genuinely haven't had a conversation with her about it.'

However, Beyoncé had been a hugely popular guest performer on *The X Factor* in the past and Simon was one of her most ardent fans. He had said on *Extra* only months previously: '[She's] ambitious, talented, competitive. She defines this new breed of what I call super pop star. They're all girls at the moment – it's like a new super species who literally want to rule the world.'

Beyoncé might not have been keen to work for Simon, though: he had offended her in the past. 'I once criticised her and I met her father afterwards. Boy, oh, boy, that was a difficult meeting,' he said. 'She came on my show about a year later in the UK – it was still obviously in her head and I apologised. I was wrong. She sang better than anyone I have ever heard sing in my life live and at one point looked over to me and went, "Criticise that." I could see it in her eyes.'

When she was put on the spot about the chances of her ever signing up to *The X Factor* – as her ex-bandmate Kelly had done on the UK show – Beyoncé said: 'It's a big commitment. It's not just a show you are doing, it's about changing people's lives. I would want to give my acts everything I had, and I don't think for the next few years that's going to be possible.'

Prior to her comeback shows in Atlantic City, Beyoncé and Jay-Z decided to renew their wedding vows. Celebrating four years of marriage that April, they were said to have held a 'moving' midnight ceremony on their anniversary. The pair were thought to have bought matching gold rings, and said 'I do' for a second time in front of friends including Oprah Winfrey and Will Smith. Days later, they whisked baby Blue off on an exotic holiday to St Barts, where Beyoncé was pictured cradling the infant in blankets as they boarded a plush yacht. At just three months old, it was the first trip of many for the tiny international jet-setter.

On her return home, the string of concerts in May saw Beyoncé effortlessly pick up her pre-baby pace, with explosions of lights, fireworks and, most significantly, high-energy dancing. Voicing his approval of her emphatic comeback from backstage at the opening gig, Jay-Z tweeted: 'Beyoncé is the best performer in the world. Period.' The audience felt the same and screamed the venue down with every shimmy and shake of her Ralph & Russo-clad derrière. 'Y'all don't know how hard I had to work,' she told the baying crowd. 'I had to lose sixty pounds. They had me on the treadmill, eating lettuce.' She also told fans: 'I gotta say, it feels so good to be back home on stage.'

Fittingly, during each concert, Beyoncé paid tribute to the late Whitney Houston, whose sudden death just weeks before had shocked the world. Blending Whitney's version of 'I Will Always Love You' with her own song 'Halo', she proved how much her former idol had meant to her. Whitney had been found face down in a water-filled bathtub after an apparent overdose, and at the time her death was announced, Beyoncé released a heartfelt statement on her website, describing the loss as 'painful':

> I remember meeting Whitney for the first time when I was fifteen. She was the ultimate legend. The ultimate woman. Not only was she confident, poised, stunningly beautiful and intelligent, but she was sincere and kind. She took the time to make everyone feel like they were very important to her. I, like every singer, always wanted to be just like her. Her voice was perfect. Strong but soothing. Soulful and classic . . . So many of my life's memories are attached to a Whitney Houston song. She is our queen and she opened doors and provided a blueprint for all of us. God bless her.

Spotted in the crowd at one of the shows was First Lady Michelle Obama, who sang along to all the hits with her and Barack's two daughters, Sasha and Malia. Michelle had made it no secret that she adored Beyoncé and had recently told *People* magazine: 'If I had some gift, I'd be Beyoncé. I'd be some great singer.' She also let slip that she even worked out to Beyoncé's music. The month previously, Beyoncé had let it be known that the feeling was mutual, as she posted a handwritten open letter to Michelle on her website. Calling her 'the ultimate example of a truly strong African-American woman', she said she was 'proud to have my daughter grow up in a world where she has people like you to look up to'. She also wrote: 'She's a caring mother, she's a loving wife, while at the same time she's the First Lady!' The letter continued: 'No matter the pressure, and the stress of being under the microscope – she's humble, loving and sincere . . . Michelle, thank you so much for every single thing that you do for us.'

Not to be outdone, Michelle responded on Twitter, saying: 'Thank you for the beautiful letter and for being a role model who kids everywhere can look up to.' She signed the tweet 'MO' – her nickname.

The exchange of admiration was particularly pertinent: the presidential election was to be held that November, and Beyoncé had also teamed up with Michelle to work on a big-budget national campaign to prevent childhood obesity called Let's Move! As part of the scheme, she had recorded a dance workout video with dozens of children, which took the form of a flash mob. 'I am excited to be part of this effort that addresses a public-health crisis,' she said. 'First Lady Michelle Obama deserves credit for tackling this issue directly.'

Chapter Eighteen

In May Beyoncé celebrated her first Mother's Day, which she marked by writing her own mum Tina an open letter.

Dear Mama, Everything I am is because of you! You are the first voice that ever sang to me. At every turn you push me to be better. You teach me to be true to myself and the ones I love. When I look into your eyes, I am sooo proud. Now that I am a mother, I truly realise all the sacrifices you made for us. My love for you goes beyond what I can say. Happy Mama's Day! Love, B.

Some time later, Jay-Z celebrated his first Father's Day in style: it was widely reported that Beyoncé presented him with a $40-million private jet. The Challenger 850 was no regular plane: it came equipped with a living room, kitchen and two bathrooms. With steep running costs, it was said that the average flight would set the couple back at least $20,000. Meanwhile, the doting dad was already reported to have bought his daughter a pair of diamond earrings and platinum bracelet. Appearing on their friend Oprah's show, *Master Class: Special Edition*, he joked: 'I imagine I'll take things I learned from my mom and things I've learned from raising my nephews and apply that. Then, at the end of the day, I just know I'll probably have the worst, spoiled little kid ever.' He also acknowledged that he would probably end up making his daughter cringe: 'Everyone imagines they'll be a great dad until their [kids are] teenagers, saying, "Get away from me, Dad. You're embarrassing me,"' he said.

In spite of so many stories focusing on the family's extravagant lifestyle, Beyoncé was always keen to stress that her main aim as a mother was to provide a normal, unstarry upbringing for Blue. Speaking to *Vogue*, she envisaged a life where her daughter could run through sprinklers, have boisterous sleepovers with her friends and make jugs of lemonade – just as she had done as a little girl.

But with the demands of her job, Beyoncé was always going to need help with Blue and it was said that two nannies were with the family constantly from the moment she was born. Inevitably, Beyoncé also relied heavily on Tina to help in the early days, and there were later rumours that she suffered from mild postnatal depression – especially when a later song called 'Mine' contained the lyric: 'I'm not feeling like myself since the baby.' The same song led some to question her and Jay-Z's marriage, as she sang:

> *Now I'm even more lost*
> *And you're still so fine oh my, oh my*
> *Been having conversations about breakups and separations*
> *. . . Are we gonna even make it?*

Beyoncé never commented on having depression or any marital woes, but she obviously found being a mum immensely rewarding, more precious than anything she had ever experienced. 'I just adore being a mother, hearing her say "Mama" and calling me when she needs something,' she said when Blue was a little older.

And when she faced the inevitable questions about the possibility of expanding her brood, there was no hesitation. 'Definitely I would like to have more children,' she told *Vogue*. 'When I was younger, there were moments when I said, "I'm not going to have children." And then moments when I wanted four. And now I definitely want another, but I don't know when.'

Although she had given birth only a few months previously, Beyoncé got a welcome confidence boost that spring when she was crowned the World's Most Beautiful Woman by *People* magazine. Taken aback, she said: 'It's overwhelming . . . It makes me feel very crunchy, which means embarrassed. My mother is absolutely the most beautiful woman in the world, she's an incredible example. I know that women are like fine wine – we get better with age.'

Far from showing off sleep-deprived skin and giant bags under her eyes, the new mum attributed her win to tending her newborn daughter: 'I feel more beautiful than I've ever felt because I've given birth. I have never felt so connected, I never felt like I had such a purpose on this earth or so proud of myself.' Revealing her ultimate beauty lifesaver to readers, she said she swore by a four-dollar drugstore cream called Aquafor Healing Ointment. 'I use it to remove eye makeup, as a lip moisturiser and on my eyelids.'

When asked which parent her daughter had most begun to resemble, she merely said: 'She looks like Blue. She's her own person . . . She's just the cutest thing.' Perhaps the *People* award left her a little delirious, because she confessed to CNN's Anderson Cooper that she considered changing Blue's nappies a real treat: 'I love changing diapers, I love it. I love every moment of it. It's so beautiful,' she said, adding that Jay-Z was also 'very good' at it.

Taking a break from her motherly role, Beyoncé attended the annual BET Awards in LA in early July, but the glitzy occasion was somewhat marred by reports of a feud between her and Kanye West's new girl-friend, Kim Kardashian. As she sat in the front row of the auditorium alongside Jay-Z, Kanye and Kim, onlookers sensed tension between the two women and it was said that they barely spoke during the whole four-hour show. Kanye had only recently hooked up with the famously curvaceous reality-TV star and this event was their first public appear-ance as a couple. But sources said Beyoncé was wary of associating herself too closely with Kim – especially as some of her most ardent fans begged her to keep her distance. They were soundly unimpressed that Kim had first shot to fame because of a sex tape, believing it jarred with Beyoncé's wholesome past.

Then came reports that Beyoncé had refused to go to the forti-eth birthday party of one of Jay-Z's long-time friends, Tyran Smith, because Kim would be there with Kanye. The bash was held in London where Jay-Z and Kanye were touring, but while Gwyneth and Rihanna both showed up, Beyoncé remained in New York. Some weeks later TMZ insisted there was no rift, saying she and Kim had been seen 'laughing and hugging' at a Philadelphia gig where both of their men played. But with dozens of conflicting stories flooding the web, the jury remained out on whether they got on or were so-called 'frenemies'.

When asked directly if there were any problems between her and Beyoncé, Kim told MTV: 'It's so not true. She's so sweet. I have no idea where these things come from. I think they like to make up these feuds. It's more interesting.' Whatever the truth, Beyoncé's relationship with the *Keeping Up With the Kardashians* star would be heavily scrutinised over the coming months, especially when it came to Kim and Kanye's extraordinarily opulent wedding in the spring of 2014.

Retreating from tales of petty squabbling, Beyoncé, Jay-Z and six-month-old Blue headed to their newly rented mansion in the Hamptons on Long Island for the whole of August. The $43.5-million home cost a staggering $400,000 per month to hire, but it boasted such luxuries as twelve en-suite bedrooms, a library, bowling alley and movie theatre, as well as a gym, spa, tennis and squash courts. In addition, the house was equipped with a virtual golf course, rock-climbing wall and skateboarding ramp. Gwyneth and Chris owned a seafront property in the Hamptons, so the actress was in close proximity to help out with mothering duties, and she updated *Hollywood Life* website on the family's progress: 'Beyoncé is doing great. She's just a natural at being a mom. And Blue Ivy is stunning, she has the most beautiful eyes . . . She just has this glow around her like her mother.'

Gwyneth stressed that Blue's future path was already set: 'For sure, she is going to be an entertainer,' she said. Whether her parents felt quite the same was another matter, but when asked years previously if she would ever let a child of hers follow in her showbiz footsteps, Beyoncé was all for it. 'Definitely if she wanted to do it, but I would make sure she knew all of the hard work that came with it,' she told CBS.

Much of their stay in the Hamptons was purely for leisure purposes, but under the guise of well-deserved maternity leave,

Beyoncé had a secret project furiously bubbling away. Unbeknown to her fans or the industry at large, she was masterminding her fifth solo album at the same time as nursing Blue. The album, simply called *Beyoncé*, was to be her most ambitious yet – and this time, she had very different ideas about how she was going to tackle it. Though it would be eighteen months in the making, the finished work would eventually go on to make music history.

In a short film that accompanied the release of the album, she reflected on those blissful days in the Hamptons, saying: 'I was breastfeeding, cornrows in my hair. Because I was spending so much time being a mother, I would take a few hours out of the day and record. In real life, I was this woman, this mother, trying to get my focus and my dreams and myself back.' Speaking of the calming effect of making music in such a tranquil spot, she added: 'It was like a camp. Weekends off. You could go and jump in the pool and ride bikes . . . the ocean and grass and sunshine . . . it was really a safe place.'

As she quietly tinkered away with the early stages of the album, she and Jay-Z got back on the campaign trail for Obama, who was soon to face the American electorate again. At a fundraiser they hosted at Jay-Z's 40/40 club in New York, they sold a hundred tickets for $40,000 per head, while Beyoncé introduced the president, saying they 'believed in his vision'. As he in turn took the microphone, he voiced his appreciation of Beyoncé's unwavering support, claiming she was the 'perfect role model' for his two young daughters. He also cracked a gag about his ties with Jay-Z. 'We both have daughters, and our wives are more popular than we are,' he said. 'So, you know, we've got a little bond there. It's hard but it's OK.'

Jay-Z and Beyoncé received another ringing endorsement from Obama, when he said on a radio show: 'They're good people. They're unbelievably successful but they really are down-to-earth folks. Beyoncé could not be sweeter to Michelle and the girls, who are big Beyoncé fans. They're good friends. We talk about the same things I talk about with all my friends.' Confirming his liking for Jay-Z's music, he said 'My First Song' was a current favourite. 'It just keeps me steady. It reminds you that you always have to stay hungry.'

Their mutual appreciation also saw Jay-Z appear in a two-minute ad praising the president, in which he said: 'For so long there was a voice that was silenced out there, as far as exercising your right to vote. I think it was silent because people had lost hope. They didn't think their voice mattered or counted . . . Now people are exercising their right and you're starting to see the power of our vote. It means something for the first time for a lot of people, having someone in office who understands how power-ful our voice can be.'

Beyoncé also wrote him a handwritten letter:

'Every day we see your heart and character, inspiring all of us to give more of ourselves. You are the leader to take us from where we are to where we need to be. You are the reason my daughter and nephew will grow up knowing that they can truly be anything they want to be.'

Celebrating Beyoncé's thirty-first birthday in September, the well-travelled family went on a low-key Mediterranean cruise, Jay-Z decking out their yacht with balloons and streamers.

Looking more relaxed than ever, a grinning Beyoncé was snapped on board drinking a glass of white wine, without a hint of makeup. On her website, she posted a series of birthday messages from her loved ones, including one from Tina, which said: 'God blessed me with one of the greatest gifts in my life on Sept. 4, 1981. Happy birthday.' Solange affectionately wrote: 'There is no one like you in the world. Of all of your mind-blowing achievements the one that first comes to mind is your kindness. Your sense of selflessness, consideration of other people's wellbeing and your beautiful generosity are all things that make me so proud to be your sister and your friend.'

One of the most touching messages came from Jay-Z's mother, Gloria, who wrote: 'B, You came into my life a sweet Southern girl . . . You've blossomed into an amazing woman. I admire how you remain grounded and humble, and you haven't let success change the person that you are. Mama Carter.' And a handwritten note from Gwyneth read: 'For dear sweet BB on the occasion of her 31st birthday . . . We love you so very much. Love Gwyneth, Chris, Apple, Moses.'

Soon after, in October, Gwyneth turned forty, an occasion she marked with a star-studded party at Elio's restaurant in New York. VIP chums in attendance included model Christy Turlington and acting elite Cameron Diaz and Ethan Hawke, while Beyoncé turned up without Jay-Z for a rare night of letting her hair down. The following evening, she also honoured her friend during a surprise cameo performance in Brooklyn on the last night of Jay-Z's tour. After singing three songs with her husband, to the delight of the crowd, she told them she wanted to wish a happy birthday 'to a special friend of mine', adding: 'Gwyn, I love you.'

But the impromptu dedication was not the only talking point of the evening. Wearing a bulky leather jacket, tiny shorts and a Brooklyn Nets cap, Beyoncé found herself splashed all over the gossip pages the next day, thanks to speculation that she was pregnant again. The latest rumour was sparked because she appeared to be covering her midriff at the concert, and came hot on the heels of another report on the website HollywoodLife.com that she was expecting her second baby. The website had declared that she was showing off a more rounded stomach than normal in a tight-fitting leopard-print dress. But, as it so often turned out, there was no truth to either revelation.

The same month, Beyoncé was forced to drop out of filming *A Star Is Born*. Though production had been delayed to fit in with her maternity arrangements, further scheduling conflicts could not be resolved and she issued a statement, saying: 'I was looking forward to the production of *A Star Is Born* and the opportunity to work with Clint Eastwood. For months we tried to coordinate our schedules to bring this remake to life, but it was just not possible. Hopefully in the future we will get a chance to work together.'

There was more positive news when she inked a whopping, $50-million deal with Pepsi in December. Her involvement with the firm had been ongoing since 2002, but this contract took things to a whole new level and was one of the biggest celebrity endorsements of all time. She could therefore afford to treat Jay-Z for his forty-third birthday that month and it was reported that she surprised him with one of the most expensive watches known to man. Called the Big Bang, the Hublot timepiece was said to have 1,282 diamonds in total and to have set her back a cool five million dollars.

The Pepsi campaign saw her face emblazoned on cans and in several TV and print ads – including a huge-budget promo called Mirrors, which featured a new song called 'Grown Woman'. In the minute-long commercial, she took on several of her past personas, wearing famous outfits such as her 'Single Ladies' leotard. The ad finished with a wall of mirrors shattering and her reciting the strapline, 'Embrace your past, but live for now.'

The deal brought a wave of criticism from those who felt it undermined her earlier Let's Move! project with Michelle Obama, which aimed to reduce childhood obesity. One commentator wrote in the *New York Times*: 'From saying, as she once did in referring to Let's Move!, that she was "excited to be part of this effort that addresses a public health crisis", she's become part of an effort that promotes a public health crisis.'

But Beyoncé was unperturbed. 'Pepsi is a brand I've grown up seeing my heroes collaborate with,' she told *Flaunt* magazine. 'The company respects musicians and artistry. I wouldn't encourage any person, especially a child, to live life without balance.' Stressing that, in moderation, the drink was not detrimental to health, she added: 'When you work out, take care of your body, rehearse as hard as I rehearsed in the commercial, I think it's great to have a Pepsi or Diet Pepsi when you want one. It's all about choices.' Under the terms of the deal, the company would promote her world tour the following year, while she also bagged the prestigious Pepsi-sponsored half-time show at the 2013 Super Bowl in February, for which preparations were already under way.

Long-standing Beyoncé devotees were just as excited by reports that she and her Destiny's Child bandmates were releasing a new compilation album at the end of January. Confirming the news on her website, Beyoncé wrote: 'I am so proud to announce the first original Destiny's Child music in eight years.' The album, *Love Songs*, featured one new single called 'Nuclear', which was produced by Pharrell Williams, as well as older songs that the trio handpicked. Michelle said the album was made 'for the fans', and said of recording 'Nuclear': 'It was a bunch of fun. It was just picking up right where we left off . . . I'm like, "Wow, this is dope." I literally got goose bumps.'

Disappointingly, the album performed poorly, peaking at number seventy-two on the *Billboard* 200 and number forty-four on the UK album chart. It seemed to highlight the different trajectory that the girls' careers had taken and that Beyoncé was in a vastly superior league as a solo star. Life had not been a bed of roses for Michelle during the intervening years and she spoke of the secret torment that followed the Destiny's Child glory days. 'I've dealt with depression,' she told the *Huffington Post*. 'I had to choose to get out of bed.' Michelle turned to exercise, therapy and positive thinking to combat her issues. 'We're taught "Just go to church and pray about it. The Lord is going to heal you." Well, in the meantime, I believe God-gifted people, physicians, doctors, therapists – that's your healing. Take advantage of it. Go see a professional so that they can assess you. It's OK if you're going through something. Depression is not OK, but it is OK to go get help. Sometimes you're going to wake up on the wrong side of the bed or some situation might have you down in the dumps, but you have to choose to be happy.'

Times had often been tough for Kelly, too, and she openly told *Essence* magazine: 'For a long time I wasn't happy, but that had nothing to do with Beyoncé. That had to do with me trying to get my life in order and make better decisions for myself.' But she could not help feeling envious of her best friend's triumphs: 'I'm seeing all these wonderful things happen for her and I am happy for her. But I want a path. I want things to pop off for me, too.'

Her own solo single from 2013, 'Dirty Laundry', gave an indication of her feelings:

*While my sister was on stage, killing it like a motherf****r*
*I was enraged, feeling it like a motherf****r*
Bird in a cage, you would never know what I was dealing with
Went our separate ways, but I was happy she was killing it
Bittersweet, she was up, I was down
No lie, I feel good for her, but what do I do now?

Towards the end of the Destiny's Child era, Kelly was also reportedly trapped in an abusive relationship, and 'Girl', one of the group's later songs, hinted at her fragile state of mind, as Beyoncé sang:

Take a minute girl, come sit down
And tell us what's been happening
In your face I can see the pain
Don't try and convince us you're happy.

Though she won a coveted spot as a judge on *The X Factor* in the UK in 2011, replacing Dannii Minogue, Kelly did not find the role easy and apparently admitted that she thought the show was a 'circus'. Rumours that she was unhappy on the ITV programme were also sparked when she failed to return from America for one of the prime-time Saturday-night live shows that October. Speaking at the time, she said: 'I'm so sick – I have no idea what is wrong with me, but I have the worst sore throat.' Despite this, there were unproven claims on social media that the illness was fake. And when she quit the show in 2012, there were further question marks over whether or not she had been axed. Simon Cowell later hired her for the US version of the show, but this was cancelled by Fox in early 2014, following poor viewing figures.

Conversely, it seemed everything that Beyoncé touched turned to gold. And after President Obama's triumphant re-election in November, she was the artist he wanted to perform at his second inauguration ceremony in January 2013. The event was held at the Capitol in Washington DC on a freezing cold day and, as before, beamed live to millions of homes the world over. Beyoncé had been asked to sing 'The Star Spangled Banner' and certainly looked the part for her big moment, wearing a demure black velvet and chiffon ankle-length evening gown by Pucci. The dress was complemented by a pair of dazzling 80-carat emerald earrings, worth $1.8 million and created by US designer Lorraine Schwartz, who had designed her famous wedding ring.

If Beyoncé was nervous, she did not show it and approached the podium with a look of steely determination. As the first notes rang out, she held the microphone close to her mouth and began singing the immortal words: 'Oh, say can you see by the dawn's early light . . .' Her voice was perfectly in tune and Obama looked on proudly with his hand clamped to his chest as crowds waved flags in the background. However, halfway through her rendition, Beyoncé appeared to have a problem with feedback and deftly removed her earpiece – though she did not fault on a note as she did so.

Afterwards, an ABC newscaster commented: 'She was clearly having some sort of audio problem – but you would not have known from her performance that she was struggling on any level.'

Speaking after the ceremony, she made no reference to any sound issue: 'It was a live television show and a very, very important emotional show for me and one of my proudest moments.' But then came accusations that she might have committed the unthinkable: that she had mimed the entire song. Sparked by the apparent technical blip, the words, 'Did she or did she not sing live?' were seemingly on everyone's lips – and provoked intense national debate both in the US and UK. Writing in the *Guardian*, journalist Jim Shelley posed the question: 'If we can't rely on Beyoncé to belt out "The Star-Spangled Banner", what hope is there for live performances? Lip-synching is killing music.' And the *New Yorker* was similarly scathing: 'How could she fake her way through a highly emotional performance at the inauguration ceremony that is supposed to be expressive of our real American values, our real American story?'

Even Beyoncé's former foe Aretha Franklin weighed in, telling ABC News: 'When I heard the news this evening that she was pre-recorded I really laughed. I thought it was funny because the weather down there was about forty-six or forty-four degrees and for most singers that is just not good singing weather. When I heard that I just really cracked up. I thought it was really funny, but she did a beautiful job with the pre-record . . . Next time I'll probably do the same.'

After multiple confirmations and swift denials that Beyoncé had mimed, the truth finally emerged: she had chosen not to sing live because she had not had time to rehearse with the orchestra. The bombshell was finally dropped by the United States Marine

Corps band, which provided the music on the day. The conductor, Colonel Michael J. Colburn, told the *Washingtonian* magazine: 'She wasn't comfortable performing without a rehearsal, and I wasn't comfortable with that either.'

At a press conference in New Orleans ten days after the inauguration, which was to publicise her performance at the Super Bowl three days later, Beyoncé tackled the scandal head-on. She began by asking the several hundred reporters to stand up before launching straight into an a cappella version of the US anthem, and was rewarded with an enthusiastic ovation.

Having demonstrated her capacity to perform the song live, Beyoncé then explained exactly why she had felt it necessary to pre-record it. 'I am a perfectionist, and one thing about me, I practise until my feet bleed,' she said. 'Due to the weather, due to no proper sound check, I did not feel comfortable taking a risk. It was about the president and the inauguration, and I wanted to make him and my country proud. So I decided to sing along with my pre-recorded track, which is very common in the music industry, and I'm very proud of my performance.'

Fortunately, most were sympathetic to her honesty and she also received a shot of good old female solidarity from singer Jennifer Lopez: 'Sometimes it happens when you are in certain stadiums and certain venues and things, they do pre-record stuff.'

During the press conference, Beyoncé went on to insist that she would definitely be singing live at the Super Bowl. 'I am well-rehearsed,' she told the journalists. 'This is what I am born for.' The drama of 'lip synch-gate' had created an even greater sense of hype around her halftime show – and, consequently, there was more pressure on her than ever before to get it right.

Chapter Nineteen

The fourteen-minute Super Bowl performance in New Orleans on 3 February was hailed as the pinnacle of Beyoncé's career, a moment she had waited for all her life. In just over eight hundred seconds, she proved to the world that she was a true superstar – from the tips of her killer-heeled Proenza Schouler boots to every strand of her wild blonde hair. The epic set began with a spectacular light show, as a giant white outline of her body emerged from a golden burst of flames and an explosion of red and white flares. And then there was Beyoncé. Appearing first as a dark silhouette, she was coiled tight as a spring, ready to give it her all.

'"Baby it's you,"' she sang, outstretching her gloved arms towards the screaming, 70,000-strong crowd as 'Love On Top' segued neatly into 'Crazy In Love'. Watching raptly from the stands, Jay-Z moved to the beat as a recording of his voice rapped out of the colossal speakers. Backed by the Mamas, Beyoncé was clearly singing live, scrubbing out any question marks still hanging over her. With 100 million viewers watching on TV in America and millions more around the globe, she could have crumpled under the weight of expectation but, instead, she shone. Her voice was full of passion, and the choreography, honed to perfection, was testament to the hour upon hour of rehearsals she and her team had put in. After stripping down to a black leather bodysuit, she stormed through 'End of Time' and 'Baby Boy' before her Destiny's Child bandmates Kelly and Michelle sprang onto the stage through hidden trapdoors. Wearing similarly revealing black leather, the reunited trio sang truncated versions of their most recent release 'Nuclear', plus 'Bootylicious' and 'Independent Women Part I' – during which they appeared to be singing amid a bed of flames. After joining her on 'Single Ladies', Kelly and Michelle left the stage to allow Beyoncé to wind up the show with the ever emotional 'Halo'. As she came off, she put on a black robe and headed straight into the arms of Jay-Z. Their tender embrace was caught on camera and posted directly on Instagram, while Beyoncé spoke of her joy at being back on stage with Destiny's Child for the first time since 2006. 'It really was a magnificent night for me and the girls,' she said, as Michelle tweeted: 'Had a great time w/my sisters tonight!! Tried to keep it a surprise!! Love you all . . . God bless!!'

Their reunion was only slightly sullied by viewers claiming on Twitter that Beyoncé's microphone had been turned up much louder than those used by Kelly and Michelle, with *CBS News* writing: 'Rowland and Williams were barely heard when the group sang "Independent Woman", as their voices faded into the background.'

Still, the press reviews that came out of the Superdome were unanimous: it had been one of the best halftime shows ever. The *Washington Post* said it was 'the sexiest since 2004' in which Janet

Jackson's infamous 'nipplegate' wardrobe malfunction was the major talking point. The *New York Times* declared Beyoncé had now 'silenced her doubters' and said: 'Amid all the loudness were small things to indicate Beyoncé was answering her sceptics, quietly but effectively. Beyoncé the machine had made her point. This was proof of life.' And the *Daily Telegraph* gave an equally glowing summary: 'Following her demure appearance at the inauguration, this was all quite aggressive, a full frontal, take-no-prisoners assault on the senses, loud, flashy, energetic and breathtakingly accomplished.'

It wasn't just the media who were blown away. More than five million tweets were sent about her performance, with Kim Kardashian posting: 'OMG Beyoncé killed it!!! And when Destiny's Child came out . . . that made my life! #Bootylicious.' Michelle Obama also described the show as 'phenomenal', writing: 'I'm so proud of her!'

Jay-Z was another to tweet his reaction, writing: 'Lights out!!! Any questions?' His post was in response to claims that Beyoncé's show had been so powerful that she had caused a power cut that occurred shortly after her set. The stadium was plunged into darkness and the football game was suspended for thirty-four minutes while the problem was rectified. Officials claimed it was due to an abnormality in the power system but others believed the extravagant lighting and video effects of Beyoncé's act were to blame. According to *USA Today*, a fire alarm went off in the press box in the upper level of the stadium shortly after she went off stage, suggesting that the pyrotechnics that had lit her set might have been too much for the stadium to handle. The electricity had allegedly also blown the system twice during her rehearsals, leaving some wondering if New Orleans' infrastructure was still weakened in the aftermath of Hurricane Katrina.

Given the precision of each and every step, it was no surprise when Beyoncé revealed that her Super Bowl performance had taken her months to mastermind. 'I'm feeling so proud. It was a really beautiful day,' she said. 'Five months of preparation and it was really great.' Some eight hundred dancers had auditioned, while her plunging leather bodysuit alone had required fourteen workers, five fittings and at least two hundred man hours to construct. Created by New York designer Rubin Singer, the outfit incorporated strips of python and iguana, silk, plastic and insets of black lace. Early in the show Beyoncé had ripped off a separate biker jacket with padded shoulders and a leather flounce skirt with a lace trim. Rubin also created all of the jackets worn by the 120 backing singers and dancers.

One minor snag was that Beyoncé's bodysuit had to be repeatedly adjusted as her waistline was disappearing due to the frenetic rehearsals. 'When a performer is working so vigorously, they're shrinking constantly, and she was losing weight every day,' said Rubin. 'We had to keep taking it in and taking it in and taking it in and doing tweaks and changes.'

Following her previous clashes with animal-rights protesters, the finished ensemble did not go down well. 'We would take a bet that if Beyoncé watched our video exposés, she'd probably not want to be seen again in anything made of snakes, lizards, rabbits or other animals who died painfully,' said PETA. 'Today's fashions are trending towards humane vegan options, and Beyoncé's Super Bowl outfit missed the mark on that score.' Other viewers took to Facebook and other social networking websites to brand the costume too *risqué*, also saying that her dancing was overly provocative for family viewing.

Though Beyoncé knew the industry well enough to recognise that her performances would attract negative as well as positive response, she had not banked on one element of the post-Super Bowl analysis. American website Buzzfeed decided to publish a set of less than flattering photos of her in mid-performance, which showed her pulling a series of Sasha Fierce-esque facial expressions. When her publicist Yvette saw the pictures, she sent an email to the website, asking them to remove some of the offending photos, specifying seven in particular. But her request backfired badly. Buzzfeed posted up Yvette's email, which said: 'As discussed, there are some unflattering photos on your current feed that we are respectfully asking you to change. I am certain you will be able to find some better photos. The worst are #5, 6, 10, 11, 12, 19 and 22. Thank you very much.' Unfortunately for her, the situation snowballed and the photos went viral, with other blogs and gossip sites champing at the bit to display Beyoncé looking less than perfect. Newspapers and magazines that had previously had no interest in the pictures were also scrambling to use them. As a PR exercise, it was one of the few that ever went wrong for Team Beyoncé.

Regardless of the minor issues, the event was generally perceived as a runaway success and her relief was clear. 'It feels good to know that the hard work paid off,' she said. 'It's a live television show, it's the biggest show in America. There are so many things that could happen – and God was on my side.' She also celebrated in unusual fashion afterwards, saying: 'I had alligator, I had turtle. I had a drink with my mother for the first time. My mother doesn't drink!'

Straight after the show, there was a fresh wave of excitement when she announced details of a new world tour. Alluding to her marital status, it was to be called the Mrs Carter Show World Tour and would begin in Serbia in mid-April. The official tour poster showed her standing by a throne and wearing a golden bejewelled corset and crown in a clear nod to Queen Elizabeth I. But, almost immediately, Beyoncé's pro-feminist tendencies were again called into question over her use of her husband's name for the tour's title. The *Daily Mail* even launched a debate, asking: 'Is Beyoncé betraying feminism by naming her tour "The Mrs Carter Show"?' Defending herself, Beyoncé argued that it was not a submissive move, simply a loving reference to Jay-Z: 'I feel like Mrs Carter is who I am, but more bold and more fearless than I've ever been.' In fairness, Beyoncé never sought to pull the wool over anyone's eyes on the issue. She was proud of being a strong, independent black woman with a hugely successful career, but the principles of marriage, babies and coexisting with a man had always been just as important. For this, she made no apology whatsoever.

In any event, punters were far from put off by the name of the tour: all eleven of her British dates astonishingly sold out in just ten minutes. But there was widespread dismay when it was announced by Beyoncé's publicist Yvette that all media photographers would be banned from the tour, except her personal snapper Frank Micelotta. The strict ruling was seen as a direct response to the 'unflattering' photo fiasco following the Super Bowl.

Early 2013 was shaping up to be a hectic time, and Beyoncé and Jay-Z had recently had the added thrill of celebrating Blue Ivy's first birthday. The *Sun* reported that her parents bought her an $80,000 diamond-encrusted Barbie doll, which was decorated with 160 gems, as well as throwing her a lavish bash in New York. According to the paper, Blue's little friends received party bags with more than $25,000 worth of goodies, including jewellery, princess costumes and playhouses.

As Blue grew older and developed more of her own personality, Jay-Z told *Vanity Fair* that she had found her musical ear. But he was unconvinced by Beyoncé's claims that the tot preferred her daddy's music to her own. 'That's not true,' he told the magazine. 'She does like her mother's music – she watches [Beyoncé's concerts] on the computer every night.' But his daughter certainly had an ear for his music too. After testing his new album on her, he said: 'She plays a song and she goes, "More, Daddy, more . . . Daddy song." She's my biggest fan.'

Now that Blue's vocabulary was expanding and her curiosity growing about the world around her, Tina's brother Larry Beyincé told gossip site Celebuzz that she was becoming a real character. 'I'll speak to her on the phone. She likes to watch cartoons and *Sesame Street*. She told me "hi" and "dog" and "moo" and "miaow" and "woof woof". And then she just said "bye bye".' Beyoncé could not have been more smitten with her daughter, telling Oprah Winfrey in a later show: 'It's so much joy and I have my best friend. She is hilarious and she is fire. I didn't expect her to be fire but, Lord, I'm [gonna] have me a time. She's beautiful.'

Around the time of Blue's birthday, Beyoncé posted a photo of herself and her daughter on a beach on her Tumblr account, in which wearing a bikini, she flaunted a hint of six-pack as they paddled in the sea. A cute snap in its own right, the picture seemed to be sending a clear message to those who had suggested that her body had been airbrushed for the latest edition of *GQ*. The men's magazine had awarded Beyoncé the accolade of 'Hottest Woman of the Century', and the so-called Ms Millennium had posed for a striking cover shoot in a cropped sport top and tiny pair of knickers that showed off a rippling set of abs. Subsequent claims that her image had been digitally enhanced therefore hit a nerve: she was fiercely proud of her body and the work it took to keep it in such athletic condition. She was said to have locked horns over the issue again when fronting a new swimwear campaign for H&M that year. Sources said she refused to allow the fashion chain to put out airbrushed photographs that slimmed her curves, and that she demanded the original, unaltered images were used for the ads. The unfair demands women faced in conforming to a certain body shape was becoming a prominent theme in her music, a subject she would explore on the new album that was still secretly in the pipeline.

Similar feminist leanings also peppered her HBO documentary, *Life Is but a Dream*, which finally aired on the American TV channel in February after months of anticipation. Revealing some of her most intimate thoughts in the ninety-minute close-up, she spoke passionately about gender inequality, saying: 'Women have to work so much harder to make it in this world. It really pisses me off that women don't get the same opportunities men do. Or money, for that matter. Money gives me the power to run the show. It gives men the power to define our values and to define what's sexy and what's feminine – and that's bullshit. At the end of the day, it's not about equal rights, it's about how we think. We have to step up as women and take the lead.'

Stressing the importance of female relationships, she said: 'I love my husband, but there is nothing like a conversation with a woman that understands you. I grow so much from those conversations. I need my sisters.' And while nothing could ever detract from her love for her daughter, she opened up about her lack of maternal instinct, saying she was not like women who have waited for motherhood all their lives. Furthermore, she confessed that she was 'scared to death' of being pregnant, but that Blue's arrival had encouraged her to show a new, sexually exposed side of herself. Expanding on this idea in *Vogue*, she said: 'I just feel my body means something completely different. I feel a lot more confident about it. Even being heavier, thinner, whatever. I feel a lot more like a woman. More feminine, more sensual. And no shame.'

Life Is but a Dream saw her reflecting deeply on her split from her father, and though she had known it was the right thing to do, it clearly still troubled her. In tackling some difficult truths, the programme had a cathartic effect on her: 'This movie has healed me in so many ways. It makes me want to cry.' But when she was asked, 'Did you get your dad back?' she replied sadly, 'No. I had to sacrifice my relationship with Dad. I had to let go.' Clearly, things would never be the same between them.

The film also featured rare home-video footage from her childhood as well as glimpses of her and Jay-Z's private life. In one scene where the pair were out for dinner in Croatia, Beyoncé had her arm draped around her husband's neck as they lovingly serenaded each other with Coldplay's song 'Yellow', playing quietly in the background. 'Jay-Jay, I love you so,' she sang, touchingly changing the words. A far cry from their scrupulously guarded manner of old, the documentary's refreshingly honest approach was well received, with *Billboard* saying of Beyoncé: 'The well-oiled, media-trained, hit-making machine has a heart. And it's huge.'

Two weeks before the hit-making machine unleashed her Mrs Carter world tour, she and Jay-Z celebrated their fifth wedding anniversary with a three-day trip to Cuba. The loved-up couple checked out the sights of old Havana and relaxed by the rooftop pool at the luxurious Hotel Saratoga. But while their holiday seemed innocent enough, as they sampled traditional Cuban music and mingled with the fascinated locals, there were angry claims that they had broken Washington's strict embargo on travelling to Cuba for tourism. Republicans called for an investigation into their trip, believing that the pair were granted special access to the country because of their close ties to the president. Facing a grilling on US news programme *Today*, Obama said coolly: 'I wasn't familiar that they were taking the trip . . . You know, this is not something the White House was involved with. We've got better things to do.' However, in August 2014, the trip was declared legal and above board with the Treasury Department's Office of Inspector General issuing a nine-page document saying the pair did not violate any US sanction laws.

Beyoncé was disappointed by the negative publicity their Cuban exploits generated. 'You know, it was such a beautiful trip,' she said. 'I met some incredible children. I visited some incredible entrepreneurs. And it was really educational for me. I learned so much about so many people and the country.'

Energised by their mini-break, the first of her 132 Mrs Carter shows kicked off in Belgrade on 15 April and, as usual, the set was a sight to behold. With a strong royal theme, she emulated various different queens through fashion, and it was her most ambitious show yet from a style point of view. Outfits were provided by almost every top-end designer, including Roberto Cavalli, Pucci, Givenchy, Kenzo, Ralph & Russo, Julien Macdonald and David Koma. Meanwhile, Stuart Weitzman designed all of her shoes, those of the Mamas and her dancers.

One of her most elaborate costumes was a gold bodysuit created by Latino duo the Blonds. With outrageous, shimmering detail around the breast area – including *faux* nipple detailing – it was hand-embroidered over six hundred hours, using around thirty thousand Swarovski crystals. She had a long and short-sleeved version made. *InStyle* magazine described it as the 'most scandalous' outfit Beyoncé had ever worn.

The choreography was more important than ever for the Mrs Carter run, and Beyoncé's long-term creative director Frank Gatson Jr was fundamental to its smooth running. 'This year's tour audition process was the Super Bowl,' he told *Dance Spirit* magazine. 'We saw eight hundred girls, and once we got down to a hundred, we paid close attention to who was professional and magical. Beyoncé was very clear on who to pick for the tour – she means business.' He added: 'She doesn't want watered-down choreography . . . She will do almost anything as long as she remains a lady. She has class with everything she does, even a booty shake. She knows technique will keep your movement classy. When you mix ballet with street movement, you get the Beyoncé brand. We call it country fried chicken with hot sauce.' But the pulsating dance moves played havoc with the costumes and tailors had to repair broken hooks and tears after almost every show.

The set list included numbers from all four of her solo offerings, while the dates that fell in 2014 were revamped to include tracks from her self-titled fifth album, which was released towards the end of the tour. With ten new songs, this in effect meant learning a whole new show – but Beyoncé took it in her stride as ever. Such was her dedication that, during her stretch of British shows, she once stayed up all night after dashing from Glasgow to London to appear at the Brit Awards. She then flew straight back to Scotland to finish choreographing the first of her two shows there. As Todd Tourso, one of the creative gurus on her team, said: 'She's completely relentless in her pursuit of perfectionism. It sounds cheesy, but that's why I'm willing to work so hard for her. When you have this type of leadership and muse and mentor, I think the sky's the limit.'

Her perfectionist spirit was perhaps more evident on this tour than at any other time. As Gwyneth Paltrow avowed: 'When she is working on stage, she has more power than any woman I've ever seen. She would never say it and has never said it, but I feel she knows with every fibre of her being that she is the best in the world at her job.' The iron will to be better than anyone else in the industry meant that as usual after every show, she would go back to her hotel room with a DVD of the performance. Before going to sleep, she would watch that show, critique herself, her dancers, the Mamas and her cameramen. The next morning, everyone would receive pages of notes to read over breakfast.

As she had told GQ, she treated her shows the way an athlete treats sport, constantly studying her every move. 'I watch my performances, and I wish I could just enjoy them, but I see the light that was late. I see, "Oh, God, that hair did not work." Or "I should never do that again." I try to perfect myself,' she said. But the military-style scrutiny provided some funny moments, with one of Beyoncé's dancers recalling: 'There was this one night in South America – it was an open stage and it was raining and a few of us slipped. She watched it on repeat, laughing hysterically. She didn't yell at us or anything, though – the whole stage was a puddle.'

Spread over six legs and eleven months, the Mrs Carter tour grossed $230 million, making it her most lucrative to date, and one of the biggest live successes of the decade. Typically, the shows astounded the critics, one reviewer writing in the *Independent*: 'What makes this show's largely enervating juggernaut breathe is Beyoncé's tireless physical effort. She has created a literal body of work.' The *Observer* described the artistry of the show as 'nothing short of breathtaking', and the *New York Times* said: 'She hit her notes and hit her marks, never showing the effort. She was a superwoman singing for every woman.'

Although Jay-Z could not be with her for the duration of the tour, she had a constant companion in Blue Ivy, telling *Vogue*: 'She's my road dog. She's my homey, my best friend.' Some of those on the tour revealed how Blue had begun perfecting some of her mum's dance moves, and that she liked to 'stick her booty out and wave it around in a twerk-esque fashion'. Though Blue kept her going as the schedule grew ever more punishing, even Beyoncé had her limits. On one occasion in May, she was forced to cancel a show in Belgium due to sheer exhaustion and dehydration.

Doctors had ordered her to rest. Predictably, the no-show fired up another round of pregnancy stories – why else would the unstoppable Mrs Carter bail out? The baby rumour mill had spun into life when she appeared at the Met Gala fashion ball in New York earlier that month, too. She wore a custom-made Givenchy gown that concealed her stomach, its bodice cinched high above the waist as if to mask a change in her shape. And after she had told ABC News that she would like more children because her daughter 'needs some company', the media believed it had all the necessary evidence to state that she was expecting again. As usual, it was a false alarm.

Her strength fully recovered, Beyoncé combined her philanthropic beliefs with her feminist ideology, headlining a major concert at Twickenham Stadium called Chime for Change. The July event, organised by Gucci, aimed to put women's rights in the spotlight, calling for improved education, health and justice around the world, especially in underprivileged countries. With a star-studded line-up, including performances from J.Lo, Florence + the Machine, Ellie Goulding and Jessie J, the concert was beamed to more than 150 countries across six continents, with an estimated one billion tuning in. During Beyoncé's set, Jay-Z came on stage to join her for 'Crazy In Love', giving her a big kiss and hug as they finished the song.

Beyoncé was extremely proud to be fronting the campaign, telling the crowd: 'This is such an incredible night for all of us. Because of you all, we have raised more than four million dollars.' She added passionately: 'Women's rights, it's something that has always been close to my heart. I know now, being a mother, it is really important that I can do what I can and use my voice. There are women around the world that don't have a voice so we have to use our voices and raise awareness and be part of something where we can leave a legacy and help improve this world.'

Madonna also spoke to the audience for ten minutes, saying: 'I keep telling people I want to start a revolution, but my revolution doesn't involve bloodshed and violence. My revolution starts with education. My revolution is about achieving a higher level of consciousness, but this cannot start without education.'

Chime for Change also featured an appearance by Rita Ora, an up-and-coming pop star who was Jay-Z's latest protégée. She had been hugely influenced by the superstar couple and told *Grazia* that she owed her burgeoning success to her mentor. 'Jay-Z made me feel really relaxed but at the same time, he made me realise I had loads of work to do. He's been doing this for years and I've just started. I hope my career can be as successful as his. He's my musical idol.' She added: 'Beyoncé told me, "Be yourself because we like being around you." I guess I'm like the little sister.' But just as happened with Rihanna, Rita soon found herself linked to Jay-Z in more than a professional sense. The unsubstantiated accusations that she had slept with her mentor left her fuming – especially when *Geordie Shore* reality star Holly Hagan tweeted: 'I've been told to say that Rita Ora has been ALLEGEDLY bukin jay z! I repeat ALLEDGELY [*sic*].' She later deleted the posts, but angry Rita tweeted: 'I stayed silent on one bulls**t rumour but this one I have to speak. Neva eva will any1 includin a red head dum z listin attention seekin whore try talk s**t about me& my family holly wateva da f*k ur name is [*sic*].'

Beyoncé apparently felt no need to address the gossip, and following Chime for Change, she made another headlining appearance at the V Festival in the UK that August. She stayed in a luxury Winnebago with Jay-Z, and the pair made headlines after putting in an order to the local branch of Nando's in Chelmsford for themselves and her hungry crew members. Their delivery consisted of 48 whole chickens, 48 portions of chips and 58 chicken wing platters – costing almost £1,500. Sadly, though, the concert was not a patch on her Glastonbury extravaganza two years previously. Though she had been billed as the ultimate crowd-pleaser, her seventeen-track set got off to a shaky start when she was twenty minutes late on stage. As the rain lashed down, the crowd became restless and angry, shouting, 'Boo-yoncé', as the time ticked by. Even when she burst on stage, bringing seven outfit changes and a new blonde bobbed hairdo, a technical hitch proved to be the last straw for many drenched spectators, who abandoned the show in droves. One unimpressed concert-goer told *Metro* newspaper: 'The sound was so terrible people were just walking away halfway through her set.' Those fans hoping to watch the show from the warmth of their homes were equally disappointed when her performance was dramatically dropped from Channel 4's broadcast at the last minute. Presenters Edith Bowman and Steve Jones hastily pointed the finger at Beyoncé herself when they told viewers she had refused to clear her performance for TV. The cancellation sparked a furious backlash on Twitter with many viewers claiming they'd been 'cheated'.

So much time away from home gave Beyoncé the perfect excuse to bail out of her father's wedding to his new partner that summer. Mathew tied the knot with a former model called Gena Charmaine Avery in Houston. Solange also gave the ceremony a wide berth.

Mathew played down his daughters' absence, telling TMZ: 'Unfortunately, Beyoncé and Solange had previous engagements, which made it impossible for them to attend.'

Meanwhile, Beyoncé's mother, Tina, had shown she was ready to move on too, going public with her new boyfriend, TV actor Richard Lawson, at a black-tie ball in New York. Although the gulf between her and Mathew was widening, Beyoncé proved just how much Tina meant to her by buying her a $5.9 million mansion in Piney Point Village, a wealthy city in Harris County, Texas. The house had six bedrooms, and was designed in ornate French and Italian style, with marble floors and a winding staircase. She and Solange followed this act of generosity a few months later by throwing Tina a decadent, masquerade-themed party for her sixtieth birthday in New Orleans. The bash at Muriel's in Jackson Square reportedly cost more than a hundred thousand dollars and saw celebrity friends such as Kelly Rowland, Jennifer Hudson and producer The-Dream all turn up in masks, while Tina arrived with Richard in a horse-drawn carriage.

Beyoncé's own birthday that September, her thirty-second, was spent in a typically exotic location. She and Jay-Z chartered a yacht in Stromboli, Italy, and spent much of their week drinking champagne onboard and swimming in the crystal clear waters. They were seen hugging and holding hands on deck, and playing with Blue Ivy – who was snapped rocking an on-trend leopard-print swimming costume.

The chance to recharge her batteries after a fraught few months was no doubt welcome for Beyoncé, but she and Jay-Z ended 2013 with one of their toughest challenges of late: embarking on a strict vegan detox. Announcing the decision in a blog on his website,

Jay-Z wrote: 'On December 3rd, one day before my 44th birthday I will embark on a 22 Days challenge to go completely vegan, or as I prefer to call it, plant-based!!' He added: 'Psychologists have said it takes 21 days to make or break a habit. On the 22nd day, you've found the way.' Stressing that the aim was a 'spiritual and physical cleanse', he signed off: 'P.S. B is also joining me.'

Beyoncé quickly got into the spirit of the diet plan, posting photos on Instagram of healthy dishes such as Portobello mushrooms and vegan mac 'n' cheese. But at a lunch date with Jay-Z while they were on the regime, she made a huge *faux pas*. Turning up for a meal of curried lentils and kale salad at the strictly 'flesh-free' Native Foods in LA, she wore an expensive Christopher Kane jacket with a fox fur collar. With the paparazzi shots quickly incurring the wrath of animal-rights activists, she once again seemed unrepentant about her personal fashion choices.

Chapter Twenty

While it was generally acknowledged that Beyoncé had been working on new music over the past eighteen months, she had managed to keep all details about her fifth album totally under the radar. So when it was released suddenly on iTunes, late one night in December 2013, it caused a worldwide sensation. A shock to just about everybody, there had been no pre-release promotion, no early single and, crucially, after previous experience, no leaks on the internet. Astonishingly, the fourteen songs on the album, titled *Beyoncé*, were accompanied by seventeen music videos filmed in total secrecy at different locations all around the world. The project's exclusive online release meant that the videos could be shared through platforms such as Twitter, Instagram and Tumblr.

She had kept the entire project so tightly under wraps that even members of her production team were in the dark on the exact timing of the album's release – midnight on 13 December. As *Rolling Stone* magazine commented: 'Beyoncé has delivered countless surprises in her fifteen years on top of the music world, but she's never dropped a bombshell like this. Queen Bey woke the world in the midnight hour with a surprise "visual album", dropped via iTunes with no warning. The whole project is a celebration of the Beyoncé Philosophy, which basically boils down to the fact that Beyoncé can do anything the hell she wants to.'

Quite why she had gone to such enormous lengths to keep the project under wraps was simple: she wanted to control the way in which people experienced her music. The idea was that her fans would listen to the record in its entirety and watch the videos, soaking up a concentrated and complete vision of her art. 'I miss that immersive experience, now people only listen to a few seconds of a song on their iPods and they don't really invest in the whole experience,' she explained. 'I felt, like, I don't want anybody to get the message, when my record is coming out. I just want this to come out when it's ready and from me to my fans.'

Though eighty songs were recorded in all, those that made the final cut were the ones that were most spontaneous – or, as she called them, 'effortless'. The album was by far her most personal. Sexually explicit in tone, she said it examined 'my insecurities, all of my doubts, all of my fears and everything I've learned'. No wonder, then, that she was more anxious than ever about the public reaction to the album. 'I was terrified. I was really nervous because this was a huge risk,' she confessed. 'I was so scared. I had already gone through all the horrible ways it could go in my mind.'

She need not have worried. Apple reported that *Beyoncé* was iTunes' fastest-selling digital album ever, with more than a million sold in just five days. Breaking a Guinness world record, it even beat One Direction's sky-high sales and made her the first woman in history to hit number one with her first five studio albums. On top of all of that, the album hit number one in a hundred countries – from Belgium to Botswana and from the Ukraine to Uzbekistan.

It received rave reviews from music critics, many of whom ranked it the best album of 2013. The *Guardian* hailed the shock release as 'Beyoncégeddon', describing it as a major triumph and 'a masterclass in both exerting and relinquishing control'. The *Los Angeles Times* said: 'What's exciting about the record, beyond its means of delivery, is how the music similarly blends the intimate and the extravagant.'

In addition to the album, she released a five-part documentary series about the recording process, called *Self-Titled*. In this she explained why the video content was so important to her. 'Music is more than just what I hear. When I'm connected to something, I immediately see a visual or a series of images that are tied to a feeling or an emotion, a memory from my childhood, thoughts about life, my dreams or my fantasies. And they're all connected to the music.'

She added: 'I think it's one of the reasons why I wanted to do a visual album. I wanted people to hear the songs with the story that's in my head, because that's what makes it mine. That vision in my brain is what I wanted people to experience the first time.'

The seventeen videos were filmed between June and November 2013 while Beyoncé travelled on her Mrs Carter tour. Locations included a Brazilian beach, a Paris nightclub, Coney Island in New York, a French château and a South American church. Sensual and often quite daring, they were visually exciting while portraying her as an independent woman, lover and mother.

Given the immense scale of the album and the videos, many wondered how on earth her team had kept it so well hidden. All those involved in the video shoots were asked to sign non-disclosure agreements, while others stayed quiet through loyalty to the star. 'The thing is, we're such a tight-knit family,' explained stylist Ty, who had the task of overseeing the videos. 'When you see the final project, you're just, like, "I can't believe we survived it,"' he said. 'We were able to pull this off, which is unheard of. It's just a celebration for the whole team.' Ty was responsible for styling Beyoncé's appearance in the videos, arranging for the clothes he had chosen to be sent to locations around the world at a moment's notice. 'I'd have it sent and pray that the pieces and the packages would be received by different hotels in other countries,' he said.

Orchestrating the filming of the videos around the tour timetable was a huge challenge for all of Team B. 'Honestly, I was, like: "You want to do what?"' recalled her brand manager Melissa Vargas. Reflecting on the recording process in the Hamptons, she added: 'It was kind of like *Survivor*. We slept in there. Everyone had a room. There was only a certain amount of people that could come, so if you were vibing with her and everything was going great, you would stay for longer. We had a chef and every single person in that house sat down at dinner with Jay and Beyoncé. It didn't matter if you were the assistant engineer, the producer, or a writer.'

But even Beyoncé confessed that towards the end of the project she worried that she was losing control. 'I was recording, shooting videos and performing on the tour every night, all at the same time. At some point I felt, like, What am I doing? Is this too ambitious?'

Much darker than previous recordings, the album's themes included desire, feminism, fear, loss, bulimia, postnatal depression, marriage and motherhood. For a hit-maker like Beyoncé, the new material was something very different. With an underlying earthiness, the lyrics were more intimate and less polished than normal. 'My message behind this album was finding the beauty in imperfection,' she said. 'I took all the things about myself that I wanted to change and put it in my music. More than the music, I'm proud of myself as a woman . . . It's about loving your imperfections and the things that make you interesting, because I refuse to let anyone put me in a box.'

A case in point was a track on the album called 'XO', which she initially recorded while suffering a sinus infection. But rather than re-record it when she had recovered, she told *Out* magazine: 'I recorded it in a few minutes just as a demo and decided to keep the vocals . . . I really loved the imperfections.'

The album also introduced a new persona called Yoncé, an invention of her long-time producer The-Dream, who came up with the name one day as they were kicking ideas around in the studio. He incorporated 'Yoncé' into a tune while her friend Justin Timberlake was casually drumming out a rhythm on an upturned bucket. 'I'm, like, "What does that mean?"' Beyoncé said. 'But I love it.'

Stressing that her identities had now merged, she added: 'I think Beyoncé is Beyoncé, Mrs Carter is Beyoncé, Sasha Fierce is Beyoncé. And I'm finally at a place where I don't have to separate [them]. It's all pieces of me, and just different elements of a personality of a woman, because we are complicated.'

A key factor in the direction and shape of Beyoncé was the involvement of a relatively unknown producer called Boots. The publicity-shy musician, real name Jordy Asher, wrote the songs 'Haunted', 'Heaven' and 'Blue' – a ballad dedicated to Beyoncé's daughter, which drew on the sense of freedom motherhood had given Beyoncé. 'I feel liberated, and I feel like I can give my heart to people,' she said, in the series of videos.

Boots sang backing vocals and played many of the instruments on the album. Their working collaboration became so strong that he was responsible for producing about 80 per cent of it. Although Beyoncé always remained totally in control, he became the driving force, increasing her confidence so that she was comfortable in opening up her emotions and innermost feelings in her music as never before.

The sexual leaning of the work was present in songs such as hip-hop track 'Partition', which included graphic lines about sex in the back of a limo, with an X-rated reference to a Monica Lewinsky moment. 'It takes me back to, like, when me and my husband first meet and he is trying to scoop me and, like, he thinks I'm the hottest thing in the world,' Beyoncé said about 'Partition'. 'And I was so embarrassed after I recorded the song . . . and I'm, like, I can't play this for my husband. I still haven't played it for my mom. She's going to be very mad at me.'

'Partition' was filmed at Crazy Horse in Paris, the club Beyoncé had taken Jay-Z to the day they got engaged. At the time, she had thought, 'I wish I was up there. I wish I could perform that for my man. So that's what I did for the video.' The erotic film played out a bored wife-turned-stripper's fantasy of seducing her husband, showing her in sexy underwear, pole dancing and virtually naked in front of the camera.

Another single from the album, 'Pretty Hurts', was a bold critique of the modern-day obsession with body image. Its seven-minute video depicted the extreme measures women go to in order to achieve ideal looks and figures, beginning at a beauty pageant with a stick-thin contestant grabbing at the flesh on her tiny frame. Beyoncé was also filmed rubbing her teeth with Vaseline – an industry trick to help girls remember to keep smiling on stage. She then emerged from a toilet cubicle, wiping her mouth to suggest she had just made herself sick as a way of controlling her weight. Singing that the 'soul needs the surgery', Beyoncé looked distraught after stepping onto a set of scales and acted out a series of beauty techniques, pretending to wax her moustache and undergo Botox. The drama then cut to her imagined bedroom, in which she began smashing up a display of trophies. A recurring motif in many of the videos, the idea harked back to her never-ending haul of accolades as a child. 'I had this image of this trophy and me accepting these awards and kind of training myself to be this champion,' she said. 'And at the end of the day when you go through all of these things, is it worth it? I mean you get this trophy and you're like, I basically starved, I have neglected all the people that I love, I've conformed to what everybody else thinks I should be and I have this trophy. What does that mean?'

Acclaimed music-video director Melina Matsoukas led the 'Pretty Hurts' shoot, revealing that Beyoncé was initially unsure about such bold imagery in the video. 'I'd written that she was in the house and had some kind of eating disorder. And at first we weren't going to do that,' she told *New York* magazine. 'But on the third day of shooting, she said, "I really want to take it further" . . . So that's when we added in the diet pills. She was, like, "Does anybody have a Tic-Tac or Advil?"'

Melina said Beyoncé was also worried about how the bulimia

scenes might be perceived and that people would think she was endorsing it. 'People will be, like, "Beyoncé has an eating disorder and is getting plastic surgery" in the headlines, you know? But I think she let that go. She's, like, "It's a character, obviously. It's a video. This is not me."'

Speaking of the trophy metaphor, Melina explained that it was 'important' for Beyoncé to destroy them. 'She loved it. She loves to do all that. She was, like, "This is so much fun." There was stuff flying everywhere. Thankfully nobody was hurt. But she goes there, which is why I enjoy working with her so much.'

One of the album's biggest hits, 'Drunk In Love', was a duet with Jay-Z that became her seventeenth solo Top 10 hit in the UK. Surprisingly for a couple who had previously guarded their privacy to the extreme, the song's lyrics described passionate sex and included one verse about making love in the kitchen. 'We just kinda had a party. It was so great, because it wasn't about any ego, we weren't trying to make a hit record . . . we were just having fun . . . and I think you can hear that,' Beyoncé said.

The relaxed mood of the video saw waves crashing on a night-time beach and Beyoncé dancing in a transparent black outfit. The promo also saw her holding another trophy, which in her documentary she said, 'represents all of the sacrifices I made as a kid, all the time that I lost, being on the road in the studios as a child'. She added: 'I just want to blow that sh*t up. I have a lot of awards, and I have a lot of these things and they're amazing and I worked my ass off – I've worked harder than probably everybody I know to get those things, but nothing feels like my child singing "Mommy", nothing feels like when I look my husband in the eyes, nothing feels like when I'm respected when I get on the stage and

I see I'm changing people's lives. Those are the things that matter. And at this point in my life, that's what I'm striving for. Growth, love, happiness, fun. Enjoy your life, it's short. That's the message.'

But 'Drunk In Love' drew considerable controversy as it contained the lyric 'I'm Ike Turner, turn up/Baby no I don't play/ Eat the cake, Anna Mae.' Seemingly innocent at first glance, the words were lifted from a harrowing scene of domestic abuse in the 1993 Oscar-nominated Tina Turner biopic, *What's Love Got to Do With It?* In the scene, Ike Turner forced Tina (whose birth name was Anna Mae) to eat cake by smearing it over her face, then assaulted a friend who tried to intervene. Though critics had lauded this album as Beyoncé's most feminist to date, many were uncomfortable with such a violent reference in a song that otherwise seemed to celebrate love and sex. Commenting on the apparent contradiction in the *Huffington Post*, writer Ellie Slee was scathing: 'Beyoncé: when you smile affectionately and sing along with that lyric, you are propagating a cycle of humiliation, of rape, of violence that is still horrifically real for women all over the world,' she wrote. 'Your body confidence, your empowerment, is admirable, and really does have a place in the beautiful, evolving feminist fight that we find ourselves in. However, it is not about picking and choosing your moments; not at this level. Trivialising domestic violence, standing by your man whilst he makes Anna Mae's cake sound like something you want to eat, is not OK.'

Such was the reaction to the lyrics that one London radio station, Bang, decided it would play an edited version of the song from which the offending verse had been removed. Eyebrows were raised in a similar fashion at another song from the album called 'Flawless'. The song had been released earlier in 2013, then titled

'Bow Down/I Been On', and featured a refrain that urged: 'Bow down, bitches.' As a result, there was confusion as to whether it was telling women to practise subservience towards men, or if it was merely being ironic. It did feature the line, 'Don't think I'm just his little wife', but for some the premise of 'bowing down' was too much to stomach. One writer in the *Daily Telegraph* said: 'It seems that overnight we've been transformed from Beyoncé's beloved single ladies, independent women and survivors into her bitches. From Beyoncé singing, "all the women, independent, throw your hands up at me" to "bow down bitches" a change is under way, and it leaves a bitter taste in the mouth.'

Seemingly horrified at the reaction she had provoked, Beyoncé clarified her intended meaning, saying the song was meant as a statement of empowerment. She took to iTunes Radio, saying: 'The reason I put out "Bow Down" is because I woke up, I went into the studio, I had a chant in my head, it was aggressive, it was angry, it wasn't the Beyoncé that wakes up every morning. It was the Beyoncé that was angry. It was the Beyoncé that felt the need to defend herself. And if the song never comes out . . . OK! I said it!' She continued: 'I listened to it after I finished, and I said, "This is hot! I'm [gonna] put it out. I'm not going to sell it. I'm just going to put out." People like it, great; they don't, they don't. And I won't do it every day because that's not who I am. But I feel strong. And anyone that says, "Oh, that is disrespectful," just imagine the person that hates you. Imagine a person that doesn't believe in you. And look in the mirror and say, "Bow down, bitch" and I guarantee you feel gangsta! So listen to the song in that point of view again if you didn't like it before.'

* * *

Beyoncé and Jay-Z's first live performance of 'Drunk In Love' came at the Grammy Awards in Los Angeles in January. It was a good night for the pair as the rapper picked up an award for his collaboration with Justin Timberlake, *Holy Grail*, and dedicated it to Beyoncé, who was wearing a revealing white lace gown. 'I want to thank God, I mean a little for this award, but mostly for that and all the universes for conspiring and putting that beautiful light of a young woman in my life,' he said. He added: 'And I want to tell Blue that "Look, Daddy got a gold sippy cup for you!"' As he and Beyoncé took the stage for the eagerly antici-pated duet, she stepped out in a leotard and leather basque, with a short, wet-look hairdo. Sitting astride a chair for the song's opening, she then began an erotic dance, singing and gyrating on the dark stage as smoke billowed around her. Dressed in a suit and bow-tie, Jay-Z rapped his verses, and the sexually charged song ended with the pair kissing before they walked off stage with their arms around each other. The duet was described simultane-ously as 'scorching' and 'chill inducing', with the *New York Post* declaring the performance 'tantalising'.

Suitably toning down her act, the same month saw Beyoncé perform at an ultra-exclusive bash held at the White House to celebrate Michelle Obama's fiftieth birthday. Playing a thirty-minute set, she wore a sequined gold minidress, while Blue Ivy was pictured in her best frilly white frock. Other guests included Stevie Wonder, Samuel L. Jackson, Jennifer Hudson, Sir Paul McCartney and the Clintons. But while guests had their phones checked upon entry and were strictly ordered not to tweet or post photos from the event, Beyoncé later uploaded some pictures of her and Blue posing with the Obamas' dog Sunny.

Blue had celebrated her second birthday in January and was treated to not one but two eye-opening parties. One saw the family head to Florida where they had booked out part of Miami Zoo so she could spend her special day surrounded by penguins, kangaroos and lemurs. That was followed with a pizza feast at a local restaurant called Joey's. At a second bash in New York, there were two special guests in the shape of Kelly and Michelle, who happily painted their faces and posed for photos alongside Beyoncé and the birthday girl. Fans hoping their attendance meant another reunion was on the cards were later thrilled when it was announced that Beyoncé and Kelly were to provide vocals on Michelle's new gospel number, 'Say Yes', in the spring of 2014. The three even shot a video together, which they failed miserably to keep secret. 'We filmed at somebody's house, and they probably got excited and called their cousins and friends and, next thing you know, the whole town was on one street,' Michelle said. 'I woke up to the news of the song being leaked and I just hate when that happens because it was an unmastered version. At the same time, I was overwhelmed by the support. I know things happen for a reason.'

Michelle stressed how happy she had been to work with Beyoncé and Kelly again, telling *People*: 'I don't care what anyone says, we miss each other. We have that spiritual bond with each other where we know when you're really tired, you need your sister with you today or you just need a phone call to let them know you're thinking about them. I call them my soul mates.'

As Beyoncé resumed life on the road, Jay-Z's own four-month Magna Carter tour had concluded, allowing him to join her for the remaining dates of Mrs Carter. He appeared on stage to perform 'Drunk In Love' with her at all six London shows, as well as at the final tour stop in Lisbon. The climax on 27 March was a highly charged evening, which left Beyoncé sobbing on stage. Addressing the crowd, she said: 'If y'all don't know, tonight makes one hundred thirty-two shows. Tonight is the last show of the Mrs Carter tour. We started a year ago and I want to say this has been such a journey. In the past year, we've been through so much together. The Super Bowl, shooting the videos, all of these shows. When I first started the tour, my baby was not even walking yet. I just want you to know that I am so lucky.' As the emotion became too much, she sobbed: 'I'm giving y'all an ugly cry. Thank y'all again. Thank you for allowing me to have a career. When I fall, you lift me up. When I'm hungry, you feed me. And I just want to give you my light. I dedicate this song to you guys.'

After the show ended, the tears swiftly turned to elation as she and Jay-Z cracked open a bottle of their favourite Armand de Brignac champagne and posed for a series of photos backstage with her dancers, the Mamas and the crew.

After the show's finale, the pair jetted to the Dominican Republic to celebrate their sixth wedding anniversary. While on the idyllic Caribbean island, Beyoncé posted photos on Tumblr of herself attempting a game of mini-golf, playing with Blue Ivy, doing a handstand in a bikini and drinking wine with Jay-Z by the sea.

But after a few days' relaxation, there was to be no let-up in their work schedule: April also saw them announce a new joint tour called On the Run. Referring to Jay-Z's recent track 'Part II (On The Run)', the twenty-stadium tour was to kick off in June

2014, with shows across America and Canada and two concluding concerts in Paris that September, which were due to be filmed by HBO for a TV special. As they both had such a strong touring pedigree, On the Run seemed like an obvious development and followed Jay-Z's assertion the previous year that a series of joint concerts was 'slowly making sense, more sense every day'.

Picking up the criminal theme of their very first single together, '03 Bonnie & Clyde', a promotional poster showed the couple posing as outlaws in sinister black balaclavas. In an unusual step, they also posted a mock movie trailer for the tour on YouTube, called *Run*, which featured cameo appearances from actors Sean Penn, Jake Gyllenhaal and Blake Lively. With gunfights, explosions and plenty of dancing girls, the theatrical clip was again directed by Melina Matsoukas – who revealed that Jay-Z was initially unsure about its premise. 'Beyoncé was definitely really excited. Jay was a bit sceptical, but we were able to kind of force him into it,' she told *Elle*. 'I think he was hesitant about "Oh, now I have to be an actor."' Beyoncé, on the other hand, relished the role. 'She's really good with action and she's a badass in real life. So why not be one in a video? It's just about having fun and creating some cool images,' added Melina. 'I think for her it's a sense of freedom. Maybe these are things she didn't think she could do a couple years ago, and now she's just, like, "I'm gonna play whatever part I wanna play and not listen to whatever people have to say."'

Unsurprisingly, tickets for On the Run sold out in mere minutes at many venues, and at the time of publication the shows were set to gross $100 million – a whopping $4.5 million for each. Although they had both played solo sell-out tours only weeks previously, the duo's on-stage antics were clearly more in demand than ever.

Chapter Twenty-one

If anyone was still unconvinced by Beyoncé's astonishing cultural reach, there can have been little doubt when an American university announced in early 2014 that it was launching a course about her influence. Rutgers University in New Jersey unveiled a module called 'Politicizing Beyoncé', which was to explore American race, gender and sexual politics through the highs and lows of her career. Teacher Kevin Allred structured the course to include analysis of her music videos and lyrics, coupled with readings from black feminists. Asking questions about whether Beyoncé's sexy image was empowering or simply stereotypical, Kevin's aim was to help students think more critically about how the media received her. 'This isn't a course about Beyoncé's political engagement or how many times she performed during President Obama's inauguration weekend,' he said, adding that there was far more substance to her than there was to the average pop star. 'She certainly pushes boundaries. While other artists are simply releasing music, she's creating a grand narrative around her life, her career, and her persona.'

However, when jokingly asked if students would get higher

grades for putting on a perfect re-enactment of the 'Single Ladies' video, Kevin told the *L Magazine*: 'I had a student who said she had memorized the dance, but I didn't let her do it for the class for extra credit. She was, like, "Can I do this for my final presentation?" and I said, "I don't think so, but we could all learn it together . . ."'

Such a story highlighted the far-reaching grasp that Beyoncé now had on modern society, and she extended her rearch in May with a new movie role that saw her voice the part of Queen Tara in the animated children's film, Epic. But the spring of 2014 also brought with it a shockingly dramatic incident, which tore apart the meticulously controlled Knowles-Carter PR juggernaut. It was 5 May and an array of the world's biggest celebrities had gathered in New York for one of the glitziest showbiz events of the year. Dubbed the 'fashion Oscars', the annual Met Gala to raise money for the Metropolitan Museum of Art's Costume Institute always attracted the *crème de la crème* of Hollywood, who would turn up *en masse* in visually stunning designer gowns that adhered to a specific theme. This year was no different, and stars who flocked to the ball included Victoria Beckham, Kim Kardashian, Rihanna, Reese Witherspoon, Sarah Jessica Parker and Kate Bosworth. Beyoncé and Jay-Z were, of course, on the guest list, as was Solange, and with its 'White Tie and Decorations' theme, Beyoncé wore a heavily embellished black kimono dress by Givenchy, which plunged almost to her navel. The decorative part of her outfit consisted of a sheer veil over her eyes, teamed with chandelier earrings and a costume ring, which she accidentally dropped on the red carpet. Sensing the perfect photographic opportunity, Jay-Z – kitted out in a white tuxedo – dived to the rescue, retrieving the ring, then bowing before her as he placed it back on her finger. As the photographers' cameras erupted in a frenzy of clicks, Beyoncé grinned affectionately at her husband's mock proposal.

The evening appeared to go smoothly, with photographer Mario Testino posting a photo on Instagram of the couple enjoying dinner, Jay-Z tenderly putting his arm around his wife's shoulders. However, when the action later shifted to the unofficial after party at the city's Standard Hotel, the night took a very different and bizarre twist. While in the hotel's Boom Boom Room the couple chatted at their own table, then Beyoncé mingled with stars like Oscar-winning actress Lupita Nyong'o. *US Weekly* magazine reported that Jay-Z later sat next to a fire-pit while Beyoncé and Solange danced with model Naomi Campbell.

But then, at around two thirty a.m., the two sisters and Jay-Z were suddenly seen making an abrupt exit from the top-floor party, heading into a lift to take them down to the ground floor. In the lift a heated row took place – and though it was never intended to be seen by the public eye, secret CCTV footage of the fiery spat was leaked to gossip website TMZ a few days later. In the jaw-dropping clip, which went viral minutes after it dropped on the site, Beyoncé entered the lift first, followed by Solange, Jay-Z and a bodyguard. Almost as soon as the doors closed, Solange could be seen squaring up to Jay-Z. Then she began pushing and attempting to hit him as he tried to keep her at arms' length. While the bodyguard attempted to restrain her, she repeatedly punched and kicked Jay-Z, even hitting him with her clutch bag, its contents spilling all over the lift floor. Though he attempted to hold Solange's foot as the kicks rained in, he did not try to push or strike her back. The video had no sound, so it was impossible to tell what the fight was about, but the incident went on for three and a half minutes, and it was claimed that the bodyguard pressed the lift's emergency stop button on the twelfth floor so that the fracas could be dealt with in private.

In the midst of the ugly scene, Beyoncé stood calmly, apparently choosing not to intervene. At one point she lifted up the long train of her dress, seemingly to prevent it being damaged in the scuffle. During a lull in the fight, while the bodyguard held Solange back, Beyoncé could be seen talking sternly to Jay-Z, but quite why she chose not to pull her sister away was one of the most perplexing mysteries of the entire incident.

As the situation calmed and the lift reached the ground floor, Beyoncé and the minder walked out of the doors first, but then Solange lashed out at Jay-Z again, striking him with her bag one last time. After the bodyguard had stepped in to hold her back once more, all four then made for the hotel exit. Photos taken from within the lobby showed the three emerging from the lift, in which Solange looked distinctly unhappy. Beyoncé appeared surprisingly calm, given the circumstances, and wore a serene half-smile, while Jay-Z seemed shell-shocked and clutched at his cheek. After leaving the hotel, Beyoncé and Solange climbed into a chauffeur-driven car while Jay-Z headed off in a separate vehicle. A source was quoted in *People* as saying that Solange looked 'as mad as hell' and that Jay-Z 'walked down the block and got in another car'.

Social media inevitably went ballistic with the video clip, the incident becoming a top trend on Twitter for days. Hashtags, including '#WhatJayZSaidToSolange', led users to post their own theories as to what had happened, and a steady influx of Photoshopped pictures poking fun at the spat also went viral. With the video becoming one of the biggest celebrity water-cooler topics in living memory, there was much analysis of why it had provoked such a massive storm of interest. Commenting on the public's fascination with the incident, the *Washington Post* asked: 'Is it the nasty pleasure of seeing what we previously only speculated about, that the marriage the Knowles-Carters present to the outside world is subject to damage and indignity, just like any other?'

Theories about what could have sparked the unpleasant brawl flooded the web in the days that followed. One report claimed Jay-Z had been flirting with a designer called Rachel Roy at the ball, which had made Solange angry. Rachel had known the Knowles family for years and used to be married to Jay-Z's former business partner and friend Damon Dash. According to one source, Solange had had a run-in with Rachel earlier in the night, during which Beyoncé was reported to have intervened, pleading with the designer not to talk to her sister. But, according to the insider, the confrontation left Solange angry, and towards the end of the night, 'she snapped,' said the source. 'When they got in the elevator, it escalated quickly the way family tensions can. It got exceptionally heated.'

Some news organisations suggested that a cloud had hung over Solange's relationship with Jay-Z since she had left his Roc Nation label the previous year to start up her own venture, Saint Records. 'She used to be on Jay-Z's label but now she isn't,' a source was quoted in the *New York Post*, adding that this could have caused a deeper family rift. 'She moved to New Orleans from Brooklyn with her son. Solange still spends a lot of time in New York, but she is further away from her family, which has created some issues.'

There were also allegations on website radaronline.com that Solange was furious with the rapper because he would not let her take part in his and Beyoncé's forthcoming On the Run tour.

'Solange had expected to be named the opening act for Beyoncé and Jay,' the site reported. 'She thought it would just be a given.' Another source alleged that Solange had become 'drunk and belligerent' at the party and was 'like a pressure cooker waiting to explode'.

Meanwhile, the *New York Daily News* offered its own unique breakdown of events. The paper claimed that the blazing row had been sparked when Jay-Z snapped at Solange after two of her friends tried to get into the party at the Standard Hotel, saying they were friends of his. A source said Solange's pals 'wouldn't leave and kept name dropping Jay-Z. They were pretending they were guests of his and not hers.' The newspaper said that when Jay-Z was informed of this, he ordered Solange: 'Don't use my name.' As a result, it was said that he decided to go to Rihanna's private post-Met Ball party nearby, which prompted Solange to ask him: 'Why can't you go home?' She allegedly then turned to Beyoncé and said, 'Why does your husband need to go to the club right now?' And when Jay-Z interjected, 'You're one to talk', Solange erupted into the rage that has now been viewed, courtesy of TMZ, many millions of times.

With so many uncorroborated stories floating around, websites began searching for clues to help solve the riddle. Buzzfeed posted a series of other occasions during which Solange had been known to speak her mind, including a time when she had hit out at a TV interviewer who had dared ask her about Jay-Z's 40/40 club. 'Please don't tie me into family and my brother-in-law's establishment,' Solange said. Another time, she had struggled to hold back her frustration over press intrusion after Blue Ivy was born. 'It has really gotten out of hand,' she tweeted. 'I've been doing my best at keeping my mouth shut . . . but the ignorance is really sad and upsetting . . . We are supposed to be superhuman and watch people we love get slandered, lied on, and ridiculed. It is one of the hardest things to accept.' In an interview, she had also spoken about her unyielding allegiance to her elder sibling, saying: 'I've had to defend myself a lot and I'm super protective of my sister. That's my sensitive subject. I've been known to like snap off a little bit behind her. You have a human reaction.'

Other websites revisited the fact that Solange had abruptly cancelled her European tour the previous summer. A statement on her website in July 2013 said: 'I am completely devastated . . . I really had to make the best decision for my mental/physical health and provide some stability for my family.' She had also admitted taking drugs in the past, and at the Pitchfork Music Festival in the US the same month, multiple eyewitnesses said she told the crowd: 'I smell a little bit of herb out there. If you have any, now is the perfect time to light it.' And way back in 2009, Solange had also tweeted: 'I don't even smoke weed that often but I'm finding that I can't remember things.' Then in 2011 she posted to her followers: 'Is weed taboo in NYC? Like, why can't I ever find any?'

With so many question marks hanging over the row, an investigation was launched into how the incriminating video footage was obtained in the first place. It was rumoured to have been sold to TMZ for a quarter of a million dollars and was by far the Standard Hotel's biggest-ever security breach. As a result, the hotel called in showbiz lawyer Marty Singer to help root out the person responsible for the leak. 'The Standard has identified the individual responsible for breaching the security policies of the hotel and recording the confidential CCTV video released by TMZ,' said Brian Phillips, the hotel's spokesman. 'The Standard has already terminated the individual and will now be pursuing all available civil and criminal remedies.'

But while the fight, quickly dubbed 'Elevatorgate', was puzzling enough, the follow-up was just as baffling. The day after the TMZ video leak, it emerged that Solange had deleted Beyoncé from all of her Instagram photos – except for one shot taken in 2013. Conversely, Beyoncé posted four upbeat pictures of herself with Solange, including snaps from an awards ceremony and a holiday album. Another had been taken the month previously at California's Coachella festival, when she had joined Solange on stage as a surprise guest and the two sisters had danced seemingly without a care in the world.

The fall-out from the fight was further complicated by a cryptic prayer that Beyoncé posted on her Instagram page: 'Help me to choose friends wisely so I won't be led astray.' It added: 'Give me discernment and strength to separate myself from anyone who is not a good influence. I release my relationships to You and pray that Your will be done in each one of them.' Curiously, Solange also tweeted: 'This might have been top 10 days ever in life,' which many assumed was an ironic response.

Just two days after the fight, Beyoncé and Jay-Z shook off rumours that the argument was due to problems between them when they were pictured courtside watching their beloved Brooklyn Nets play the Miami Heat. Both looked happy and relaxed at the Barclays Center in New York and were smiling in photos, while Jay-Z was seen hugging Solange's son, Julez. However, eagle-eyed observers suggested that Beyoncé's wedding ring tattoo looked distinctly lighter in shade and that it could be in the early stages of being lasered off. Only weeks previously, she had shared a Tumblr snap that showed a plaster on the same finger. A source was quoted in the media as saying: 'Jay's been telling his friends that Beyoncé is getting her ring tattoo removed, the one they got when they were married. He just sort of shrugs it off, though, saying, "Nothing is for ever."'

Four days after the argument, Beyoncé and Solange showed all was well between them as they both attended Destiny's Child star Kelly's wedding to her manager Tim Witherspoon in a low-key ceremony in Costa Rica. According to an insider, they flew on a private jet together – but, interestingly, Jay-Z did not join them.

As the days went by without any conclusive explanation for the argument, the drama took another twist when the family at last broke its silence and issued a statement: 'As a result of the public release of the elevator security footage from Monday, May 5th, there has been a great deal of speculation about what triggered the unfortunate incident. But the most important thing is that our family has worked through it. Jay and Solange each assume their share of responsibility for what has occurred. They both acknowledge their role in this private matter that has played out in the public. They both have apologized to each other and we have moved forward as a united family.'

The family also denied that Solange had been drunk: 'The reports of Solange being intoxicated or displaying erratic behaviour throughout that evening are simply false.' And they added: 'At the end of the day families have problems and we're no different. We love each other and above all we are family. We've put this behind us and hope everyone else will do the same.'

Seemingly desperate to show a united front, the family were then photographed out enjoying an al fresco lunch at a restaurant called Petite Amelie in New Orleans. Beyoncé posted up a series of pictures of the occasion online, showing her and Jay-Z with Blue Ivy, Tina, Solange, plus her boyfriend Alan Ferguson, and Julez. Further unconfirmed reports in the aftermath of Elevatorgate said that Solange and Jay-Z put any bad feeling to one side as they went jewellery shopping together at New York store Mr Flawless.

Despite the carefully constructed image of unity, the whole incident had unquestionably dealt a severe blow to the Knowles-Carter brand, and it seemed that their publicists faced a major uphill struggle in trying to clean up the PR disaster. Crisis communications expert Howard Bragman told CNN: 'Jay-Z and Beyoncé have all the money and power in the world, and they couldn't keep it under wraps apparently. So that tells you.' He stressed that the only way to avoid such horrible pitfalls was to keep right out of the public eye. 'You go in your private limo with a chauffeur that's signed a non-disclosure agreement, you go to a private home behind gates, you never go out in public. Once you step out of that cocoon, you're fair game, and there are paparazzi and media that have a price on your head like a hunted animal.'

As the family tried to pick up the pieces post-fight, the débâcle descended into farce, with a skit of the incident acted out on TV's *Saturday Night Live*. Actress Maya Rudolph from *Bridesmaids* played Beyoncé in the sketch, with *SNL* regular Jay Pharoah starring as Jay-Z – who joked that his wife wasn't there because 'she's off making another sexually aggressive music video about a monogamous relationship'. Re-enacting the CCTV footage with audio, they claimed that it was all a big misunderstanding and that Solange had merely been attempting to get a spider off Jay-Z.

It was not until two months later that Solange finally spoke about the bust-up with her brother-in-law. In an interview with *Lucky* magazine in July 2014, she referred fleetingly to the showdown as 'that thing' and insisted there was no longer any ill will between them. 'What's important is that my family and I are all good,' she said. 'What we had to say collectively was in the statement that we put out, and we all feel at peace with that.'

But resolved or not, the family's earlier tensions still gave way to waves of speculation over the state of Beyoncé and Jay-Z's marriage. Fresh reports suggested that in the lift Solange had been attempting to protect Beyoncé from her husband, and that she was unhappy with how he was treating her sister. Suddenly, a throwaway comment that Jay-Z had made in 2010 resurfaced and seemed worryingly relevant. 'I don't think there is such a thing as a perfect relationship,' he had told *Kingsize* magazine, when asked about his and Beyoncé's secret at the time. 'It is unrealistic and hoping for too much. I don't think it is worth all that pressure. We also have our struggles and problems.'

Yet more doubts were cast on their relationship when they failed to show up for Kanye West and Kim Kardashian's much-hyped wedding in Italy in late May. All kinds of excuses for their no-show drifted around the internet, including one theory proffered by hollywoodlife.com that they had steered clear to avoid bumping into Kim's good friend Rachel Roy, who had been at the heart of the initial 'Elevatorgate' conspiracies. A source told the website at the time of the wedding that they were also reluctant to get swept up in Kardashian fever: 'They wouldn't mean it as a diss, they just don't want to go and would rather stay home with Blue Ivy, prepare for their tour and just relax. A wedding like this would be a complete process that they really aren't interested in getting involved in . . . Beyoncé doesn't want the kind of celebrity that Kim Kardashian has nailed down as her own thing.' Other reports in the *New York Post* claimed they shunned the ceremony 'because it was too low-rent for the Jay-Z/Beyoncé brand'. The paper's source added: 'Beyoncé wasn't going to allow a Kardashian to socially climb her.'

It was also suggested that they might have felt awkward about going because Beyoncé was said to have turned down Kim's request to be a maid of honour. She also declined an invite to Kim's baby shower – although made up for it by sending the impending arrival a $15,000 Swarovski-studded high chair designed by Carla Monchen.

And though the pair opted to lie low in the Hamptons instead of flying out to the extravagant nuptials in Florence, Beyoncé also posted Kim a public message of congratulations via Instagram. Next to a photo from a *Vogue* shoot, which featured the couple with their baby girl North West, she wrote: 'Wishing you a lifetime of unconditional love. God bless your beautiful family.' The message was signed with an emoticon of a bee.

At least their absence from the $12 million bash at the Forte di Belvedere was a pleasing result for those Beyoncé fans who still wanted her to shun Kim's friendship. In 2013, a Change.org petition called 'Beyoncé cannot attend Kim Kardashian's wedding' had been created. It said: 'As you all know by now Kim Kardashian and Kanye West have sadly been in the news for their engagement . . . Now we must do all in our power to stop Beyoncé from attending.' One fan who signed the petition was concerned that

Beyoncé would be drawn into the *Keeping Up with the Kardashians* media circus: 'She needs to stay away.'

Meanwhile, Beyoncé had another friend to attend to in the shape of Gwyneth Paltrow – whom she had branded 'incredible' and 'a great friend on every level' in *Life Is but a Dream*. Gwyneth was going through a tough time after announcing her split from husband Chris Martin in the spring of 2014 and was adjusting to life as a single parent. Famously, the actress had stated that she and Chris were 'consciously uncoupling', with a statement on her website, Goop, saying: 'It is with hearts full of sadness that we have decided to separate.' The *Sun* reported that as both Gwyneth and Beyoncé felt in need of some R-and-R, they planned a four-day spa retreat together in California, with yoga classes, meditation and hikes.

Despite this, a counter-story suggested that the two women had fallen out: they had not been seen together in public for some time. According to *Heat* magazine, Beyoncé reportedly did not want her name linked to a celebrity charity sale on Gwyneth's website. Beyoncé was said to have donated a pair of Stuart Weitzman stiletto boots to the Goop initiative, but did not want that fact to be publicised. 'She would have been fine if they had just sold her stuff anonymously,' a source was quoted as saying in the magazine. 'She doesn't feel the need to parade all her charity work for people to see, so she was annoyed when the email went out.'

Despite the uncertainty over the status of the pair's friendship, the US tabloid *Star* maintained that Gwyneth was giving Beyoncé advice on her own marriage – even suggesting that she and Jay-Z visit her esteemed guidance counsellor.

Chapter Twenty-two

The week that Beyoncé and Jay-Z opened their On the Run tour in late June, they released a rehearsal video on to the internet, showing them backstage holding hands, hugging and sharing a series of affectionate glances. The three-minute clip also showed two-year-old Blue Ivy waiting backstage and telling them, 'Good job!' after the first concert in Miami.

However, the tour's launch was dogged by an intensification of gossip about their alleged marital strife, with some reports even claiming that they were leading 'separate lives'. Though they remained typically silent as the rumours stepped up a gear, the showbiz press launched a full-on assault at the pair, with both their personal and professional lives coming under fire. As their relationship was scrutinised, many websites said the tour was 'crumbling' and 'suffering' – despite projected figures that suggested On the Run could be the second best selling tour of all time. The number-one spot is held by U2, but their tour had extended for nearly two years from 2009 to 2011, covering 110 shows – almost six times as many as Beyoncé and Jay-Z planned.

Then came murmurs that the recent elevator fracas had simply been an elaborately devised plot to drum up ticket sales. But, as usual, when the heat was turned up on her, Beyoncé simply let her music do the talking. When the tour kicked off on 25 June at Miami's Sun Life Stadium, more than seventy thousand spectators were wowed by the joint spectacle. One of them was newlywed Kelly, who was sporting a very visible baby bump. She had recently announced she was expecting her first child with new husband Tim by posting a picture of a tiny pair of baby trainers on Instagram.

At each of the two-and-a-half-hour shows on the tour, the couple performed more than forty songs, taking it in turns to hold the stage, then share the spotlight for their various collaborations. The show presented them as gun-wielding Bonnie and Clyde-style fugitives and, according to the *Miami New Times*, they appeared to be 'trying to escape the media, their place in pop music, the haters, the bullshit – even sometimes each other'.

Though the tour was symbolised by the sinister-looking black masks that each wore for the posters and promo video, Beyoncé's friendship with Kim Kardashian was again questioned when the reality star hinted that the duo had pinched the fashion statement from her husband. Posting an Instagram photo of Kanye wearing a similar mask the year previously, Kim captioned the photo with a set of hashtags implying he was streets ahead of them in the style stakes. She wrote: '#ThrowbackThursday #LastYear #StyleIcons'. Some weeks later, Kim seemed to take an even more direct shot at Beyoncé and Jay-Z when she posted a photo of her and Kanye kissing in a lift which, she captioned '#Elevatorkiss'. Still, Kanye attempted to lay rumours of Kim and Beyoncé's rift to rest months later when he told New York radio station Power 105.1: 'They love each other. They respect each other.' He also insisted that he and Kim played Beyoncé's music to their toddler North and added: 'When Beyoncé was working on her album she had pictures of Kim on the wall because Kim represents powerful women.'

In general, On the Run won rave reviews from entertainment critics. Commenting on the first night in Miami, AllHipHop.com said: 'Early on, it becomes apparent that this is a totally integrated performance. Sure, it gives Beyoncé time for her phenomenal costume changes, but the co-ordination is not just remarkable, it's the absolute best way that two of the world's best performers can deliver a show that proves why they're on top together. People are definitely infatuated with them as a power couple, first and foremost. A lot of people look at them as a royal family of sorts and idealize them in a lot of ways to represent true love and a fairy tale coming true.'

According to the *Guardian*, 'The tour played into both of the pair's strengths. Jay brought the Brooklyn bravado and Bey brought the southern strut.' Just as impressed, the *Boston Globe* said: 'Few performers could pull off a production of this scale and scope. There is not an ounce of fat on this tour. Nor is there much to behold beyond its stars: no long catwalks, elaborate sets, or even a visible band. With Beyoncé and Jay-Z, two natural-born entertainers, you do not need much more.'

With the critics happy, fans were sent into raptures when a big screen on the stage showed never-before-seen home-video footage of their wedding. Beyoncé looked radiant in the white dress that her mother had designed for her big day while Jay-Z wore a classic tuxedo. As the pair sang a medley of 'Forever Young' and 'Halo', the clips showed Jay-Z putting Beyoncé's sparkling wedding ring on her finger as they exchanged vows, and she was also seen getting her 'IV' wedding tattoo done. Footage of Blue Ivy appeared on the screen, as well as a picture of 'The Carters' written in sand. Another shot showed a pregnant Beyoncé showing her bare, swollen stomach, surely putting those much discussed surrogacy and fake pregnancy rumours to rest once and for all. The show also featured a raunchy performance of Beyoncé's graphic song 'Partition', during which she recreated one of the *risqué* dances from the video. Footage of the song filmed at their concert in Cincinnati, Ohio, was beamed into the 2014 BET Awards, with Jay-Z dripping sweat as he opened the song, before his wife sauntered sexily on stage. With her blonde hair blowing in the wind, she grabbed a pole and slid up and down it provocatively, before showing off her flexibility as she arched herself over a chair. The same BET Awards show saw her win the gong for Best Female R&B/Pop Artist, as well as Best Collaboration, with Jay-Z, for 'Drunk In Love'.

Though the concerts were not Beyoncé's most ambitious from a technical point of view, her stage outfits were still works of creative brilliance. For her first look to perform '03 Bonnie & Clyde', she wore a fishnet and leather Versace black bodysuit, complete with a plunging neckline, a fishnet mask and high-heeled boots. The designer said the looks were inspired by the 'gangster, hip-hop feel' and the opening outfit symbolised 'a sexy bandit on the run'. Other costumes included a police-style denim jumpsuit by Diesel, detailed with Swarovski crystals, while Michael Costello created a black Victorian lace bodysuit for her. 'My inspiration comes from Beyoncé because I'm a true diehard Beyoncé fan, but I think it's her hair and the way that she moves – I try to use that and mimic that into the clothing,' Michael said, 'whether it's a sequin, a button, or a dramatic sleeve. If you see the dramatic sleeves I did for the Beyoncé lace Victorian bodysuit – the black one – I wanted something she could move in and look stunning in when she's on stage.'

But by far the most talked-about outfit was a black Alexander Wang 'bondage' bodysuit, cut away so daringly across the hips that it resembled nothing more than a thong across her rear. It was a brave look that was rather comically described as an 'assless leotard' and a 'butt cage'.

Slightly more modest was a Givenchy bodysuit, finished with sparkling stones and crystals. Creative director Riccardo Tisci told *People*: 'The embroidered bodysuit took almost a thousand hours to make at the haute-couture house in Paris. They hand-stitched each of the three-D stones, crystals, stars and paillettes one by one.' Givenchy also constructed a monochrome American flag skirt for Beyoncé, which was hand-sewn over five hundred hours. Riccardo revealed that Jay-Z was very involved with his wife's stage looks: 'He came to the fitting,' said Riccardo. 'His eye is so sharp. He loved everything.' Jay-Z kept his look simpler, wearing a variety of suits and hoodies, plus his trademark black sunglasses and beloved gold chain – which weighs eleven pounds and is worth a staggering quarter of a million dollars.

Meanwhile as the tour got under way, Beyoncé's esteemed makeup artist Sir John revealed that the secret behind her flawless stage glow was an intense exfoliator. He told website style.com that he used a glycolic peel with a fruit enzyme on her – as often as twice a week. 'The goal in any girl's routine is to increase cell turnover so that you need less foundation and concealer,' he said. 'Beyoncé hardly has to use any.'

Though she and Jay-Z both looked the part and their act was as slick as anticipated, the image of togetherness they portrayed on stage was not enough to stop the continuing claims that they were in turmoil away from the bright lights. Just prior to the tour debut, there had been fresh reports that Beyoncé was expecting their second child. But this time it was not some straightforward proclamation of a star couple's blissful baby joy. *Life & Style* magazine's front cover screamed, 'Pregnant & betrayed,' referring to wholly unproven allegations in rival title *In Touch* that Jay-Z may have been unfaithful.

Given Beyoncé's svelte appearance on stage during On the Run, there seemed to be little substance to the latest pregnancy claims, but the rumour mill carried on churning. In July, an accusation surfaced online about a 'short-named' R&B singer, who was alleged to have had an affair with Jay-Z. The association was made between him and Lady Marmalade singer Mya, who emphatically denied a fling. 'Never did, never was, never will,' she told a fan on Instagram, when asked about the possible relationship. 'Illegitimate, thirsty sources with no facts and that's the "media" for you – especially today,' she added, before comparing herself to Jesus and saying she had been made a scapegoat. 'False rumors are crafted for ratings & numbers. And miserable, unhappy people need someone to judge to deter the attention away from their own misery and feel better about their miserable lives. If they did it to Jesus, they'll do it to anyone. God bless.' Neither Beyoncé nor Jay-Z commented on the material that was flooding the media, but speculation heightened after an incident during their Cincinnati show on 28 June when Beyoncé dramatically altered the words of her 2006 song 'Resentment'. Instead of singing 'Been ridin' with you for six years' as she had in the original, she sang: 'Been ridin' with you for twelve years/Why did I deserve to be treated this way by you?' It was very quickly noted that she and Jay-Z had been together for twelve years, while much was made of the fact that she also changed the line, 'Like I couldn't do it for you like your mistress could,' to 'Like I couldn't do it for you like that whack b***h could.'

Then, in a later performance in Philadelphia at the beginning of July, Beyoncé openly sobbed through the same song. Ironically wearing a long wedding veil and lacy white trouser suit, her tears were interpreted as a sign of cracks in the power couple's veneer. After the song, a video followed, in which her voiceover told the audience: 'Love is an act of endless forgiveness.'

Still, it was an evening of mixed messages because this time she decided not to change the 'Resentment' lyrics, and later in the show, Jay-Z lovingly pulled her close and kissed her fully on stage. While the column inches attracted by the two performances of the song stacked up, it was impossible to gauge whether Beyoncé's tears and thoughts on forgiveness were simply to illuminate the emotional song or if they had a deeper, more personal resonance about her marriage. Certainly, there had never been any evidence to suggest that Jay-Z had been unfaithful to his wife, but Beyoncé was upset that their marriage was being questioned so publicly and so relentlessly. An insider was quoted in *Grazia* magazine as saying: 'She's been uncharacteristically anxious and has been cutting herself off from those close to her. She can't bear the constant speculation. She's used to being perceived as having the perfect life and is struggling with all the negative attention.' She was also thought to have been hurt by allegations that Jay-Z had become overly close to his protégée Rita Ora. The singer herself blasted the insinuation earlier in the spring, telling radio station

Power 105.1: 'Don't you dare disrespect Beyoncé like that ever again in your entire life. You should know better than that . . . That's just straight up disrespect. You can't even go there.' In July, Beyoncé showed there was no rift as she posted online pictures of herself modelling Rita's new designs for Adidas. Rita replied: 'My big sis, the queen to you . . . rocking my first Adidas loves Rita Ora collection! #unstoppable out for you August 26th. #thankyou #myfamilia #iloveyou.'

In August, an American rapper called Liv again got people talking when she released a tracked called 'Sorry Mrs Carter.' It was widely held that the song alluded to some kind of flirtation with Jay-Z, though the lyrics said they 'never screwed'. However, the words also said: 'I bet he wish I just stayed and played my part/Imagining what could have been with no regards.' Liv made references to several Beyoncé songs in the track too, rapping: 'Girls can't run the world fighting over men/All my single ladies better keep in mind.' A few days later, as if to lay claim to her man, Beyoncé then posted pictures online of her wearing nothing but an oversized sports top emblazoned with the word, 'Carter' and the number four.

With so many negative stories circling, there were claims that normally rock solid Beyoncé was unravelling behind the scenes, with a source telling *Heat* magazine: 'It's been an incredibly rough few weeks for Beyoncé. She doesn't know what to believe and is doing her best to not let anyone see how much pain she's in. It feels like everything is crumbling around her.'

As if that were not enough, there was an additional stream of bleak reports stating that she and Jay-Z were preparing to announce a separation after On the Run concluded. The *New*

York Post quoted a source, who said: 'There are no rings, if you haven't noticed.' The source also claimed that Jay-Z was the one 'doing all in his power to keep the couple together'. Days later, the same paper then claimed that Beyoncé had been looking at New York apartments 'on the sly' without Jay-Z, saying she had checked out a $21.5 million penthouse in the district of Chelsea. With almost daily updates, the *Post* claimed that the pair were staying in different hotels as they travelled around the US. 'They're not just staying in different hotel rooms, but they have booked separate hotels, and they arrive separately to each show,' an insider was quoted as saying. The tabloid also suggested that the couple might not even make it to the end of On the Run. It said that Beyoncé, Jay-Z, concert promoter Live Nation, TV firm HBO and a small team of lawyers had assembled for an emergency meeting to discuss the escalating situation. The executives were reportedly said to be keen on releasing a statement about the rift, but Beyoncé and Jay-Z were apparently against this. Furthermore, in the event of a split, the *Post* said that Jay-Z was 'adamant' that Beyoncé should not do a TV tell-all with Oprah, which would see her 'pretending to be the victim'.

Meanwhile, as the tide of rumours raged in the background, Beyoncé released a remix of her 2013 song 'Flawless', featuring singer Nicki Minaj, which referred directly to Solange and Jay-Z's infamous lift fight. In one of the verses, Beyoncé rapped: 'Of course sometimes shit goes down when there's a billion dollars on an elevator.' Whether or not the lift drama was directly responsible for the apparent ructions in her marriage remained unclear, but such a blatant reference to the incident suggested it was far from forgotten. The stories of the couple's rift were not limited to the US press, and the *Daily Mirror* reported, with a little less finality, that they had sought marriage counselling on tour 'to keep communication open and make sure there are no misunderstandings'. Gwyneth apparently also gave them advice on breaking up in the most amicable way. It was said that she urged them not to rush into divorce, but to 'consciously uncouple' and remain the best of friends just like she and Chris Martin had done. Beyoncé was also said to have stayed at her friend's $10 million Brentwood house without Jay-Z when the tour took LA.

Some months later, in January 2015, Gwyneth was interviewed by US 'shock jock' Howard Stern, and for the first time revealed that she offered support to her friends in the wake of the elevator saga. Asked by Stern if she had contacted them, she said: 'I never say, "What's going on?" If any of my friends have anything like that, I call right away. Absolutely. If someone's clearly going through something, I always go straight for it.'

For a star who has always played her personal cards scrupulously close to her chest, the closest Beyoncé had ever come to actively discussing any relationship hiccup was in an interview with *Harper's Bazaar* in 2011. Apparently confessing that her and Jay-Z's union was far from perfect, she had said: 'Like anything great and successful in your life, marriage takes hard work and sacrifice. It has to be something both you and your husband deeply want. The best thing about marriage is the amount of growth you have because you can no longer hide from your fears and insecurities.'

In more recent times, she had suggested that life without Jay-Z was wholly unthinkable. During a TV special in 2013, her friend Oprah Winfrey commented: 'You balance being the fierce woman with a woman who adores and loves her man.' Beyoncé's reply was unflinchingly steadfast. 'Absolutely,' she said. 'I would not be the woman I am if I did not go home to that man. It gives me such a foundation.'

With such unprecedented interest in the true status of their marriage, each On the Run concert presented a fresh opportunity for the outside world to search for clues about what was really going on *chez* Carter-Knowles. During their show in Chicago in the last week of July, the pair's body language was analysed, with the *Journal Sentinel* saying: 'It wasn't until Beyoncé's "Drunk In Love", about halfway into the two-and-a-half-hour event, that the couple even touched, with Jay giving Bey an awkward from-behind hug.' Such an occurrence would normally barely register, but this was a couple who could scarcely draw breath during this period without it making news headlines. Though the powerful pair were used to their lives being under the microscope, this level of scrutiny swamped anything they had ever faced before. Their way of dealing with it was to say nothing.

During the same show, which was watched by a grinning Michelle Obama and her daughter Sasha, Beyoncé again changed the lyrics to 'Resentment'. The *Chicago Tribune* commented that the gig was not just a concert, but 'a soap opera and morality play, a life-imitates-art-imitates-life slice of meta theatre about a supposedly troubled couple talking to each other through their songs'.

As the tide of unsubstantiated gossip washed endlessly over them, the couple went to great lengths to show that everything was well between them. In Chicago, they ate dinner with Blue at a city steakhouse, declining the offer of a private room and instead opting for a booth alongside other diners. The pair were said to be very relaxed and ordered tuna tartare, steak and salmon, plus a couple of glasses of rosé wine. Beyoncé also smiled for fans' photos as she visited her favourite store, Topshop, in the Windy City. Their seeming togetherness came hot on the heels of a stream of family snaps, which Beyoncé posted on Instagram during the tour. After the Chicago show, she put up a snap of herself clinking glasses at sunset with an unidentified male, thought to be Jay-Z. Another photo captured her floating peacefully in the ocean with her arms outstretched and her fingers making a heart shape. One shot showed her and Jay-Z silhouetted in the water, holding hands as a small boat cruised by. More family pictures appeared on her website, showing her standing alongside Jay-Z and Blue Ivy at an art exhibition in New York; she and Blue were wearing matching vintage-style floral frocks. A further image pictured Beyoncé grinning while lying on top of a surfboard – a cheeky sexual reference to the lyrics of 'Drunk In Love', in which she sang about a surfboard and 'Grindin' on that wood'. Another shot was posted of Jay-Z holding their daughter on a tropical beach, which she captioned: 'My favourite hue is JayZ Blue.' Such candid snaps did not appear to be the handiwork of a woman who was falling apart at the collapse of her relationship. On the contrary, Beyoncé was continuing to paint a panorama of an idyllic life with Jay-Z – which hardly seemed worth the effort if, as the doomsayers were predicting, their marriage was on its deathbed.

After her and Jay-Z's emotional 'homecoming' concert in Houston, Beyoncé indulged in a spot of nostalgia and shared photos of them hanging out at the same city roller rink she had regularly skated at during her youth. And during a day off, when the tour swept into New Orleans, the pair were seen on an intimate lunch date at Cochon restaurant. That same evening, they had a laid-back dinner with Solange at an eatery called Kingfish, with an eyewitness telling *People*: 'They seemed to be having a nice time and were really relaxed and super low-key.' After finishing the US leg of the tour in San Francisco, Beyoncé posted an Instagram photo of Jay-Z and Blue boarding their private jet, along with the words: 'Thank you San Fran! Your city is beautiful. It was the perfect place to complete the best tour of my life!' During their stay, the pair booked out the $30,000-a-night Presidential Suite at the St. Regis Hotel, while they were seen looking happy together during a jovial dinner with rapper will.i.am at Tosca Café.

On leaving San Francisco, the couple escaped the relentless media glare by taking a break in Malibu. Badly in need of a rest ahead of their final planned On the Run shows in France in mid-September, Beyoncé shared a photo of her sipping wine in the sunshine, with Jay-Z's reflection visible in a window. But even this caused minor outcry, as it was suggested that the photo had been digitally altered to make her look slimmer. So-called 'experts' on the techniques of Photoshopping pointed out that the table, sofa and her phone seemed slightly curved and distorted in the snap; said to be a tell-tale sign of poor editing. Given her strong pro-female stance and self-pronounced love of her own curves, it was understandable that some fans felt confused and put out by the idea that her picture had been manipulated somewhere along the line.

During the tour break, a black and white promo clip for the pair's two Parisian concerts was also released, in which Beyoncé serenaded Jay-Z with the song 'Bang Bang (My Baby Shot Me Down)'. Originally penned in 1966 by Sonny Bono and performed by Cher and later Nancy Sinatra, the song was seen as an odd choice for the concert teaser as it has long been presumed to concern an abusive relationship.

But if they were distressed by the fact their every move and gesture now prompted international debate and much reading between the lines, they did not let it detract from their daily life – or their stage performances. 'If there is trouble in Paradise, it is certainly not the focal point of this tour,' commented the *Boston Globe*. 'The so-called queen and gangster would never let the seams show.

After so many unanswered questions about the Knowles-Carter union over the months, perhaps it was fitting that the first person to comment directly was Beyoncé's closest ally: her mum. While out for lunch in Beverly Hills with Kelly Rowland in August, she was confronted by a TMZ reporter and in video footage said: 'Haters gonna be haters, there's nothing we can do about that.' And when asked if things were good between her daughter and Jay-Z, she said: 'Everything's perfect… they're good.' Pressed on her feelings about all the rumours, Tina had the last word, adding defiantly: 'I just don't even read the bull.' Shockingly, dad Mathew later had his say, suggesting that the divorce rumours were merely a publicity stunt to boost On the Run. He told Houston radio station 104.1 KRBE that it may have been hyped 'to ignite that tour.' He added: 'It's called a Jedi mind trick. The Jedi mind trick fools you a lot of times.' He even suggested that the elevator incident was not all it seemed, saying: 'All I know is the Jedi mind trick. Everyone's talking about it. Ticket sales went up. Solange's album sales went up 200%!'

With such a fraught summer filled with endless whispers and conspiracy, Beyoncé experienced additional turbulance when she discovered that she might have a second secret half-sibling.

Mathew Knowles was hit with another paternity suit as it was claimed he had fathered the child of an ex-lingerie model from Houston called TaQoya Branscomb. According to Buzzfeed, estate agent TaQoya alleged that a baby girl born in 2010 in Harris County, Texas, was his, and that she was insisting he take a DNA test.

Coincidentally, a photograph surfaced just days later in which TaQoya was seen posing happily for the camera with Solange. TMZ stated that the pair had met in 2008 through a stylist friend and had socialised together a few times since. But as news of the paternity suit filtered through, Solange denied ever knowing TaQoya, with her spokesperson saying the snap was just a 'random fan photo'.

The new paternity claim followed the revelation back in 2010 that Mathew was the father of Alexsandra Wright's son – a scenario that had not played out well over subsequent years. Alexsandra had ferociously criticised him during a TV interview, alleging that he had never met his son Nixon, while also claiming that she relied on food stamps because he owed $32,135.90 in child support.

Family dramas and purported marriage wobbles aside, Beyoncé at least received a dose of cheerier news when it was revealed in July that she was up for eight MTV VMAs at the annual ceremony. Leading the pack by a mile, the late August event saw her win three of those categories; best collaboration for 'Drunk in Love' and Best Video with a Social Message as well as Best Cinematography for 'Pretty Hurts'.

Singing her heart out in a hugely ambitious 15-minute medley of every song from her *Beyoncé* album, she wore a jewel-studded leotard and danced before a huge 'Feminist' sign, getting the entire crowd to their feet by the end of her set. However, with Kim Kardashian seated on the opposite side of the auditorium during the bash and aides apparently keeping them apart, rumours of a rift were far from curtailed.

To top off Beyoncé's amazing night, she received the prestigious Michael Jackson Video Vanguard Award – whose previous recipients include Justin Timberlake, Britney Spears, Janet Jackson, Madonna, and of course, the King of Pop himself. As Jay-Z handed her the award up on stage, he proudly said: 'The recipient of the Michael Jackson Vanguard Award and the greatest living entertainer – Beyoncé.' Hugging and kissing him, she openly wept with joy and said: 'I'm so full. Thank you. I have nothing to say but I'm filled with so much gratitude. I thank God for this moment. I love y'all so much. Little Blue I love you, my beloved I love you, my fans I love you, MTV I love you. Goodnight.'

Wearing a shiny gold dress and coordinating pumps, Blue – who avidly watched her mum's performance while sitting on Jay-Z's knee – gave her own unique seal of approval to the world, saying: 'Yeah, Mommy.' So in spite of the torrent of stories insisting that the power couple's marriage was soon to come to an end, they seemed every inch the happy family on this triumphant evening.

Chapter Twenty-three

September 2014 brought the conclusion to the On the Run tour, with the couple's two much-hyped shows in Paris taking place. Both gigs attracted more rave reviews, while Beyoncé was joined on stage by Nicki Minaj for 'Flawless (Remix)', which sent the audience into raptures. But rather than a fresh bout of speculation about her and Jay-Z's marriage being in trouble, the headlines took a different tack this time. Highlighting again the often maddening contradictions inherent in the couple's life, the press stated with even more finality than on previous occasions that they were expecting a baby. This time, the rumour erupted after concert-goers noticed that during the song 'Beach is Better,' Jay-Z changed the lyrics from 'I replace it with another one' to ''cause she pregnant with another one'. Inevitably, social media went ballistic with the latest development, especially as the two French shows saw their biggest display of on-stage affection yet. Gazing tearfully at her husband, Beyoncé said: 'I'm your biggest fan. I love you so much. Give it up for Mr. Carter!' while Jay Z replied: 'I wanna say it's been an honour and a pleasure sharing the stage with you. I couldn't dream for anything else to be in a stadium with the woman I love, who I believe is the greatest entertainer of our time. Make some noise for Beyoncé. Thank you Paris, France. What a beautiful night! I will never forget this.' Despite such a public declaration of love, the pregnancy rumour was thrown swiftly into doubt when eagle-eyed fans later pointed out that Beyoncé was holding a glass of champagne in celebratory post-gig photos. In turn, this prompted a debate on how many alcoholic drinks are permissible in pregnancy, with others instead suggesting that her glass was filled with water, not fizz.

Though no baby confirmation was forthcoming, it was then mooted that she was looking curvier of late. As if by magic, it seemed that the fevered reporting of the previous few weeks had never even existed. With talk of a split and messy divorce evaporating into thin air, it was claimed that the pair held a special 'commitment ceremony' on the French island of Corsica in the midst of a trip to celebrate Beyoncé's thirty-third birthday. According to *Grazia*, they recited a new set of vows, before tucking into a lavish feast prepared by their private chef. The magazine claimed they then embarked on a 'second honeymoon', chartering a $500,000 yacht around Italy. Upon their return to Paris it was suggested that the jet-set pair were house hunting and checking out lavish apartments worth millions. Such a reversal of public perception again highlighted the difficulty in trying to second guess her and Jay-Z's relationship, as well as how tightly guarded their entire world is.

Hot on the heels of their phenomenally successful tour came reports that the 'Bey'n Jay' juggernaut would continue with the release of a joint album. According to the *New York Post*'s Page

Six column, the recording was planned for 2015 and would follow the same secretive principles as Beyoncé's last offering – with no prior marketing or promotion. Meanwhile, fans were full of excitement when a new, super-deluxe version of her self-titled album was released in November. The 'Beyoncé Platinum Edition Box Set' comprised of two CDs and two DVDs featuring new songs, '7/11' and 'Ring Off', as well as four previously unreleased remixes with collaborators such as Nicki Minaj, Kanye West and Pharrell Williams. The package also included a live DVD containing 10 songs from the Mrs Carter Show World Tour and a photo booklet, while the album's original 14 songs and 17 videos completed the luxurious bundle.

Away from her music, the fashion world was left salivating when a new clothing line for one of Beyoncé's favourite stores, Topshop, was announced. Set to include footwear and dance and sports accessories, she said: 'I could not think of a better partner as I continue to grow the Parkwood business. I have always loved Topshop for its fashion credentials and forward thinking.' Sir Phillip Green, Topshop's owner was equally enthusiastic about the new venture, saying he found Beyoncé's creative flair 'inspiring.' He added: 'We have much to achieve in just under a year, but we are all up for the challenge, and look forward to delivering athletic streetwear in an inventive and exciting way.' But in spite of her various projects rolling along, Beyoncé kept a low profile during the latter stages of 2014, and appeared determined to avoid any big press interviews. This was unsurprising given that any such opportunity would surely give rise to a barrage of questions about her marriage. It was then mum Tina who took the spotlight, as she gave a rare and touchingly honest talk during a speech at a 'Women and Money' lunch in Houston. Opening up about various hardships in her life, including tough times at school, she admitted that her marriage to Mathew became 'tumultuous' once Beyoncé had been conceived. 'After I got pregnant, my marriage just got really bad and I knew I had to do something,' she said. She found salvation in setting up her beloved hair salon, and stressed: 'I would never be totally dependent on someone. I would never give up on myself.' Tina then revealed how her divorce from Mathew was 'very sad,' and admitted that dating again at her age was the 'scariest thing in the world.' Confessing that Beyoncé and Solange got her dressed for her first date with partner Richard Lawson, she joked: 'I changed clothes five times.' In her speech, Tina also spoke of the strong messages in Beyoncé's music. 'My daughter wrote a song called 'Survivor' some years ago and it's my favourite song by them because it says "When the times get bad, I'm going to work harder".'

Tina was, of course, a key figure on an important day in November when Solange married her partner Alan Ferguson. Far from keeping the event ultra-private, photos of the bride and groom's nuptials appeared all over social media during their three-day, white-themed party in New Orleans. Of course, the extra-special VIP guest was Beyoncé; and suggesting the mysterious elevator upset was now water under the bridge, Jay-Z was also very much part of proceedings. However, poor Solange's big day was almost ruined when she broke out in painful-looking hives after the formalities. Speaking to *Entertainment Tonight* later, Tina revealed: 'She went through the wedding and the sit-down dinner and she was just fine.' But as the party took to the streets, her skin erupted. 'She was dancing so hard, I think she just got over-heated... the seafood, I think she had a reaction to it. So her face broke out in these welts.' Luckily, it was her big sister who came to the rescue – armed with a hefty dose of antihistamine. 'Beyonce took her back to the hotel and gave her Benadryl,' Tina said. 'And in two hours, she showed up at the reception and did the dance with her son and just danced all night and had a ball.' So relieved was Solange that she even tweeted: 'Shout out to Benadryl yo, lol.' One of the highlights for Tina was the exchange of words between Alan and her youngest daughter. 'Oh my God, the vows they were the most beautiful thing,' she told *Entertainment Tonight*. 'There wasn't a dry eye in the place, they were just so heartfelt.'

The ceremony evidently inspired Tina, for she followed Solange up the aisle just months later when she wed boyfriend Richard. In fact, the idea had originated a few months earlier from none other than Blue Ivy, who had asked Richard directly when he was going to make an honest woman of her grandmother. On being confronted by the inquisitive youngster, Tina revealed that Richard said: 'Oh, Blue, soon. Do you approve?' And according to Tina, she answered in the affirmative. 'That's the first time we talked seriously about getting married,' she told *People* magazine. On the day, 300 guests including bridesmaids Beyoncé and Solange, plus Jay-Z and Blue Ivy, boarded a glitzy super-yacht called Eternity at Newport Beach in California. They carried on the familial theme by all dressing in white for the nuptials, with Beyoncé wearing flowers in her hair and Blue Ivy donning a tiara. Beyoncé later shared photos online of Blue dancing with her daddy, while in another humorous shot the whole family posed with their tongues sticking out. Speaking about the special day, Tina told *People*: 'It couldn't have been more perfect.' She added: 'There was a time when I doubted if I would find love again. But I was determined to be happy, and God sent somebody into my life… You can find love at any age. You just have to go for it.'

Although Tina and her daughters had much to celebrate during this period, Mathew was notably absent from these key family events. Tensions between Beyoncé and her father seemed to be running as high as ever, especially when a leaked email allegedly from Mathew emerged during the infamous Sony hacking scandal of late 2014. The email had apparently seen him approach Universal Pictures the previous year and concerned a proposal to make a film about the ups and downs of Destiny's Child. But given his strained relationship with the band, it seemed unlikely that this was an idea any of them would have leapt at.

Indeed, it was later reported that the Destiny's Child girls were busy planning their own ten-year reunion – set to include a tour and an album. But crucially, it was claimed that they would not use their former band name, precisely because they did not want Mathew to have any involvement in such a venture, nor make any money from it. A source was quoted in the *Daily Mail*, saying: 'The problem is they can't figure out how to nix Mathew from the deal. They all want more than anything to give the fans one last run of the group, especially since they all have their own individual success, but don't want to deal with Mathew.' Seemingly testing the water for such a reunion, the three girls later put on a surprise performance together at the Stellar Gospel Music Awards in Vegas, where they sang Michelle's number 'Say Yes' before a wildly appreciative crowd.

The end of 2014 saw Beyoncé and Jay-Z schedule in some

romance as they jetted to Iceland for a short break. Celebrating Jay-Z's forty-fifth birthday in style, the pair checked into a private luxury resort and spa beneath Langjokull glacier called Trophy Lodge. Said to be 'fit for a king', the small resort is made up of cosy log cabins and the duo enjoyed snowmobile rides over the icy landscape, dips in the famed hot springs, and sipped champagne as they watched the mesmerising Northern Lights. But the trip was kept short as there was an important pre-Christmas occasion back in New York to attend; the Duke and Duchess of Cambridge were on their first official visit to the Big Apple and were keen to check out Jay-Z's beloved basketball team Brooklyn Nets. A frenzy of camera bulbs lit up the Barclays Center arena as William and Kate chatted to Beyoncé and Jay-Z courtside, and headlines the world over delighted in the merging of pop royalty with *real* royalty. Sadly however, it was not the greatest night for the Nets as Jay-Z's beloved team lost to the Cleveland Cavaliers. Any disappointment was quickly forgotten though as he, Beyoncé and Blue Ivy left the festive freeze of New York to escape to the warmer climes of Thailand. Sparing no expense for the ultimate Christmas treat, they booked out a $25,000-per-night villa at Phuket's swish Amanpuri resort and got busy sampling local culture, with Beyoncé posting up a series of shots on Instagram of historic temples and lush paddy fields. They also enjoyed elephant rides during a visit to a wildlife park, while tiara-wearing Blue was awestruck by a tiger cub which the family observed being bottle-fed. But as has often been the case with Beyoncé, animal rights activists were deeply unhappy with pictures of their exploits. World Animal Protection's Dr Jan Schmidt-Burbach remarked: 'When you look behind the scenes, holiday snaps like these support an industry that relies on animal cruelty.' Unperturbed, their travels continued into Cambodia and Burma with Beyoncé and Jay-Z hitting the streets on mopeds and mingling seamlessly with the locals. As usual, much was made of Beyoncé's fashion choices, with many jumping to the confusion that her array of loose-fitting print dresses and kaftans was hiding a baby bulge. The star herself did little to dissuade the gossip when she posed for a photo half-buried on a beach, with a big, sandy bump moulded around her middle.

Once back in New York in mid-January, the baby talk continued – especially when Beyoncé turned up for a Nets game wearing a baggy hooded trench coat. Remaining typically silent on the issue, it was left to Michelle Williams to address the latest chatter. Asked about her megastar friend while appearing on *The View*, she said rather tetchily: 'You know, when she was pregnant, people said that she wasn't pregnant.' And commenting on the recent bump in the sand, she groaned. 'First of all, if you look at the picture, the baby bump is probably where her knees probably really are… Just stop it, stop it.' Michelle wasn't the only one to shoot down the rumours, as Angie Beyincé also came out of the woodwork, saying she had only recently enjoyed a very boozy girls' night with Beyoncé and Michelle – during which they 'FaceTimed' former bandmate Kelly. Still, if anyone was going to spur Beyoncé into feeling broody again it would surely have been new mum Kelly, who welcomed her son Titan Jewell in November 2014. At the time, Beyoncé had shared her joy at being an 'aunty' again, captioning a picture of the newborn on Instagram: 'There's no better feeling than holding my beautiful nephew. I thank God for the honour of witnessing my sister's journey into motherhood. I've always dreamt of our little ones growing up together. I'm so thankful for our bond. Baby Ty, I love you so much.'

While her extended holiday during the previous few weeks left work projects distinctly on the back-burner, the start of 2015 brought the prospect of more trophies for Beyoncé, with another six Grammy nominations. This made her the most nominated female in the history of the awards, with her total nods standing at fifty-four. Two of these were for 'Drunk In Love' with Jay-Z, which came despite the song being lambasted by potential Republican presidential candidate Mick Huckerbee. In his memoirs released in late January, *God, Guns, Grits and Gravy*, he said the track was merely 'Jay-Z and Beyoncé's foreplay,' and suggested the rapper was 'crossing the line from husband to pimp by exploiting his wife as a sex object.' Though he did at least concede to Beyoncé's 'amazing talent,' fans were furious that he branded her music 'vulgar, misogynistic, and violent,' and seemingly called into question her role as a mother. Not content to leave it there, Huckerbee also stuck the knife into Barack and Michelle Obama for permitting their daughters Sasha and Malia to listen to Beyoncé. 'With the first lady so concerned about making sure her daughters' bellies don't ingest unhealthy food, how can she let their brains ingest obnoxious and toxic mental poison in the form of song lyrics?' he questioned.

Still, when the 57th Grammys rolled around on February 8th, it was Beyoncé who rather typically had the last laugh. She won three of the six categories she was up for – Best R&B performance and Best Song for 'Drunk In Love' as well as Best Surround Sound Album for her self-titled work. Though it was largely considered to be triumphant British newcomer Sam Smith's night, Beyoncé's achievements could not be ignored; in notching up her 20th Grammy win overall she had surpassed even Aretha Franklin's accomplishments. As she prepared to go up on stage, she kissed Jay-Z and then accepted one of the trophies from Smokey Robinson and said: 'I'd like to thank my beloved husband. I love you deep. My daughter who's watching, Blue, I love you. And I'd like to say thank you to my Beyhive. Thank you guys for riding so hard.' Later in the evening, she performed a spine-tingling gospel song, 'Take My Hand Precious Lord', written by Reverend Thomas A. Dorsey. The song formed part of a tribute to civil rights campaigner Martin Luther King which tied in with one of the season's big-hitting film, *Selma*. However, the entire bash was almost overshadowed by a mock 'stage-invasion' by none other than Kanye West. Imitating his controversial interruption of Taylor Swift at the VMAs in 2009, the rapper walked on stage while singer Beck was collecting his Best Album gong, and then swiftly returned to his seat while the crowd roared with laughter. In later interviews, Kanye even suggested that Beck should have given up his Grammy, saying: 'Beck needs to respect artistry, and he should have given his award to Beyoncé.' Although she was the picture of good grace as the cameras zoomed in on her during Kanye's stunt, sources claimed she was not pleased. One report insisted that she ditched interviews after the awards so she didn't have to address the incident, and another insider was quoted as saying: 'For Kanye to jump on stage without it being planned or part of a discussion is exactly the type of drama Beyoncé did not want.'

Meanwhile, many of the showbiz reporters on the Grammy

red carpet were hungry for gossip about her and Jay-Z's rumoured album together, and it was the couple's producer Noel Fisher – also known as Detail – who appeared to confirm plans when accosted by *Billboard* magazine. 'I'm working on a couple of new projects that I don't want to unveil,' he said. 'And then me and Beyoncé and Jay-Z are actually doing something together this year.' Pushed for further information, he added: 'When you think of Jay and Bey together, you think "album". You should already know.' And asked if it will hit stores in 2015, he said somewhat cryptically: 'In my imaginary mind, I will work to say it's true.'

Seemingly relishing her return to the stage, Beyoncé appeared before another audience just two nights later, this time partnering up with Ed Sheeran for a Stevie Wonder 'All-Star Grammy Salute' hosted by CBS. The pair performed a rip-roaring clutch of the music legend's hits, including 'Master Blaster' and 'Higher Ground', with Beyoncé wearing her usual skyscraper heels which she teamed with a thigh-skimming black and gold dress. After the gig, she and Jay-Z were joined by their new pal Ed for dinner in Los Angeles – during which she presumably tucked into strictly healthy, vegan fare. For February also saw her launch a new food delivery service, based on organic meals that were free of gluten, soy and dairy. Devised in collaboration with personal trainer Marco Borges, the 22 Day Nutrition plan promised dieters that it would take just three weeks to break bad eating habits. With sample dishes including curry fried rice and vegetables as well as almond berry breakfast loaf, Beyoncé said of the regime: 'All you have to do is try. If I can do it, anyone can.'

The same month saw the release of the much-hyped film *Fifty Shades of Grey*, the soundtrack of which included Beyoncé's 'Haunted' from her self-titled album as well as a sultry rendition of 'Crazy In Love.' As the build-up to the release of the raunchy film reached fever pitch, director Sam Taylor-Wood revealed that she had given Beyoncé a slightly uncomfortable sneak preview during what was their first ever meeting. Chatting to the *LA Times*, she said: 'As the scene opened there was no context. There wasn't the slow meeting and the interview and the coffee shop, it was just, "Here's a hardcore sex scene, hey, nice to meet you"... I suddenly felt myself recoil. I suddenly thought, "This is really explicit, and I don't even know this woman."' However, Sam's embarrassment was short-lived. 'When the scene finished, Beyoncé just went, "Wow, that was hot". So I thought, "OK, that was fun. That was a good day at the office."'

But days after the film was released to the delight of huge audiences all over the globe, Beyoncé again hit the headlines when more than 200 alleged untouched photos from her 2013 L'Oreal campaign were apparently leaked on a fan site called The Beyoncé World. The pictures appeared to show her in pre-Photoshop mode, with pimply skin that seemed far removed from her normally flawless complexion. However, many staunch members of the Beyhive attacked the shots and claimed they were not real, prompting the website to take them down. It said in a statement: 'Due to the disdain of the Beyhive, we have removed the photos. We don't want to cause any drama, nor do we wish to start fan wars. Some of the things we have seen posted were just horrible, and we don't want any part of it. We were just posting the photos to share the fact that our queen is naturally beautiful, at the same time she is just a regular woman.' Unsurprisingly, Beyoncé herself made no comment on the latest Photoshop saga.

Despite the unwelcome pics, she quickly deflected attention away from the debacle with the release of a new single, 'Die With You'. And as is so often the case, she chose to shun standard release methods and instead made the track available on Jay-Z's brand new music streaming service, Tidal. A rival to the likes of Spotify, the strictly artist-owned system was launched in collaboration with Kanye West, Rihanna and Coldplay. But with its £20 monthly fee, it swiftly drew criticism from those in the music world who felt Tidal was a cynical ploy designed to make rich musicians much richer. However, it was claimed in the business press that Tidal got off to a shaky start, with the app soon dropping out of the iPhone top 700 downloads chart. With consumers appearing reluctant to shell out for the service, speculation began doing the rounds that Jay-Z and Beyoncé would release their joint album exclusively on Tidal - a move that would surely reverse its fortunes in a flash.

The release of the 'Die With You' single coincided with Beyoncé and Jay-Z's eighth wedding anniversary, which they spent in the typically idyllic climes of Hawaii. After apparently leaving Blue Ivy back home with Solange, the couple basked in the sunshine as Beyoncé delighted in posting up a stream of Instagram 'selfies' featuring a variety of risqué swimwear – which, it must be said, showed absolutely no hint of a baby bulge.

Though the past 18 months have often been tricky for Beyoncé with the drama of her personal life frequently taking precedence over her professional endeavours, the honours have continued to stack up. One notable accomplishment was the announcement of her own exhibit at the Rock and Roll Hall of Fame and Museum in Cleveland, Ohio.

Featuring her Givenchy gown from the 2012 Met Gala and her heels and hot pants from the 'Crazy In Love' video, other items on display included her black 'Single Ladies' leotard and Super Bowl outfit. Nestled among artefacts such as John Lennon's psychedelic *Sgt. Pepper's* jacket and Kurt Cobain's electric guitar in the museum's Legends of Rock section, curator Meredith Rutledge-Borger told Associated Press: 'When we looked at the amount of stuff that she was willing to send, we just thought, The only way we can really showcase these items is to put them in the Legends of Rock area in the museum, which really is the spot that we have to pay tribute to legends of rock, which Beyoncé has proven herself to be. We felt that [she] really needed to take her rightful place alongside Aretha Franklin and the Supremes and Janis Joplin.' Speaking from the singer's Parkwood enterprise, Lee Anne Callahan-Longo, from Beyoncé's management team, said: 'For an artist to be able to have a presence where all of her idols and mentors live, it is a big deal.'

Being showcased among her idols in such a setting was far more important to Beyoncé than Lee Anne could begin to articulate. Ever since she had first shown promise as a gap-toothed child singing shyly in her mother's kitchen, she had wanted nothing more than to match the dizzy heights of those she so revered musically. As she vowed to CNN's Star Jones in 2007, she would stop at nothing until she reached that summit. 'I'm working at doing things that are different and not being like every other artist. I'm working on my art and becoming stronger; hopefully an icon.'

Of course, Beyoncé secured icon status a long time ago, but it would be folly to assume she is content with her lot yet. As each award and professional achievement stacks up, she simply comes up with a brand new ambition. 'I keep making new goals because I'm never satisfied and I always want to grow,' she told Star Jones. 'I'm not worried about selling millions and billions of records because, thank God, we've done that. Now I'm working at being a legend and being around for twenty more years.'

With such a determined 'can-do' attitude, Beyoncé was the perfect face to front up a major new celebrity campaign in 2014 called Ban Bossy. Aimed at empowering women, she joined forces with the likes of Victoria Beckham and Michelle Obama for the project, which was founded by the American Girl Scouts and LeanIn.org. 'Girls are less interested in leadership than boys because they worry about being called bossy,' she said in the promo. Looking directly into camera, she then delivered a resonating punchline that seems to sum up the whole ethos of Planet Beyoncé: 'I'm not bossy, I'm the boss.'

It was a perfectly fitting mantra, so it was hardly surprising when the 'boss' was named the world's most influential person by *Time* magazine in 2014. Proudly gracing the cover of the prestigious edition, Beyoncé said: 'Shooting for *Time* magazine was definitely one of the goals in my life. It's something important for me as an artist because it's not about fashion or beauty or music – it's about the influence I've had on culture.' Writing for the magazine, Facebook CEO Sheryl Sandberg evaluated the star's position: 'Beyoncé doesn't just sit at the table. She builds a better one,' she said. 'She raises her voice both on and off stage to urge women to be independent and lead. In the past year, Beyoncé has sold out the Mrs Carter Show World Tour while being a full-time mother. Her secret: hard work, honesty and authenticity. And her answer to the question, "What would you do if you weren't afraid?" appears to be "Watch me. I'm about to do it."'

As if she needed any more proof of her appeal, Beyoncé was also cited as the most searched for female star on Google last year, while she was branded the most powerful celebrity on earth in *Forbes* magazine's Celebrity 100 – which ranks fame based on money and media reach. Taking into account the astonishing sales of her album *Beyoncé* as well as her cash-spinning Mrs Carter tour, the magazine estimated that she had earned $115 million in the preceding twelve months. Appropriately enough, Jay-Z also made the top ten.

With her influence continuing to expand so steeply, a throwaway comment she made to *GQ* in 2013 was becoming even more apt: 'I now know that, yes, I am powerful. I'm more powerful than my mind can even digest and understand.' But in making such a lofty claim 'Queen Bey' also insisted that she had earned her right to rule, pointing again to the number of sacrifices she had made early on in her life. 'I've worked harder than probably anyone I know, at least in the music industry. So I just have to remind myself that I deserve it.'

It was also compelling that her power had begun to be reinforced through parody. In May 2014, *Saturday Night Live* featured a gag stating that Beyoncé-worship was now obligatory in America. With actor Andrew Garfield taking part, the sketch stressed that 'refuseniks' would be tracked down and eliminated by government bodies known as the 'Beygency' if they did not comply. Though it was a joke, it reflected exactly how many had come to view her: as an entire belief system rather than a humble pop star. Beyoncé responded to the skit by writing 'Haaaaaaaaaaaa' on her Instagram page, alongside a large pink-and-black graphic, saying, 'The Beygency'.

Despite the continuing furore surrounding her private life, it seems that nothing can derail Beyoncé from her ambitious path. At the age of just thirty-three, she has so far won 473 awards and been nominated for 521, yet this could be the mere tip of the iceberg. Asked what she wanted to achieve by the age of forty, she previously told *Access Hollywood*: 'I would love to direct, continue to learn videos. Maybe by then my own short film . . . I'd love to continue to grow as an entrepreneur.' But when quizzed on what she hoped for by the age of sixty, she joked that the 'Single Ladies' dance might finally be beyond her. 'I will not be doing the Oh-Oh-Oh dance, that will not be cute,' she said. 'I think my priority will be my children and hopefully my grandchildren by then – and my record label or production company or whatever else.'

There is no doubt that family is every bit as important to Beyoncé as her career and, fundamentally, she has succeeded in her mission to have both – all strictly on her terms. Doing things 'her way' is what has set Beyoncé apart from so many of her contemporaries, and her refusal to be moulded or pushed into a corner against her will separates her from the cynical, marketing-led pop industry. Yes, she is a mainstream artist, but she often eschews mainstream convention to propel herself to the top of the league. She releases her music when and however she chooses to; she records volumes of videos that must make her rivals' heads spin, and each time she steps on stage she is transported to a parallel universe that other acts can only dream of inhabiting.

Crucially, Beyoncé has never craved fame for fame's sake, and gut-wrenching hard work has always been the motivating force in her world. Even though she could easily sit back, retire and watch the royalty cheques roll in until the end of time, she would not hear of it. There is unfinished business: she knows she can always do better, work harder and achieve more. In that, she is surely one of the ultimate role models for our time.

Of course, like any figure in the public eye, there are those who balk at what she does and what she represents, but there is no denying the breadth of her fan base. Men, women and children of all ages adore her, and her gay and ethnic following is equally immense. Quite *why* Beyoncé is so universally admired is up for debate, but she seems to offer something for everyone. As a pop legend, sex bomb, style icon, mother, feminist and philanthropist, she is homely yet achingly glamorous, traditional yet innovative, chaste yet daring. The contradictions wrapped up in being Beyoncé mean that she ticks a lot of boxes. Comparisons are also frequently drawn between her life and the good old American dream, but in reality the secret of her appeal remains impossible to define. If it was more obvious, others would clamour to replicate it – but for now, at least, Queen Bey's lofty position on the throne looks mightily secure.

Though there is no guarantee that Jay-Z will remain a part of her future, we can only assume that the unshakeable principles she represents as a strong, independent woman will never waver. However the next chapter plays out, Beyoncé will be in control of her destiny and she does not need to explain herself to any of us. As she herself pointed out, while floating serenely on her back in the sea, in her *Year of 4* documentary, 'I don't have to prove anything to anyone. I only have to follow my heart and concentrate on what I want to say to the world. I run my world.'

Picture Acknowledgements

© Corbis: 8/ photo Luca Chelsea (above).© Getty Images: 4/ photo Frederick M. Brown, 5/ photo Samir Hussein (above), 5/ photo Kevin Mazur Wire Image (below right), 6/ photo Jeff Kravitz (above), 7/ photo Christopher Polk (middle). © Rex Features: 1/ photo David Fisher, 2/ photos Matt Baron BEI (above & below), 3/ photo Brian Rasic (above), 3/ photo Startraks Photo (below left), 3/ photo Snap Stills (below right), 5/ photo James McCauley (below left), 6 (below), 7 (above), 7/ photo Antoine Cau SIPA (below), 8/ photo Frank Micelotta (below).

Every reasonable effort has been made to contact the copyright holders, but if there are any errors or omissions, Hodder & Stoughton will be pleased to insert the appropriate acknowledgement any subsequent printing of this publication.

Do you wish this wasn't the end?

Join us at www.hodder.co.uk, or follow us on
Twitter @hodderbooks to be a part of our community
of people who love the very best in books and reading.

Whether you want to discover more about a book
or an author, watch trailers and interviews, have the
chance to win early limited editions, or simply browse
our expert readers' selection of the very best books,
we think you'll find what you're looking for.

And if you don't,
that's the place to tell us what's missing.

We love what we do, and we'd love you to be part of it.

www.hodder.co.uk

 @hodderbooks

 HodderBooks

 HodderBooks